Close Calls with Nonsense

Also by Stephen Burt

Poetry

Parallel Play
Popular Music

Nonfiction

The Forms of Youth: Twentieth-Century Poetry and Adolescence
Randall Jarrell and His Age

Close Calls with Nonsense

Reading New Poetry

Stephen Burt

Graywolf Press
SAINT PAUL, MINNESOTA

Publication of this volume is made possible in part by a grant provided by the Minnesota State Arts Board, through an appropriation by the Minnesota State Legislature; a grant from the Wells Fargo Foundation Minnesota; and a grant from the National Endowment for the Arts, which believes that a great nation deserves great art. Significant support has also been provided by the Bush Foundation; Target; the McKnight Foundation; and other generous contributions from foundations, corporations, and individuals. To these organizations and individuals we offer our heartfelt thanks.

Published by Graywolf Press
2402 University Avenue, Suite 203
Saint Paul, Minnesota 55114
All rights reserved.

www.graywolfpress.org

Published in the United States of America

ISBN 978-1-55597-521-0

2 4 6 8 9 7 5 3 1
First Graywolf Printing, 2009

Library of Congress Control Number: 2008935602

Cover design: Kimberly Glyder Design

Cover photo: Ulrik Tofte, Getty Images

To Jessie and Nathan, again and always.

Contents

III.

IV.

V.

Preface

In Favor of One's Time

If you have ever brought home unassembled furniture, you likely know how important good instructions can be—how frustrating when the instructions require instructions, and how irrelevant the instructions can seem once we have put together the shelves or chairs. The aesthetic criticism of poetry has something in common with those instructions, at all times but especially in our time, when so much poetry comes in flat packs and in pieces, relying on us to put it together ourselves. If the essays collected here make no sense absent this foreword—if these introductions to poets and poems themselves need introductions—then most of them have not done what I hoped they would do. And yet, just as most people seem to like the prose asides we hear when poets read their poems aloud, most people who read books about poets and poems seem to like a little introductory generalization, or justification, to go with the exposition and appreciation to come. If you are averse to statements of principles—if you want to start putting together those chairs, those poems—feel free to skip this foreword now.

Most of the essays, reviews, and arguments here have to do with American poets; most of them take up one poet at a time. The first and last pieces make claims instead about poetry, or contemporary poetry, in general; some of the ones in the middle address poets and poetry from outside the United States. Some of the poets I try to describe in these pages stand among the most famous, and the most popular, in the English-speaking world: others are lucky to sell five hundred books. Some stand near the beginnings of their careers; others died before I was born. All the essays describe poets or poems that I have been glad to reread. The length of the essays has something to do with the depth of my admiration, but at least as much to do with what editors—who allow, understandably, more space for grander names, and less for descriptions of unknown writers—accept. I have written reviews I regarded as negative, and reviews that attracted hate mail even though I thought of them as largely positive. I do not regret them, but I have not collected them here: such pieces do their work upon their first appearances, losing, often enough, what value they have after the waves that they track have hit the shore. With some regret (since most of them concern lesser-known writers), I have excluded almost all short reviews of single books, including all my one-page columns for *The Believer*; I have also compiled an American book, omitting, with one exception, essays written for non-American audiences about poets (e.g., David Constantine, Daniel Huws, Robert Minhinnick) whose work remains unavailable in the United States.

Most of these essays, most of the time, show how poems and poets differ one from another: I try to explain what seems to me (as Gerard Manley Hopkins had it) "counter, original, spare, strange"—and yet, if reread, characteristic—in a particular poet's body of work. These essays nonetheless share some working hypotheses. They imply, most of the time—and they ask you to assume, at least some of the time—that there is a human endeavor called lyric poetry, one that changes, of course, as history changes all things, but that also reflects a continuity of human relations (relations among human beings, and relations between us and our language) since at least Sir Thomas Wyatt and Shakespeare, if not indeed since the Vedas and the psalms. Lyric poetry in this view consists in short pieces of language (spoken, or sung, or written, or all three) in which the psyche finds the language and the sounds to fit its own internal states; through that language we can imagine that we know what it is like to be a particular person, or kind of person, or else what it is like to be ourselves.

To say so is to say that we have emotions, and selves. It is not to assume that those selves are autonomous, nor to assume that lyric poems do nothing else. As a Swiss Army knife may enfold several blades, along with several other tools, a poem may have many dimensions, many possible functions, folded into its words. Without any blades, though, we do not have a knife (though we may have a tool), and without any idea of a person whose interior states find language, we do not have a lyric poem (though we may have a poem of another kind). To say that there are things called lyric poems, and that they have common features from antiquity (even if they also diverge as history, and literary history, move on) is also to say that people and their inner lives have common features over time, and that poets describe them. In a poem called "Elements of Composition," A. K. Ramanujan, the major English-language poet of India, described "millennia of fossil records / of insects that do not last / a day": in them we see "body-prints of mayflies" in petrified mud—we recognize them, in other words, as mayflies—long after the individual insects have died. As mud is to mayflies, so poems are to human beings; they preserve impressions that future observers may therefore recognize as akin to what they know firsthand. A. E. Housman, in *A Shropshire Lad* (1896), made a similar point:

Then, 'twas before my time, the Roman
    At yonder heaving hill would stare:
The blood that warms an English yeoman,
    The thoughts that hurt him, they were there.

There, like the wind through woods in riot,
    Through him the gale of life blew high;
The tree of man was never quiet:
    Then 'twas the Roman, now 'tis I.

Such a poem as Housman's does not simply reflect assumptions about the endurance of feelings, and of symbols for them: its resonance for us (as long as we find it resonant) constitutes evidence for the claim it makes, insusceptible to mathematical proof, but made more plausible each time we hear an old song.

These essays, if they work rightly, are not only like instructions (the ones we get with flat-packed furniture); they are also like introductions (the ones we get when meeting new people), meant to bring poems and poets together with people who might become, as it were, their friends ("hermeneutic friends," in Allen Grossman's phrase). Today's poems, today's people, are in part like, in part unlike, the people and poems of the past. Are poets now, and poets long ago, trying—at least sometimes—to do the same things? Are our poets trying to make the same sort of things that Catullus, or Christina Rossetti, made? The answer—at least sometimes—seems to be yes; the best evidence is there in the poems. But not all living poets would say so: some of them seem, and sound, cautious, vexed, or uncertain as to whether they have "selves," coherent and bounded interior lives, at all, and (if they do not) as to what or who speaks in their poems. Those uncertainties have become, for some of my favorite contemporary poets, a recurrent subject: I try to show here—in Rae Armantrout, in Denise Riley, and in several of their peers—how those uncertainties turn into matters of style, and how their new, fractured, challenging styles reveal (whatever the theories they also entertain) the attitudes and emotions a person might hold.

If you read the not-so-good poetry of the present—the books that line library shelves, or (if you have been reviewing poetry for a while) the books that come in the mail—what you will see is, often, technical failure: amusia, useless dissonance, clashing figures of speech, semantic redundancy, and other problems of the sort that get hashed out in creative writing classrooms, where so many first books (including some good ones) begin. If you read the forgotten poetry of the past, though, you will find something else: smooth—even too-smooth—technique, poems that succeed on their own clean terms, but that make you say, "Life isn't like that; any life is stranger, and more complicated, than this poem admits life can be." To read poetry sensitively and critically we have to be able to make both kinds of objections—and to learn, from poets and from other readers, when the poem was right, and our first impressions were wrong. Life is more capacious and more complicated—fortunately—than any one writer's version of it; otherwise there would be no room for new literature to grow. In saying why this poem works and that poem doesn't, we draw finally on our sense of what life is like, what versions of the world and the people in it we are willing to entertain—even if those versions contradict one another, or (as in Whitman) contradict themselves.

I have tried to show why I like what I like, and why I like some poets and poems more than others. I have tried to avoid both the sense that every poet of interest is "great," that all are equally original, and the opposite paradigm by which aesthetic criticism is first of all a rating system, placing poets in order of supposed importance, as if criticism were akin to constructing brackets for basketball tournaments, or (worse yet) to judging cases at law. Except in such specialized contexts (and they are special, neither ideal nor typical) as the making of syllabi and anthologies (where strict limits of space and time require, willy-nilly, rankings), the business of critics is not to assign stars, or to pick winners in poet vs. poet contests. It is to say what interests us, what seems trustworthy, inventive, memorable, new; to say, when appropriate, why a work fails; to show how we read, what we choose to reread, and why.

The answers to such questions differ from poem to poem. To believe that any appreciation implies a unified theory of value in art, to believe that a critic must develop one, is to commit at least one logical fallacy: it is to assume that just because "poem" and "poetry" refer to a relatively stable, relatively well-defined class of things, we must appreciate or deprecate all such things for the same reason, must ask them to serve the game goals. In fact, I go to Pope for this, to Keats for that, to Dickinson for a third thing, and would not willingly part with any of the three. The same holds for contemporary poetry: I do not seek ingenious compression and riddling wit from Les Murray, nor from Bernadette Mayer; I do not look for extended, shamanic engagements with the raw forces of the id from Kay Ryan. I do not look for deft comfort amid centuries-old techniques when we read Denise Riley, nor do I look for intellectually ambitious embodiments of poststructuralist feminism in Richard Wilbur. Yet all these desiderata (comic treatments, oneiric reenvisionings, and so on) are to be had in some of the poets just named. The map of poetry in English, in this respect, resembles the map of the New York City subway: many trains run to many destinations, and some routes overlap for much of their lengths, but not all trains run at all times.

Hostile or skeptical readers—and I hope this book finds some—will and probably should accuse the essays collected here of wishful thinking. How (such readers may ask) can poets and poetry be (as my favorite living poets are) at once innovative and traditional, alert both to the troubles of modern language, and to the resources of centuries past? How can the poets now in midcareer equal—in invention, in memorability—the best poets of generations past, lacking as we do (as almost all of us do) the classical educations and the polyglot fluencies that most of those earlier poets possessed? How can a mode of criticism (mine) that emphasizes poems as separable objects do justice to poets who want us to see their works in some other way—as continuous projects, for example, whose goals are primarily mystic, or sociological? How can I recommend a poet whose inventive language I admire if I reject her politics, or his religion? How can I believe it worthwhile to spend yet more time with a stack of first books, when I could instead reread Emily Dickinson, or learn Russian, or learn to cook?

The last of those questions has, ultimately, no answer, though if we ask it in a narrower form—about the literature of the present as against the great literature of the past—answers do emerge: all the poets I praise here have added something to the resources of the language, have made forms in words for experiences and attitudes not given effective shape in English before. How those experiences arise, and how much they owe to biology, to politics, or to economics, are inquiries for other kinds of books. This book tries to say instead what poets do with experience once they have it (and by "experience" I mean everything from a broken leg to a bright idea), to show how they represent what happens to them, in language, for themselves and for us.

One of Frank O'Hara's more quotable poems is called "In Favor of One's Time": "it's more difficult than you think to make charcoal," O'Hara says there; "it's also pretty hard to remember life's marvellous / but there it is" (by "it" he means both memory and life) "guttering

choking, then soaring / in the mirrored room of this consciousness."
He is partly kidding, as usual, but he is partly not kidding: there is no
reason we must attend to the flickerings of other people's inner lives,
but if we can do so—and literary criticism can help us do so—our own
lives will hold more marvels, and be more fun. O'Hara seemed to believe, as T. S. Eliot believed (it was one of the only beliefs they shared),
that it makes no sense to ask which very recent works are great, but
plenty of sense to ask which are good, and, when a work of art seems
good, to try to say why. O'Hara believed, too, that comedy was not inferior to tragedy, ephemerality not necessarily inferior to monumentality, that fun and wisdom were both worth seeking in art, and both
available in the works of his own era. This book covers a span of years
that begins before O'Hara's birth and concludes right now. Although it
includes introductions to poets whose places in history seem secure—
William Carlos Williams, for example, and O'Hara himself—most of
it describes poets and poetry that we cannot know the future will read:
poetry, more or less, of our own time. This book, I hope, make a case
in favor of that time: I leave it to others to make the case against.

I remain grateful to the editors who accepted, encouraged, and in some
cases commissioned the pieces collected here: to Mary Jo Bang and
Timothy Donnelly at *Boston Review;* to Jeremy Harding and Daniel
Soar at the *London Review of Books;* to Mick Imlah at the *Times
Literary Supplement;* to Heidi Julavits, Ed Park, Meehan Crist, and
Andrew Leland at the *Believer* (and to Dana Goodyear for bringing me
to their attention); to Margaret Todd Maitland at *Ruminator Review;*
to Ethan Paquin of *Slope;* to Meghan O'Rourke and Juliet Lapidos at
Slate; to John Tranter as editor of *Jacket;* to David Wheatley and Justin
Quinn of *Metre;* to Peter Forbes, Robert Potts, and especially David
Herd of *Poetry Review;* to Anna Rabinowitz at *American Letters and
Commentary;* to Willard Spiegelman at *Southwest Review;* to Tim
Kendall and John Redmond of *Thumbscrew;* to J. D. McClatchy of
the *Yale Review;* to Dwight Garner of the *New York Times;* and—
among the editors of volumes and the organizers of public events—to
Eric Haralson and Duncan Dobbelman; to Oren Izenberg and Robert
von Hallberg of the University of Chicago; to Juliana Spahr, Claudia

Rankine, and Lisa Sewell for their work with Wesleyan University Press; to Rod Mengham of Cambridge University and to Nick Halpern in contexts too numerous to count. I hope that the work here also makes clear, should anyone go in search of such debts, how much I owe both intellectually and personally to certain poets, critics, scholars, and editors: to Langdon Hammer, to Stuart McDougal, to Michael Scharf, to Kelly Everding and Eric Lorberer, to Andrew Osborn, to Monica Youn, to Jennifer Lewin, and most of all to Helen Vendler, whose guiding spirit may be apparent herein. I am indebted as well, of course, to Graywolf Press and the people there, especially to Jeff Shotts, who has played shepherd (if not indeed sheepdog) to this flock of wandering essays, and also to Fiona McCrae, Mary Matze, and Polly Carden, among others. Most of the joy in my life outside literature, and much of the joy within it, comes from the life I share with Jessica Bennett and with Nathan Bennett Burt: she knows, and when he is older he will know, how much of the sense, the verve, and the wisdom of our lives together has made it into the writing I now undertake.

Close Calls with Nonsense

I

Close Calls with Nonsense

How to Read, and Perhaps Enjoy, Very New Poetry

Sheepish Introduction

Invited to offer a "defense of poetry," Randall Jarrell complained fifty years ago that poetry doesn't need to be defended, it needs to be read. Since then, fewer and fewer Americans (at least in proportional terms) have read it. When successful young poets compare themselves to their friends who haven't yet published a book, they may feel lucky; when they compare themselves to Jonathan Safran Foer or Zadie Smith or—but pick your own Best New Novelist—even the most-celebrated serious young poet can find it hard to know she exists.

This essay will not, exactly, tackle that problem; it will, instead, tackle one of its sources, by helping you enjoy those young poets' books. I write here for people who want to read more new poetry but somehow never get around to it; for people who enjoy Seamus Heaney or Elizabeth Bishop, and want to know what next; for people who enjoy John Ashbery or Anne Carson, but aren't sure why; and, especially, for people who read the half-column poems in glossy magazines and ask, "Is that all there is?"

History Lesson (Part One)

Most of the new North American poets I've liked lately share a surface difficulty: they tease or demand or frustrate; they're hard or impossible to paraphrase; and they try not to tell stories. These poets agree in their tastes, but not in first principles, and they come from all over: many hold degrees from prestigious graduate writing programs (Iowa, Columbia, Brown); some don't. Some publish with self-consciously small, "underground" presses (Edge, Flood, Roof, Subpress); some with well-established independents (Alice James, Coffee House, Graywolf, Hanging Loose); some with university presses (Arizona, Iowa, Wesleyan); and some with the hoary New York trade houses. Some live in Brooklyn, some in Chicago, at least one in Seldovia, Alaska; many migrate annually, going where the (academic) jobs are. Descriptions of poets in terms of schools or regions or first principles have rarely been less useful than they are now.

Literary history, however, has rarely been more so. There is a story behind the evasive oddity of much contemporary poetry, a story that begins forty years ago; it's oversimplified, sometimes inaccurate, and unfair to some older poets it includes, but it's a story that many young poets believe, and it might help you see what they try to do.

Despite the achievements of very famous modernists (T. S. Eliot, William Carlos Williams), by the mid-1950s most American poetry seemed predictable, passé; its elaborate stanzas reflected the safety of professors' lives. (Kenneth Koch epitomized and parodied their output in one line: "This Connecticut landscape would have pleased Vermeer.") Rebels in San Francisco, in New York City, and in North Carolina translated poetry from French and Spanish, wrote tiny song-like poems or enormous ambitious ones rather than midsize, controlled, formal work, and published in obscure magazines they ran themselves (such as Cid Corman's *Origin*) rather than in well-established ones tied to academia. Some of these more adventurous poets, like Frank O'Hara and John Ashbery, hung out with abstract painters; others, like Allen Ginsberg and Gary Snyder, hung out with, or were, the Beats. In 1959 Robert Lowell, once deemed an academic formalist, published *Life Studies,* whose poems (and prose) described in painful, self-inculpating detail Lowell's eventful life. Its broken, apparently rambling forms looked shockingly new (they were) and easy to imitate (they weren't, though many so-called confessional poets tried).

The next year brought the War of the Anthologies. Donald Hall and Robert Pack's *New Poets of England and America* (1958) had already presented the formal verse of the 1950s as practiced by a then-new generation—Anthony Hecht, John Hollander, James Merrill, the young Adrienne Rich. Donald Allen's *The New American Poetry* (1960) publicized the so-called rebels, Ginsberg, O'Hara, and Snyder among them. Allen grouped his New Americans by style or region: the New York poets (Ashbery, Koch, O'Hara), the Black Mountain poets, the San Francisco Renaissance, the Beats. The next decade generated more schools and styles, which spun apart from one another as their exponents grew up. Few of these schools acquired stable names; they included urbane mandarins (such as Merrill); the tersely spiritual, influenced by Spanish-language poetry (such as James Wright); the Black Arts poets (Amiri Baraka; post-1966 Gwendolyn Brooks); tormented, engagé writers influenced by French film (the Adrienne Rich of 1969's *Leaflets*); and a heroically populist kind of free verse poet connected to antiwar protests and to feminism (the Adrienne Rich of 1973's *Diving into the Wreck*).

By 1975, Ashbery, Rich, and Merrill had won major prizes. Many young people learned to write their own poems by imitating one of the three; others were imitating Lowell's "confessionalism" or Elizabeth Bishop's emotional reserve. Increasingly, they were doing so in college courses, as creative writing programs proliferated. These programs encouraged a realistic, accessible, personal sort of verse: students wrote poems other students could understand, and they wrote what they knew—their own lives. Outside the classroom, American feminism and African American cultural politics encouraged similar trends: successful anthologies carried names like *Naked Poetry* (1969) and *No More Masks!* (1973).

Writers who preferred their poems less "naked," and more challenging, formed their own magazines, reading series, small presses, and social circles. The best-known such circle now gets called "the Language poets," after the mimeographed magazine *L=A=N=G=U=A=G=E*, which Charles Bernstein and Bruce Andrews ran from 1978 to 1981. While its poems and poets differed considerably, all avoided the easy epiphanies, the focus on personality and emotions, and the storytelling that (in their view) made so much sixties poetry (especially protest poetry) complicit with the social order it hoped to oppose. Some of these poets' academic champions liked that argument (others just liked very difficult poems). Many more critics liked the friendlier, less aggressive difficulties in Ashbery, whose *Self-Portrait in a Convex Mirror* (1975) and *Houseboat Days* (1977) established his continuing prominence.

History Lesson (Part Two)

Ashbery won prizes and poetry critics admired him, but ordinary American readers did not buy his books: in fact, as the 1970s became the 1980s, ordinary American readers, the ones who kept the literary novel afloat, seemed to buy less and less poetry of any sort. Not only did sales decline, newsweeklies and book reviews assigned fewer column inches to poetry than they had ten or twenty years before. Even the university seemed to lose interest, as European theorists (Michel Foucault or Jacques Derrida) replaced modern poets (Lowell or Stevens or Eliot) at the center of many English departments, and "creative writers" established their own academic fiefdoms.

Could poets regain their lost audiences by making their work more traditional, or easier to understand? The so-called New Formalists of the 1980s, led by Dana Gioia, thought so. Because they wanted to conserve old ways of writing, New Formalists were frequently assumed to be politically conservative: some were. (Gioia himself later accepted George W. Bush's invitation to run the National Endowment for the Arts.) Whatever the New Formalists' successes as writers, they clearly failed to restore poetry's popularity. By the late eighties, contemporary verse seemed at home only in the academy, where most well-funded journals and programs promoted autobiographical free verse. Sick of those models, some students sought something new—something more open to personal emotion, to story and feeling, than language poetry, but more complicated intellectually than most of the creative writing programs' poets allowed.

For many, that something was the work of Jorie Graham, whose third book, *The End of Beauty* (1987), flaunted its philosophical ambitions, sporting abstract terms, endless sentences, fragments, elusive references, even the occasional _____ where a noun belonged. Yet the book also included familiar myths (of Adam and Eve, Orpheus, Persephone), American locales (Grand Forks, North Dakota), and a clear sense of voice and personality. Graham's teaching job at the Iowa Writers' Workshop made it even easier for nascent writers to discover and imitate her style, and the styles of poets (Michael Palmer, for example) whose devices Graham sometimes shared. By the early nineties, difficult writers with small-press links had become well-known teachers themselves, among them C. D. Wright and Keith and Rosmarie Waldrop at Brown, and Bernstein at Buffalo. Donald Revell at Denver (later at Utah, now at UNLV), and Richard Howard at Houston (now at Columbia) supported new poets with projects unlike their own, poets who looked to Allen's New Americans, to the Language poets, and, behind them, to Gertrude Stein, Emily Dickinson, or George Oppen for devices that could challenge or free them.

These trends made the 1990s the first decade since T. S. Eliot's 1910s in which the emerging styles proved harder for neophytes to understand than the old ones. New styles (and new cliques) required new magazines, and the magazines came—in print *(Apex of the M, Conduit, Fence, Jacket, jubilat, lingo, No, Spinning Jenny, Turnrow, Volt)* and on the Internet *(Slope, Jacket, Web del Sol);* new editors adapted older journals to newer styles *(Boston Review, Colorado Review, Denver Quarterly)*. University presses (Wesleyan, Iowa) that would have sniffed at Language poets in 1980 began to publish their work, and work by their students and imitators. Some poets cared very strongly for independent, or nonacademic, publishing practices: endless debates about "selling out," about what counts as "mainstream" and "independent," continue to detain insiders, while print- and Web-based journal editors, making the medium part of the message, try to invent new collaborative forms. Although *The End of Beauty* hasn't a prayer of matching sales figures for *Nevermind,* people who listen to lots of rock music might do well to make an analogy between the post-Graham poetry world and post-Nirvana indie rock: in each case a big success from the early 1990s scrambled both the commercial field (as it seemed to record labels and radio stations, to publishers and magazines) and the self-definitions of artists in what had been a discrete set of "mainstream" and "underground" styles.

As with rock and roll, the names for trends and schools now fifteen years old have limited use when applied to the art being made now. Yet it's surprisingly hard to discuss contemporary poetry without naming camps and schools: sometimes, people won't let you. The first time an editor asked me to survey contemporary American poetry in general, I needed a hook for the piece: I took the advice of a friendly rock critic and invented the Elliptical school, an ex post facto name for some of the newish poets whose background I've just sketched. "The Elliptical Poets," I wrote, "seek the authority of the rebellious"; they sounded "desperately extravagant, or tough-guy terse, or defiantly childish." They broke up syntax, but reassembled it; they tried (as had Graham) to adapt Language poets' disruptions to traditional lyric goals (expressing a self and its feelings), and tried (as Graham did not) to keep their poems short, songlike, or visually vivid. I named Elliptical poets' poetic ancestors, and their preferred rhetorical devices, and quoted exemplary poems; I also named the poets themselves, starting with Mark Levine and Lucie Brock-Broido, and extending to C. D. Wright, Susan Wheeler, Karen Volkman, Claudia Rankine, and others.

Since 1994 I have published (not counting unsigned work) more than 150 essays, articles, and reviews about contemporary poets and poetry, from eight-thousand-word arguments to five-hundred-word reviews. "The Elliptical Poets" garnered more American reaction than any ten others combined. (My spouse, who maintains a Web site for my work and hers, once discovered that the overwhelming majority of our hits in one three-month period came from searches for "Elliptical.") Some of the feedback I got was jazzily positive, even thankful. Some of the feedback was negative but attentive: readers pointed out (as my essay acknowledged) that some of the poets I grouped together were hardly friends, and that the books that founded the putative school had come out years apart. Outweighing both the supporters and the disputants, however, were the curious: students who planned term papers on the Ellipticals, academics who wanted to hear more about it, poets who wondered if they belonged in the school. Gelett Burgess, the American humorist who composed "The Purple Cow" ("I'd rather see than be one"), gave his quatrain an equally catchy sequel:

Ah, Yes! I Wrote the "Purple Cow"—
I'm Sorry, now, I Wrote it!
But I can Tell you Anyhow,
I'll Kill you if you Quote it!

I'm not sorry that I wrote "The Elliptical Poets": if it created new readers for Mark Levine, or Brock-Broido, or Wright, it did what I meant it to do. At the same time I wondered whether anyone would notice a broader, more careful introduction to the contemporary poets I liked—poets who share tactics, interests, and a generation, but who often have not met, and who would not fit comfortably (let alone consciously) into any school. You are reading that introduction now.

How to Read Very New Poetry

The most important precepts are the simplest: look for a persona and a world, not for an argument or a plot. Enjoy double meanings: don't feel you must choose between them. Ask what the disparate elements have in common: Do they stand for one another, or for the same thing? Are they opposites, irreconcilable alternatives? Or do they fit together to represent a world? Look for self-analyses or for frame-breaking moments, when the poem stops to tell you what it describes. (Classic Ashbery poems tend to end with these: "I shall keep to myself. / I shall not repeat others' comments about me"; "A randomness, a darkness of one's own.") Use your own frustration, or the poem's apparent obliquity, as a tool: many of these poems include attacks on the assumptions or pretenses that make ordinary conversational language, and newspaper prose, so smooth.

Ask what kind of nonpoetic speech or text a given line evokes: Does the poem seem to quote, or remind you of, an adventure story? A tell-all memoir? A bureaucrat's memo? "Madame Deluxe's Instructional Manual and Marriage Guide for the Year 2000" (the title of a very

funny poem by Tenaya Darlington)? A high school yearbook, as in
C. D. Wright's "Autographs"? Here are four lines from Wright's poem:

> Site of their desire: against a long high wall under vapor light
> Most likely to succeed: the perpetual starting over
> Inside his mouth: night after night after night
> Directive: by any means necessary

Wright's take on "senior superlatives" invokes the mingled and conflicting stories that mark many Americans' high school years, with their
new passions and their incompatible hopes: the two-page poem concludes with its own "Mantra: no one has been hurt, no one has been
killed // P.S.: have a wonderful summer and a wonderful life." Many
other new poems pretend to be personal letters; almost every literary
magazine these days seems to contain at least one poem that opens
"Dear ——," flaunts a dateline, or offers a fictive return address.

Look for the patterns you might seek in visual art. Especially if
the poem avoids grammatical sense—if it looks like a canvas strewn
with phrases—try treating it as if it were such a canvas. Why place the
phrases in this, and no other, array? What sort of person would juxtapose them, and why? Do they imply a hierarchy of importance, or a
temporal order ("I noticed first this, then that")? Take Monica Youn's
"Hand to Mouth":

> the fields flooded with milk
> the herbs shining on the mountain
>
> the strong   salt soil   my dear
>
> you stoop to pinch off eatings
>
> while behind you a vast
> task is rising
>   a skein of use

Fields, herbs, milk, scenery: Youn begins by depicting a place to relax. As
the poem shifts from an aerial view to a close-up, though, the mountain

resort gets less comfy: in "salt soil" little or nothing can grow (compare ancient Carthage, demolished and sown with salt). "You" thought you had a vacation, or a romance in which your partner made no demands: in fact, though, you've landed amid "vast" responsibilities, which feel like a "skein" (a tangled web, a trap). Youn's poem of single, suggestive words simulates changes in how we view a landscape: those changes map the unpleasant surprises human relations can also bring.

If some poems resemble pieces of visual art, other poems resemble games whose rules you can learn. Their patterns can be as abstract as the alphabet, or as socially grounded as fighting words. Harryette Mullen's prose poem "Denigration" runs teasing variations on a racial slur:

> Did we surprise our teachers who had niggling doubts about the picayune brains of small black children who reminded them of clean pickaninnies on a box of laundry soap? How muddy is the Mississippi compared to the third-longest river of the darkest continent? In the land of the Ibo, the Hausa, and the Yoruba, what is the price per barrel of nigrescence?

(The Ibo and the Hausa live in Nigeria; the river is the Niger.) Other poets' games reuse traditional forms. The sestina (six six-line stanzas each with the same six end words, concluding with a three-line coda) lets poets show off and act playful, even hokey or self-satirical, without penalty. It has therefore become both a leading form for light verse and a form for poems about poetry. Such gamelike poems focus on artifice (and personality) at the expense of "sincere" or "natural" speech. That artifice can carry meaning in itself: often it tries to demonstrate that selves, personalities, egos, are themselves artificial, effects of a social matrix. Nonetheless, contemporary poems like these hold together if we can imagine a personality behind them. The poem carries, as people do, a social or regional or ethnic context; it leaps, as a person's thoughts do, from topic to topic, and it lacks, as real people usually lack, a single story line or motive that defines it. Being like a person, such a poem can also ask what exactly makes us persons, how we know a person when we see one, or how we tell one another apart.

These questions, and the techniques that go with them, can (like any technique) be made into routines; some of the most celebrated "difficult" poetry of the past ten years seems to me derivative, mechanical, shallow, soulless, and too clever by half. But that's no reason to dismiss the whole lot. The two poems below strike me as very good, and unheralded, examples of the new poetry I've just described: you can use them to try out the ways of reading I've tried to recommend.

Let's start with a trip to the beach. Here is "Aqua Neon" by Ange Mlinko, from her first book, *Matinees* (1999):

> You shouldn't live your life in anticipation of so much
> 'cause now nothing can fill you
>
> which can be found in the modern supermarket
> where sensation as food is also found.
>
> Endless stairwells leading to terminals leading to planes
> distracting the sky to itself with skylights athwart hills
>
> meeting one gaze straying nowhere if no bag falls
> to burst with free clothes in the streets where the avid
>
> giftwrap of a crowd's swept away by police.
> This is expectation, stupid.
>
> And on the seashelly stretch your bare feet gingerly cut peach flesh
> find no relief, either from running or stopping
>
> after you said we can sleep on the beach
>
> if we drink all night and drive in the morning.

"You" begin as a generic reader, receiving the poet's advice, and end as a friend or lover on a road trip to the sea. The hunger your "anticipation" produces should make "you" seek not consumer goods, not ordinary supermarket "sensations," but a psychological as well as a physical getaway. Yet once you head for the beach (by airplane) you'll remember that many people must work to get you there. Airplanes "distract" the sky because the view from the airplane distracts the passengers; on the boardwalk, town cops disperse "avid" crowds ("gift-wrapped" because they accompany the beach, which is the true gift, and because their dress is gaudy, like wrapping paper). You can run, rather than walk, along that beach, once you know that it will cut the "peach flesh" of your feet (shades of J. Alfred Prufrock); is the pleasure worth the labor, or the pain?

With her chatty, speedy lines, Mlinko has written a poem about the defects, the attractions, and the inevitability—for certain temperaments—of the student slogan "Work hard, play hard"; it's also a poem about the aqua, neon, peach, day-and-night atmosphere of certain (East Coast) beach towns, set on the day Mlinko and friend arrive. Or so I think: I'm surer of the personality and the places than I am of the story that I've just told, and I'm also sure that story is one among several Mlinko's poem allows. The point is the sense of the world the poem produces; that sense of the world comes largely from the particular phrases, the sense of line, and the way abstracts ("sensation") match concretes ("neon") and offhand phrases match familiar behaviors ("drink all night and drive in the morning"). Mlinko's casual tone might reflect her stated admiration for Frank O'Hara—not coincidentally, Mlinko (who holds a graduate degree from Brown) once helped run the Poetry Project at St. Mark's Church in the Bowery, in downtown New York: the Poetry Project has long made O'Hara its patron saint.

Mlinko offers both a likable persona and a sense of place; Allan Peterson relies mostly on the latter. Many of his poems reinvent the Anglo-American, nineteenth-century tradition of landscape poetry to fit both his adopted home in Florida and his alienated, abstracting temperament. One such reinvention is "From Now On," taken from his first book, *Anonymous Or* (2001):

A force like water turns the mill wheel.
A cocktail of current turns the dream.
But that is useless now.
No one remembers a mill wheel and dreams

are described as random activity,
hearts more turnips than Valentines.
Frances is awake and beating the organic mattress flat
to take back what it borrowed of her body overnight.
Things sap us while they work,
so no more sweet descriptions of flowers as flames,
even though the azalea is burning inside the window.
No more sanding my knees looking for shark teeth,
though sleepless oceans thrash the shore.
I will try harder than water.
I will be telling you the worst.

The oddball grammar, with its string of copulas and a passive con-stuction ("is useless," "dreams / are described"), alerts us to a lack of agency in the poet's life. Frances may beat the mattress, but "I" take ac-tion only in the future tense: "my" surroundings instead control me, in a way that seems dreamlike, though dreams now lack meaning (seem "random"). Nature seems to want something from Peterson, but what? Perhaps nature wants him to admit—as he finally does admit—that he and Frances live a domestic life, one without "flowers as flames," with neither amorous immediacy nor danger. The worries endemic to that life involve housekeeping ("beating the organic mattress flat"), frugal eating and practical gardening (turnips), and, by extension, money. Can he hope for anything else, or anything more romantic, from now on?

Peterson's line breaks make the poem resemble a series of indepen-dent sentences (even proverbs, "sayings"). You can't get blood from a turnip, one saying runs, but can you get love from one? Can you keep love if you tell your lover the worst? Perhaps, but only if he or she shares your attraction to oblique ways of stating distress, ways as oblique as "no more sanding my knees." Peterson has tried to make this problem sound as strange as it feels once we encounter it in our own lives—as strange, and as hard to solve: the indirections help the poet keep going, just as indirections, changes of subject, distracting jokes, can do in real life.

If Peterson makes a good example of the difficulty, the indirection, that pervades American poetry now, he also illustrates what we ignore if we look at poetry in terms of cliques and schools: Peterson holds a graduate degree in visual art, taught for decades at a junior college in Florida, and wrote poetry for twenty years before his first collection appeared. Not coincidentally, the poets with the fewest hip connections, farthest from the metropolitan centers, are the likeliest to get overlooked: they can win competitions, as Peterson's volumes did, but aren't likely to sign on to manifestos, found cool magazines, win academic awards, or turn up at glittering po-biz events.

What I Miss in What I Like

In pursuing certain virtues—colorful local effects, persona and personality, juxtaposition, close calls with nonsense, uncertainty, critiques of ordinary language—the current crop of American poets necessarily give up on others. I miss, in most contemporary poetry, the arguments, the extended rhetorical passages and essayistic digressions, I enjoy in the poems of the seventeenth and eighteenth centuries (and in W. H. Auden and Marianne Moore). I've started to think that I'm not the only one. Associated since her first publications with the post–Language poetry small presses, Jennifer Moxley exists in an upside-down world relative to most poets of previous generations: for her, slipperiness and linguistic resistance are normal, expected; self-revelation, explicit argument, and confident clarity seem odd, daring, and new. Moxley has come out on the other side, so to speak, of the most radical projects in contemporary writing. She sounds, often, clunky; oddly Wordsworthian; frequently fascinating; and deliberately naive. Take this passage from "Grain of the Cutaway Insight," the first poem in Moxley's second book, *The Sense Record and Other Poems* (2002):

> Long lost friend, with whom I once
>
> spoke into the night of books and
>
> left, thinking to myself on my short
>
> walk home of all the things I wanted so
>
> to tell you

in a poem, I am lonely

in the in-*commiserate* word,

its small sound remains

an incipient dis-harmony

sounding through dissembled day's

would-be routinization.

American poetry also harbors a few youngish poets devoted more straightforwardly to argument and wit; the best of them remain both easy to like and easy to understand, if you already like the poetry of the past. Some of those more traditionally minded poets want to be heirs of Merrill; others (Greg Williamson, Robert Shaw) might consider themselves heirs of Robert Frost. And then there is Kay Ryan, whose concentrated, rhyming, epigrammatic forms let poets who should know better regard her as minor. Here (from *Say Uncle* [2000]) is "Grazing Horses," her expertly oriented extended metaphor for mental and emotional disorientation:

Sometimes the
green pasture
of the mind
tilts abruptly.
The grazing horses
struggle crazily
for purchase
on the frictionless
nearly vertical
surface. Their
furniture-fine
legs buckle
on the incline,
unhorsed by slant

they weren't
designed to climb
and can't.

Ryan's horses no longer know, and cannot stay, where they are; they stand for a disorientation so total as to affect one's identity. What does it mean to be a person, to remain the same person you were, after you've had this kind of experience? Ryan's poem admits that we don't know: it approaches, through one consistent metaphor, some of the questions more obviously difficult poets tackle through their disorienting styles.

The science fiction writer Theodore Sturgeon once said that 90 percent of anything is no good: contemporary poetry is not, and never has been, an exception. No poet can whiten your teeth, improve your dating skills, or make you taller. Nor will poets decide the next election. Reviewers, moreover, participate necessarily in the game by which everyone in the "book world" (academics included) pretends that this year's work must hold more interest, show us more about human life, than did work from 1850 or 1961. (That's why few kinds of writing seem so dated, so clearly wrong, as old book reviews.) "If you don't need poetry," Frank O'Hara quipped, "bully for you." Yet poetry lets us imagine that certain arrangements of words, and nothing else— no camera, no lights, not much action—can tell us what it's like to be other people, and (in another sense) what it's like to be ourselves. In poems, we believe that language alone can reveal what Proust called "the intimate composition of those worlds which we call individuals and which, without the aid of art, we should never know." These poets have found modes of writing—ways to put language in order—that did not exist before, that present otherwise unknowable individuals, and that seem to fit our experience now: I think we'll be reading some of them for a long time.

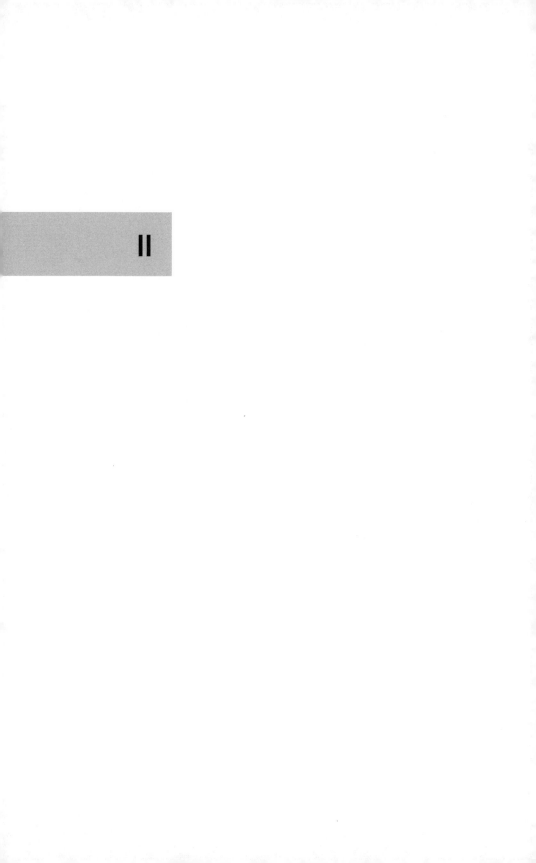

II

Rae Armantrout

Where Every Eye's a Guard

You're in the family kitchen. Mom and Dad have been arguing—
no, fighting—for over an hour, louder than the TV. As you overhear
them (you can't avoid it), you realize that anything either parent tells
the other can be reinterpreted, misinterpreted, and turned against its
speaker. In the meantime, TV commercials invite you to reinterpret
their endless pitches. ("Buy Wonder Bread," one familiar ad implores.
But what makes the bread wondrous? What will this white bread
make you wonder about? Could it be one of the ancient world's Seven
Wonders? Would Mom or Dad even understand questions like these?)
As you begin to transcribe bits of their quarrel, bits of your TV show,
bits of commercials, you discover that the language in each sounds like
language in all the others, and it all seems designed to sell you stuff—
designed, that is, for the benefit of the seller, and without your own interests in mind. As you try to put the bits together, you see how hard it
has become to trust any of it; could all language be this unreliable?

You go on making linguistic collages like this, adding verbal armatures of your own. In them you explore your growing suspicion—
of yourself, of your parents, of money, of the whole American system
in which everything that seems to matter comes with a sales pitch and

a price tag. Your growing fascination with rearranged words seems to give you the power to see through things, to find the machinery or the hidden contradictions under all kinds of economic-linguistic-artistic facades. After you've been doing this for a while, you realize (emotionally) what you might have known (intellectually) all along: these see-through dialects of fraud and bad faith, these corruptible, companionable, always-already-commercial phraseologies, are all there is. If you want to express any feeling, articulate any reaction, you will have to do it in the same languages that you have been mocking and disassembling: there is no authentic alternative, no uncorrupted language reserved for true sentiment. Moreover, you will have to do it while mocking those languages, since your sentiments and reactions now seem as suspect to you as anyone else's: you, too, live in the culture of cash-credit-and-carry, and your skeptical X-ray vision cannot be turned off.

Although bits of it derive from her brief memoir *True*, the foregoing is not a history but a fable, designed to help new readers comprehend—and enjoy—Rae Armantrout's strange, original, and corrosively self-critical poems. Armantrout grew up in suburban San Diego; her unsympathetic parents devoted themselves to evangelical Christianity and to cowboy stories. ("My mother has always been a myth-maker, of sorts," Armantrout writes in *True;* "I began to experience all this myth-making as repulsive.") Throughout high school she and a friend pursued fantasies of life as Mexican outlaws; in college, at San Diego State University and at Berkeley, she enjoyed the late-sixties counterculture, meeting her future husband, Chuck Korkegian, and her first poetic collaborator, Ron Silliman. With Lyn Hejinian, Barrett Watten, and others, Armantrout and Silliman helped set up the Bay Area small-press and journal scene of the 1970s, in which "Language writing" took shape. Armantrout moved back to San Diego in 1978, when she was expecting a child; she has lived there ever since.

As you will see if you read her *Collected Prose* (which sets *True* beside several interviews), or if you read *A Wild Salience* (the only collection of writings about her), Armantrout shares the concerns of other Language writers. She considers commodification, cultural capital, and the links between power and taste. She undermines our expectations about identity, unity, prose sense, logical and emotional direction; sometimes she identifies those expectations with economic or sexual inequity. (Her work, she says, can "focus on the interventions of capitalism into consciousness.") Armantrout's ear, her choice of models, and her unusual temperament—a kind of universal solvent for words and ideas—together let her embody all those concerns (and more) in remarkable, compact poems.

Armantrout's stanzas and lines derive from William Carlos Williams, Emily Dickinson, George Oppen, Lorine Niedecker, Robert Creeley, and perhaps Denise Levertov (Armantrout's teacher at Berkeley)—in that order. "Williams was the first poet I read seriously," Armantrout tells Lyn Hejinian in an interview. Williams and Dickinson together taught Armantrout how to dismantle and reassemble the forms of stanzaic lyric—how to turn it inside out and backward, how to embody large questions and apprehensions in the conjunctions of individual words, how to generate productive clashes from arrangements of small groups of phrases. From these techniques, Armantrout has become one of the most recognizable poets of our time.

Extremities (1978) shows Armantrout's interests before she had gathered them into a style. These earliest poems (like those of her San Francisco friends) often depend on collage: some look like collections of scraps of paper (resonant scraps: "the charmed verges of presence"). One early poem deserves special attention:

We know the story.

She turns
back to find her trail
devoured by birds.

The years; the
undergrowth

These six lines—the whole of her poem "Generation"—exhibit features that would typify Armantrout's poems. She invokes a story, or a constellation of stories, that we already know (the babes in the wood, Hansel and Gretel) in order to say that it's probably not the whole story. Her short lines and jagged rhythms give the breaks maximum prominence. Those breaks, in turn, emphasize partial syntax and semantic alternatives: "she turns" . . . into a swan, or a tree, or to religion? No, she merely turns back. This stranded, frustrated, and frustrating protagonist, caught in the midst of a story with an obscured beginning and no good end, makes available (without enforcing) a feminist moral: why do our fairy tales like to put women in trouble? At the same time, Armantrout's sparse arrangements of isolate phrases remind us how much of this "story" we tell ourselves, how much what we think we learn is what we already "know."

A less guarded early poem, "Tone," follows Williams's stanza form and Williams's interest in small objects: one section reads,

> Not pleased to see the
> rubber band, chapstick, tin-
> foil, this pen, things
> made for our use
>
> But the bouquet you made
> of doorknobs, long nails for
> their stems sometimes
> brings happiness

Like Williams, Armantrout appreciates small, ignored, manufactured things, and feels relatively little attraction to nonhuman nature. Unlike Williams, she's anxious about "use." "'When names perform a function,'" a "stubborn old woman" explains in a poem called "A Story," "'that's fiction.'" Armantrout's wary, oppositional temperament, her resistance to fictions and functions, was hers from the start: all she had to do was find her own forms for it.

By *Precedence* (1985) those forms had arrived. The quotation-filled, deeply unpredictable stanzaic poems that dominate her work from this volume forward explore her suspicions of everything, including her own modes of suspicion. Often they seem to begin after somebody else has stopped talking. Asked to speak first, these poems would not know what to say: they, and she, need received forms and ideas to work against. Consider "Double," the first poem in *Precedence:*

So these are the hills of home. Hazy tiers
nearly subliminal. To see them is to see
double, hear bad puns delivered with a wink.
An untoward familiarity.

Rising from my sleep, the road is more
and less the road. Around that bend are pale
houses, pairs of junipers. Then to *look*
reveals no more.

Armantrout seems here to describe her move back to San Diego. More than that, though, she describes the (to her, deeply unreliable) process of looking and making. Poetic vision is always double vision, impressions of fact always mediated by anticipations of form; here these anticipations seem to obstruct, or even to prevent, any knowledge of a real house or road.

Armantrout's characteristic tones involve exasperation, or tense anticipation, or knowing, beleaguered menace. "Go ahead," a recent poem asks of us, "say anything," as if it already knows what we might say. If this unease means that her poems depend on the expectations she likes to undermine, it also gives them their peculiar negative powers, as in one sequence called "Fiction": "When the woman's face contorted and she clutched the railing for support, we knew she would die for this was a film with the set trajectory of fiction." Against these predictable trajectories Armantrout can set infants and toddlers, who give her poems the alien, nearly incomprehensible perspectives she seems to enjoy: "She planned to give birth to a girl who resembled her husband's family or perhaps no one at all. An utterly new countenance."

Of course, no language, no sentiment, can remain "utterly new." We do not make up the words we use; instead we take in and send out language in mostly unexamined pieces, "regular self-deluded everyday phrases," as Rachel Blau DuPlessis puts it in *A Wild Salience.* Almost anything we say can thus sound (to a sufficiently guarded ear) like a set of unacknowledged quotations: for example, "When he awakened / she was just returning from / one of her little trips." To learn to read Armantrout is to learn to hear quotation marks around that last line, and then to ask whether quotation marks belong on the other lines, too. It is also to learn to separate speech from speaker, denotative meanings from ulterior motives, a tactic that seems recherché until the same poem offers examples:

> Now the boss could say
> "parameters"
> and mean something
> like "I'll pinch."

Here—and throughout Armantrout's work—the unreflective use of ordinary spoken language proves inextricable from economic exploitation (so that Armantrout seems in exposing the first to attack the second): the boss can repurpose his words, and his employees, because he's the man who signs the checks. The point of such a clipped style, such wiry frames around so many phrases, is not just (as it would be in John Ashbery, or in John Tranter) that we have seen these words before, that they come to us from other speakers; it is, rather, that those other speakers themselves receive these phrases, and the attitudes they connote, from a system larger than they are, one that can do us harm.

Almost as much as she likes implicit quotations, Armantrout likes oxymorons, couplets, or sentences that catch us in bad assumptions: "'Ha, ha, you missed me,' / a dead person says" ("Home Federal"); "Moments later / archeologists found him" ("Covers"). Archaeologists find people "moments later" all the time (when, for example, their children get lost in crowds), but it's hardly in their line of work, which involves finding things, and people, centuries or millennia after their loss. Armantrout's lines imply a puzzle or paradox, one we must overrule our expectations to process. Category mistakes, bad puns, cartoonish coincidences—these spark poems, too, because they let Armantrout suggest that all symbols are as arbitrary or unreliable as those the mistakes expose. In this vertiginous mode, Armantrout can sound less like other "Language writers" than like an improbably terse stand-up comic:

I made only one statement
because of a bad winter.

Grease is the word; grease
is the way

I am feeling.
Real life emergencies or

flubbing behind the scenes.

As a child,
I was abandoned

in a story
made of trees.

The poet-critics Steve Evans and Jennifer Moxley joke that Armantrout keeps getting labeled "the 'lyrical' language poet"; Armantrout
herself has shown a weighty ambivalence about "lyric" as a term for
her work. If a lyric poem is a short work whose form embodies a single
consciousness, then it's hard not to think of her work as lyric. Yet
she seems to pry open or disassemble the coherent self and consistent
voice on which most versions of "lyric" depend. "Statement" equates
Armantrout's "given name" with the tags she gets at a hospital, or
from a child—"Thirty-One Year Old / Prima-Gravida, // The Pokey-
Puppy." Our sense of self comes (it implies) not from any reliable voice
or consistent being-in-the-world, but from slippery guesses and temporary hypotheses. "Identity is a form / of prayer" she conjectures in
a poem called "My Associates." Armantrout sometimes finds a coherent "I" or a reliable "you" as hard to credit as a beneficent deity. The
same poem continues:

"How do I look?"

meaning what
could I pass for

where every eye's
a guard.

"I think that if I didn't 'write against norms,'" Armantrout says in one interview, "I wouldn't be writing." Her self-making (not only in her poems but also on the evidence of her autobiography) has been a series of resistances to easier, less guarded versions of world and self. Interiority, for her, consists in a demonstrated capacity to interrogate the images the culture throws at us, the images we discover—to our distaste or surprise—inside ourselves, too. In *True,* Armantrout recalls taking LSD and discovering her own distinctive persona, a psyche distinguished at its core by its mistrust of discoveries, distinctions, cores:

> I clearly saw that most of what I called "me" was a system of defensive barricades (the sort of "tough-mindedness" and macho posturing I'd attributed to my old heroes . . .) and that what was "inside" them was what?—shame? fear? my mother and father? This was a premature encounter with "deconstruction," I think, but one which I almost immediately began to find interesting. . . . In retrospect, I think that I did have a "real" self, of a sort. I was the person who would think such an experience was interesting and would want to do it again. I was also the one who couldn't stop trying to talk about it.

That ambivalence about "a 'real' self" (not a denial but an ambivalence) gives her works much of their oddity. Armantrout likes to watch—and resist—the way her conscious mind and her ingrained tastes segment a chaotic and potentially continuous world into discrete parts. ("I too / am a segmentalist," a recent poem admits.) She notices, and objects to, the almost involuntary force with which she gives almost all her poems closure: even when they involve quasi-independent sections, they end with the finality of a slammed car door.

Some of those closures come through accounts of dreams. "A real dream," Armantrout writes in "Birthmark: The Pretext," becomes "interesting . . . to the extent that there is a stranger in my head arranging things for me." The poet in "The Plot" "can't get to sleep" because her temperament prevents her; she remains "conscious of the metaphoric / contraption." Descent into sleep is for Armantrout a surrender to the cultural unconscious; though the realm of dreams may feel like a foreign country, its language and assumptions turn out to be those by which Americans live, rendered bizarre because newly exposed. "The Plot" concludes:

> Why is sleep's border guarded?
> On the monitors
> professional false selves
> make self-disparaging remarks.
> There's a sexy bored housewife,
> very Natalie Wood-like,
> sighing, "Men should win"—
> but the only thing that matters
> is the pace of substitution.
> You feel like trying to escape
> from her straight-arrow husband
> and her biker boyfriend
>
> You can't believe
> you're on Penelope's Secret.
> A suitor waits
> for ages
> to be hypnotized
> on stage.

What sort of world is this, in which everyone stands around like a TV host, or like an actor in an old film? It is the world of sleep, where America's mythopoetic icons return to Armantrout in dreams. This dreamscape (driven by what she calls "substitution"—what Freud called "condensation and displacement") turns American women into Penelopes, each forever waiting for her man, and American men into self-deceived Homeric suitors, doomed if Daddy ever comes home.

Armantrout's ideas, and her odd, brusque sounds, can make it harder to notice her other talents, and in particular her keen eye. Her lines slow perception into separable units, like frames of a film; in doing so, they can scrutinize and demystify it, or render it newly vivid. "Leaving" explores the Pacific coast using techniques that A. R. Ammons might have recognized:

> With waves
> shine slides over
> shine like skin's
> what sections
> same from same.

In the best of the academic pieces in *A Wild Salience,* Bob Perelman identifies Armantrout's roots in imagism: her poems at once depict objects, as accurately as they can, and show how any depictions rely on the assumptions (never neutral, never fully self-justifying) we bring. "Disown" quotes such assumptions, then trashes them in order to see old suburbs anew:

> "Run down," they say,
> "buildings."
>
> Wave of morning glory
> leaves about to break
> over the dropped plastic
> bat, the empty shed.

Williams's fans may notice the break on "break"; they may notice, too, how Armantrout's terse revaluation of urban disarray derives from the earlier poet's championing of sheds, stoops, bits of green glass glimpsed in the street.

George Lakoff and other cognitive scientists have proposed that our daily thoughts and decisions depend (as Mark Turner put it) on "small spatial stories": we *make room* in schedules, let people *into* our lives, *move up* in the workplace. At least since *Engines* (1983), her prose collaboration with Ron Silliman, Armantrout has liked to literalize and exaggerate these metaphors: "To understand is to 'follow'" *(Engines)*; "Bird calls rise / and drop / to an unseen floor" ("Theories"). What if these "small spatial stories" prove as deceptive as the Home Shopping Network? "When I'm metaphorical / I'm happy," Armantrout says in "Ongoing," though she knows she of all people cannot stay happy that way. "Metaphor should make us suspicious," Armantrout tells Hejinian, "but we can't do without it." Nor can Armatrout do without dramatizing her suspicions. Often she juxtaposes symbols high and low, respected, trashy, or trivial, in order to show that all of them work the same way. In "Here," she writes: "It's supposed to be beautiful / to repeat a motif / in another medium," so Armantrout repeats a motif in which percussion represents strength:

> There's a boy down the street,
> firing caps
> as my son did
>
> while a church plays
> its booming
> recording of chimes.

The boy's spontaneous play repeats the action of earlier, older boys; the church's "booming / recording" strikes an atheistic listener as both boastful and doubly fake—not just a false God, but false bells to boot, no better than the "[b]ig masculine threat" (to quote an earlier poem) of the boy's cap gun.

Those sardonic (and partly spondaic) lines about booms and bangs should also call attention to Armantrout's ear. Her irregular, two-to-four-beat lines and stanzas not only match the intellectual processes she describes (doubt, disbelief, resentful or respectful endurance), but also match the rhythms of that process (two steps forward and three steps back; denial, consideration, belief, denial). In "Sets," an elegant, arc-shaped stanza follows "Time's tic: / to pitch forward / then catch 'itself' / again." These successive approximations of fictions are for Armantrout the only way by which we perceive anything. Even those perceptions become suspect for Armantrout (in an odd echo of Henri Bergson) because they will always involve metaphor—forward and back (which turn time into space), "pitch" and "catch" (which invoke gymnastics or baseball).

Armantrout's jagged lines, always ready to switch from one idea back to the next, also let her juxtapose treatments and figures other poets would have to handle separately. The title poem in *Necromance*

(1991) considers a woman in a mysterious "land" (perhaps California) who "washed / dishes in a black liquid / with islands of froth— / and sang." Many poets could portray a beleaguered housewife, an oil spill, the land of the dead, or a Homeric siren: Armantrout's trick is to do all four at once. In doing so she also asks how much her word choice, our word choice, creates the events and reactions we try to interpret. Even looking and naming seem to her dangerous: the names we give to things and roles and people allow those things and people to be controlled, to take their places in markets and other systems of (conscious or unconscious) exploitation. (Later in that poem "precision / is revealed as / hostility.") The poem feels, by the end, like a defense of the sirens, as if they had developed their fatal singing out of a justified annoyance at sailors who, whenever a ship passed, whistled and stared.

Necromance also highlights Armantrout's terse but unmistakable feminism, which during the 1980s led her to scrutinize and disassemble beauty and femininity. Armantrout's focus on gender, and her drive to demystify, also led her poems to highlight so-called women's work; "Articulation," for example, announces:

> The one making coffee
> or doing the driving—
>
> that is the real
> person in your life.
> Now that one is gone
>
> or has tagged along with you
> like a small child
> behind Mother.

For a supposedly abstract (and a genuinely difficult) poet, Armantrout has quite a lot to say about motherhood, both (in Adrienne Rich's division) as an experience and as an institution. "Crossing" considers the assumptions ancient myths and children's games might share:

> According to legend
> Mom

sustains the universe
by yelling
"Stay there
where it's safe"
when every star
wants to run home
to her.

What does this unsentimental analogy say about "primitive" peoples? about mothers? about our reliance on other, supposedly grown-up leaders? "Getting Warm" could not exist without Armantrout's feminism, nor without her years of child rearing; the poem compares her own poetics to primary language acquisition:

If she's quiet
she's concentrating on the spaces
between cries, turning
times into spaces.
. . . .
She is in the dark,
sewing, stringing holes together
with invisible thread.
That's a feminine accomplishment:
a feat of memory, a managed
repletion or resplendence.

"She" may well be a baby, or a poet (writing Armantrout's sort of verse), or anyone (especially any woman) performing a demanding, "invisible" task.

Armantrout has lately become less interested in debunking per se, and more interested in embodiment, memory, and time—though these are changes in emphasis and degree, visible only on repeated rereadings of her recent work. The end-stopped couplets of "Manufacturing" dissect and examine visual experience, comparing its snapshot moments to the uneasy ongoingness of thought, hearing, and recollection:

The eye asks if the green,

frilled geranium puckers,
clustered at angles

on each stem,
are similar enough

to stop time.

It has asked this question already.

How much present tense
can any resemblance make?

Most of her poems after 1989 include at least one of these key words: *parent/mother/mommy*, *memory/remember/recall*, *repetition/ repeat/recur*, *nostalgia*, *person*, *self*. The words, and the topics they represent, interact: as we grow up, we learn (if we can) to depend on memories of our own experiences, rather than reacting against our parents' experiences. At the same time, our visions of parenthood and childhood change, especially if we become parents ourselves. In "Native" (also a poem about the suburbs), Armantrout notices these processes in her own life and asks (with a chilly pun on "dead") where it ends:

At what point does
dead reckoning's

net
replace the nest

and the body
of a parent?

To enjoy Armantrout one has to like her choppy surfaces, accede to her demands that we read slowly, and appreciate her overarching worries about figuration, mediation, symbolism in general. At the same time, Armantrout's poems offer psychological truths and sad ironies wholly separable from her commitment to difficulty and disjunction. Ever been part of a couple who felt like this?

Each finds
his mate pre-

dictable

but believes his own
rigidity

must excite
his partner

Note the pun on "rigidity"; note, too, the abnormally rapid, short (even for Armantrout) lines—as if she knows we've been there, too. Her recent poems seem more willing than the rest to let in such clear psychological language, perhaps because they are less angry and more sad, less aware of injustice than of loss. ("From the first / abstraction," the last poem in *Veil* [2002] has it, "loss / is edible.") Poems about Armantrout's dying mother make isolated images yield clear, almost Larkinesque ironies:

"Schools of fish are trapped
In these pools,"
Say the anchors

Who hang
On nursing home walls.

Armantrout's poetry of retrospect, cast back over her own life and career, can be even sadder, and clearer. "Our Nature" rebukes

our self-consciousness
which was really

our infatuation
with our own fame . . .

our loyalty
to our old gang

from among whom
it was our nature

to be singled out

Although lines like those will gather new admirers with wider exposure, most of Armantrout's poetry is not for everyone: it's usually
dissonant; almost never mellifluous, unambiguous, or strongly narrative. The sounds and tones of its stanzas are memorably crafted, but
its large-scale arrangements can seem opaque: it can be hard to know
why four segments, say, of a thirty-two-line poem require the order
they have and not another. Armantrout's current influence on younger
poets grows in part from her merits, and in part from their disillusion-
ment with other available models (other "Language writers" included).
It grows, too, from the timeliness of her obsessions: Armantrout has become the poet of our contemporary frustration with what we might call
the social construction of everything. After Darwin, Freud, Gombrich,
Derrida, Foucault, Bourdieu, Diebold, and the past few wars, we know
how little we can be authors of ourselves, how much we act in scripts
we cannot write (let alone direct). That feeling of helplessness may not
be new (it's arguably in Homer), but our constant consciousness of it is;
so, perhaps, is our awareness that the scripts we live out have no cosmic authority, reflect no god we have not made.

"An objection / so pervasive," Armantrout says in "Light," "cannot
know its enemy." We could pose the same objection to her: does she
really want to live without symbol systems? To this her poems reply:
do you really want to keep trusting the symbols you see? If we cannot be authors of ourselves, Armantrout's harsh, funny, self-conscious
poems suggest, we can be our own demanding critics, seeking closer
accounts of whatever we've done. Few readers—few poets—feel as
strongly as Armantrout the relentlessness of our given scripts; few resent them as productively as she does. Her best poems' titles recap her
obsessions: in *Veil* those poems include "Double," "Through Walls,"
all the selections from *Necromance,* "Covers," "A Pulse," "Leaving,"

"Greeting," "Birthmark: The Pretext," "Articulation," "About," "Here," "Theories," "Whole," "Our Nature," and "Manufacturing." It may be objected against them all that if nothing can be done about symbol systems in general, if we are doomed to live amid them, we might as well learn to like them, rather than constantly try to pry them open or to investigate their wiring. It would be just as pointless to object, against Gerard Manley Hopkins or Wallace Stevens, that we can do nothing about growing old.

Lightsource, Aperture, Face

C. D. Wright and Photography

C. D. Wright's poems compare themselves to many things, and to many works of art: they take forms from high school yearbooks ("Autographs"), procedures from silent films ("Treatment"), or titles from famous jazz albums ("More Blues and the Abstract Truth"). Most often and most insistently, however, her poems invoke and liken themselves to photographs, and to the work photographers do. Many poems reflect collaboration with a particular photographer, Deborah Luster, whom Wright first met in the 1970s at the University of Arkansas in Fayetteville. "We fall in and out of step with each other's projects without much inducement," Wright says of Luster: "We spring from the same hills and hardwoods." All three of Wright's book-length poems—*Just Whistle: A Valentine* (1993), *Deepstep Come Shining* (1998), and *One Big Self* (2004)—grew out of her work with Luster, whose photographs appear in the first and third, and on the cover of the second.

Although some of Wright's work fits familiar poetic genres (love lyric, ode), much of it matches, instead, kinds of photography. *Just Whistle* organized itself around nudes; *Deepstep*, around landscapes and documentary work; *One Big Self*, around the portrait. All these books—*One Big Self* most of all—place their photographic language at the service of literary and ethical goals. For Roland Barthes, "Every photograph is a certificate of presence," of the presence of a person; Barthes found in the photograph "the absolute Particular," "the *This* . . . the Occasion, the Encounter, the Real," although he also saw in each photo a memento mori. Wright describes apertures, lenses, frames, light levels, and sight lines; lists facts; and presents poetic lines as if they were photographic captions, in order to evoke the presence of the real persons whom she wants her work to acknowledge. To see how Wright uses photography is not just to see her poetic goals; it is also to see how her style—at once "experimental" and earnest, disjunctive in its assemblages and realist in its attitudes—realizes those goals, what she, and nobody else, has done with poems.

Almost all of Wright's prose about photography also describes her hopes for her own writings. "The goal is to see better not just to do it better," Wright told Bob Holman in a recent interview. "My eye is what I work off . . . working with a photographer, spending time looking has changed my orientation. I look for the line of the eye." Wright's mostly prose collection *Cooling Time* (2005) praises Luster, who "can . . . render the map in the back roads of a face nailbright"; *Cooling Time* also lauds Sally Mann, who "sees the cleavage in the ground; she sees the writing in the trees; she sees the light in the blackwater, the trunk leaking, the columns disappearing." Wright construes both photographers' work as seeing, and as discovering metaphors (or metalepses): script in foliage, streaming water in tree bark, or a map in the roads of a face.

Other poems name photographers' techniques. The prose lyric "Dearly Belated" instructs a young poet: "Take a wide-angled pan of the fields. Not [sic] lift your arm to shield the light. . . . Then zoom." *Deepstep* includes—more than once—the etymology of "photograph," Greek for "light writing": "A photograph is a writing of the light. *Photo Graphein*"; "*Photo graphein* of an old plaid couch in a field." Wright, too, the repetition suggests, is making a special and luminous kind of writing, one distinguished from other kinds of text inasmuch as it resembles (and raises the same aesthetic problems as) photographs. "What No One Could Have Told Them" catalogs or captions images from the life of Wright's son ("How the bowl of Quick Quaker Oats fits his head"): two follow-up poems, "Detail from What

No One Could Have Told Them" and "Additional Detail," focus on single images from "What No One . . . ," much as photographic enlargements would. Even scenes in Wright's poems that make no use of technical terms or approaches from photography often emphasize such photographic matters as angles of view, light sources (one or many?), light-dark contrasts (sharp or diffuse?), shadow, and hue. Consider the couple depicted in "Humidity": "They are at a point in space," she writes, "where animate dark meets inanimate darkness," and only "Flares from refineries ignite their faces. / There are no houses no trees . . . / Pods of satellite dishes" (as if seen through the windshield) "focus on an unstable sky."

Wright's poems often deploy photographic language in order to show by analogy what she wants her poems to do. *Tremble* (1996), Wright's most self-consciously lyrical book, begins with a poem whose title, "Floating Trees," might describe several of Sally Mann's photographs, though in fact Wright "took it from another photographer's exhibition." Although the poem's title suggests landscape, its opening lines instead show a domestic interior: "a bed is left open to a mirror / a mirror gazes long and hard at a bed // light fingers the house with its own acoustics." Another poem from *Tremble* bears the title "The Iris Admits the Light the Iris Will Allow." Both poetry's work and the camera's work, for Wright, imitate and enhance the work of a human eye.

To make familiar in her poems the work of a camera is also to make odd the work of an eye. A passage from *Deepstep Come Shining*, for example, describes recovery from an eye operation (a treatment for glaucoma). Wright upends the cliché in which photographers make the camera their eye; instead, the postsurgical eye is a strikingly unfamiliar sort of camera, one whose registries of light and dark the patient must learn to connect to the world she has known:

After the iridectomy
the slow recognition of forms

A shirt on the floor looked like
the mouth of a well

Spots on a horse
horrible holes in its side

The sun in the tree
green hill of crystals

To see the world metaphorically—as this patient has—is like looking at photographs, and it is like being a photographer, too: it is, finally, like being the sort of poet Wright's stanzas tell us that she is. "The eye is a mere mechanical instrument," *Deepstep* complains, as if trying to prove itself untrue, or to prove that the eye, like the camera, works in all sorts of good and bad ways depending on how we learn to see, on how the machine is used. (The chemical compound silver nitrate, essential in photographic film, is—*Deepstep* points out—both "poisonous" and useful in medicine.)

Seeing in Wright's way, seeing what Wright's lens can show, seeing photographs as Wright can see them, is like making a vow, and like touching a person. "A Series of Actions" (whose title might describe a Muybridge portfolio) ends with a four-way analogy among an opening door, a lens, an eye, and a hand, juxtapositions familiar from Herbert Bayer's much-reproduced surrealist photograph, which the closing lines evoke: "Light inside the space // The door opening as the palm / of an eye." Wright sees hands in eyes, and intimacy in hands, again in "Rosesucker Retablo #1" (a poetic response to one of Luster's photographs): "As you enter the eye   in this palm / Chuparosa   bind me   to your secrecy." "Because Fulfillment Awaits" uses the technical terminology of photographs to laud the visible spirit of the human being, or beings, which stand behind the poems: "Even in touching retouching / steeped in words," she cautions, "one tends to forget   one forgets / the face   the human face," even as "One wants / to create a bright new past   One creates it." Here we see a poet's worries about the revisions almost all poets undertake. To retouch a photograph is to alter the print, to make it something more or less than a record of appearances. Wright warns herself and her readers not to "forget" the human face a portrait, or a poem, may call to mind. At the same time she implies that the right "retouching"—like the right "touching," the right kind of physical contact—can so alter a person's consciousness as to change her sense of her own past.

Both text and pictures in Wright and Luster's first collaboration, *Just Whistle,* take as their point of departure the photographic nude. "I wrote a long twisted erotic poem and [Luster] was trying out some toxic French technique . . . and we put that together," Wright recalls. Luster treated her prints of women's bodies and body parts with a bleaching process called *mordançage,* whose "negative/positive reversal," Luster wrote, creates a "penetration zone," an "edge of line and relief." The results appear intimate and mysterious, blurred and altered: "Along these edges the bodies are gnawed and wounded; parts of arms, legs, hair are eroded and fall away into the surrounding space. The bodies, due to chemical reaction and physical rubbing, lie in wracked relief." Wright's chiasmus rearranges Luster's words: "THEY SLEEP // with tenderness, wracked . . . wracked / with tenderness."

Photographs "of nude bodies within a private space," the art historian Graham Clarke writes, have frequently relied on "female stereotypes in relation to male fantasy and expectation," making women's bodies "a sealed world open to the power of the male gaze." The bodies in *Just Whistle,* however, become not transparently knowable objects for a male gaze but unstable experiences seeking ways to understand themselves. Wright begins with "The body, alive, not dead but dormant"; two pages later, "The pantied one said nothing, not even its own newly enlivened name, its own naked name, the memory fulgurant, sheet lightning of other bodies." The paired men and women (could some be women and women?) find themselves in familiar bedrooms (or bathrooms) that Wright makes strange by withholding names and details, much as Luster's treated nudes withhold the clear lines (and story lines) other nudes might convey: "The one watching the other one a long time before it got up, the one shoving a pillow under the plums of the other, the one not removing the panties even *in situ.*"

Nor are Luster's the only sexually charged photographs to which Wright refers. Wright's poem "Book Titled *The Ballad of Sexual Dependency* Found in the Hydrangea in front of Zorabedian's Stone" speculates about a "photograph ripped out" from the volume she found:

> Odds are a thousand-odd to one
> the absent photo   was a crow shot
>
> O the ballad of sexual dependency
> is very old and intensely sad

Nan Goldin's famous 1986 collection, *The Ballad of Sexual Dependency*, portrays her friends, acquaintances, and sexual partners from East Coast art, punk, and drag scenes. Wright's book is also a sort of ballad, a partly songlike, partly narrative poem, about sexual oddity and sexual dependency; a crow, or a crowlike spirit, flies in and out of her text, a source of darkness analogous to Luster's *mordançage*. Wright returns to Goldin at the close of her volume: "bent to pluck the book of photographs, this ballad is known by all, crow shot ripped out of the middle, it is very old and intensely sad, the panties excoriating in their own precious time."

Against simpler, or more judgmental, ideas about the photographic nude, *Just Whistle* suggests that bodies, poems, and (the right sort of) erotic or nude photographs all emulate one another. Scopophilia, mystery, curiosity, and even discomfort are always already part of our sexual lives, and books, photographs, poems, and bodies may all provide an important opening to the right reader or viewer:

> The body would open its legs like a book
> letting the soft pencils of light
> fall on its pages, like doors
> into a hothouse, belladonna blooming there:
> it would open like a wine list, a mussel, wings
>
> . . . .
> The whole world would not be lost.

Such "openings" (almost always marked as female) recur throughout the book, as Wright likens the writer's eye, the vagina, the mouth (hence the speaking voice), a baby's first cry, the origin of the universe, and the "aperture" of a camera:

> aperture to the aleph, within which all, the overstocked pond, entrance to vast funnel of silence, howling os, an idea of beautiful form, original opening, whistling well, first vortex, an idea of form, a beautiful idea, a just idea of form, unplugged, reamed, scored, plundered, insubduable opening, lightsource, it opens. This changes everything.

The apostrophe, "the figure of voice, the sign of utterance" from which (in Jonathan Culler's account) lyric itself has grown, the "O" through which poems acknowledge human persons, prompts analogies at once to women's generative powers, and to the light-accepting "eye" of a camera. That eye does not, however, see things objectively, but rather "scored," marked by the consciousness that takes, and perhaps alters, the picture. And the "O" of the lens, the vagina, the poetic apostrophe, and the origin of the universe also becomes the "O" a mouth makes in signaling a companion—hence Wright's title: *Just Whistle: A Valentine.*

Deepstep Come Shining relies on documentary almost as much as *Just Whistle* relies on the nude. *Deepstep* grew from an automobile journey through rural Georgia that Wright and Luster took in the mid-1990s; the book includes no photographs except the cover. (The book shares its title with Luster's exhibit *Come Shining.*) Wright opens her poem by evoking the car, the road, and the photographer's way of seeing, with its attention to composition and light levels: "Beyond the windshield the land claims saturate levels of green. Illuminating figures and objects. Astonishing our earthliness. I was there. I know." In evoking the photographer's look at the landscape, Wright also attacks American blindness to the fate of the poor, to disabled veterans, to other troubled groups: "The baby sister of the color photographer had a baby girl in the hills. Born with scooped-out sockets in the head. Born near the tracks they sprayed with Agent Orange. The railroad's denials, ditto the army's." Such iterated sentences or sentence fragments suggest captions for photographs: sister, girl, hills, sockets, tracks, institutional desk, and typewriter or pen.

Deepstep (like *Tremble*) sets scenes as if they were photographs, balancing objects with people, light with dark, with special attention to mirrors and sightlines. Consider this descriptive paragraph (framed, as a photograph might be, by a white page):

> In the ceaselessly decomposing smoke of a pool hall. Seven green tables are racked under seven naked bulbs. The jukebox in the din calls the man a blanketyblankblank. If not the exact words the exact tenor. The plate glass casts glimpses of everything that has ever happened. The genesis of direction breaks and scatters.

Other similarly laid-out paragraphs also note luminance, outlines, and silhouettes: "Private-party love. By one sixty-watt bulb. And it be blue. The cool produces an halation . . . Some modeling on the side of the face. When directly below the bulb."

To think of documentary photography, the American South, and American writing together is to invoke James Agee and Walker Evans's *Let Us Now Praise Famous Men* (1941), still the best-known such juxtaposition. "The photographs . . . and the text," Agee and Evans's much-quoted preface asserts, "are coequal, mutually independent, and fully collaborative." *Deepstep* both names and quotes Agee ("the swerve of smalltown eyes"). So does *Cooling Time:* "What of what Agee named 'the sorrow, the effort and the ugliness of the beautiful world'?" Agee thought photography superior to writing in that photographs, unlike writing, constitute experience, embodiment, evidence. "Words cannot embody; they can only describe," Agee declared. "But a certain kind of artist, whom we will distinguish from others as a poet rather than a prose writer, despises this fact about words or his medium, and continually brings words as near as he can to an illusion of embodiment."

For Agee any writing that seeks to manifest persons, to respect and to reproduce their presences, approaches the condition of poetry. Yet poetry, inasmuch as it adopts those goals, must approach (or envy) the condition of nonverbal arts, and especially of photography. "If I could do it," Agee mused, "I'd do no writing at all here. It would be photographs; the rest would be fragments of cloth, bits of cotton, lumps of earth, records of speech. . . . A piece of the body torn out by the roots might be more to the point." The Wright of *Deepstep* articulates (and avers, like Agee, that she cannot quite satisfy) testimonial hopes much like Agee's own: "In the hopeless objective of receiving the marvels that come to one by sight, sound and touch, merely in order."

Blind people and damaged eyes, including the blinding in *Lear,* are motifs throughout *Deepstep:* "Once the eye is enucleated. Would you replace it with wood, ivory, bone, shell or a precious stone. . . . So Gloucester had to smell his way to Dover." Geoff Dyer begins *The Ongoing Moment,* his eloquent book about art photography, by discussing pictures of blind people: "The blind subject is the objective correlative of the photographer's longed-for invisibility." Blind subjects, he argues, let art photographers, from Paul Strand to Garry Winogrand, ask how a camera, a mechanical thing that only seems to see, can do justice to suffering human persons who may not (if they are blind, who cannot) see what we have made of them. For Wright these questions apply to literary art in general, even though a page is not (quite) a lens. Inasmuch as we overlook (for example) the Southern rural poor, we, too, have damaged or missing eyes, and the best replacements for damaged or missing eyes are not bones or stones but cameras, used in a particular way, and literary works that function like cameras: not to depict social problems in general but to illuminate particular persons, to make them present to us.

Deepstep moves from exteriors to interiors, from landscapes to portraits, from the documentary or journalistic power of a photograph (showing us what we would not otherwise see) to its memorial or anamnesic powers (preventing the living from forgetting the dead). "Remember me to all of them," says somebody in Wright's poem: "Bite everybody on the lips for me." The people in *Deepstep* often want their portraits made, their presences recorded: "Patty lives here. She's one of the Jumping Foxes, the Double-Dutch Champs. Can you take her picture while we're here." These poems-as-pictures tell us that they can look back at us even when their subjects cannot see: "Blur in. Blur out. Just a hypothetical blind woman brought out of completest dark.

Looking at a face." Wright accepts "the commission to be a friend / to the lost people," adding, "I want to / magnify."

Here the photographic genre is not only documentary but also portraiture: the ethical imperatives behind certain kinds of portraiture give Wright her ethical charge. When Wright gives a mission, or "commission," for photography in general, often she seems to have faces and portraits in mind. Wright's catalog essay for *Come Shining* emphasizes Luster's portraits:

> Most of the time she photographs lives unattributed, mixed in with artist friends and photo-willing kin; otherwise, the unattributed . . . photographed only for purposes of identification: driver's license, mug shot, open coffin. Some without a graduation or wedding picture to their credit. People get sidelined. Her photographs tell you this is an occasion, *their* occasion. And the occasion adds significance. Most subjects will rise.

Both *Come Shining* (the exhibit and its associated booklet) and *Deepstep Come Shining* (the book of Wright's poetry) derive their title from Bob Dylan's 1967 song "I Shall Be Released"; *Deepstep* quotes the song. "I see my light come shining / From the west unto the east," Dylan sings; "Any day now, any day now / I shall be released." For Wright and Luster, the project of portrait photography, of turning light on chemically treated paper into representations of people and places, becomes a project of releasing people from bondage. It should be no surprise, then, that Wright's essay concentrates on Luster's portraits of prisoners. She regrets that prison rules prevent these subjects from experiencing the full dignity, and the literal weight, that their portraits ought to bear:

> Nor will the prisoners likely see themselves on metal plates—but only on photographic paper, as is permitted them—and might therefore never fully grasp that these portraits are intended as keepsakes, that they be not 'buked and scorned and forgotten, but cherished and remembered. Living men and living women in natural light. We are still one; one of a kind.

One Big Self: Prisoners of Louisiana marks Wright and Luster's most ambitious collaboration. The large volume collects Luster's photographs of prisoners in three Louisiana correctional institutions. With them (but on separate pages) come Wright's prose and verse inspired by the photographs, by the interviews that accompanied their taking, and by Wright and Luster's Louisiana travels. Luster's mother was murdered in 1988, and Luster testified at the killer's trial: that experience shadows these portrayals. Most of the volume, however, concerns the claim each prisoner has on our attention, not as a convict, but as a human being. The epigraph and title come from film director Terence Malick: "Maybe all men got one big soul where everybody's a part of—all faces of the same man: one big self." Both Wright and Luster use the tools and terms special to photography to manifest such claims.

Photography and prisons share a history, one not altogether benign. The bibliography appended to *One Big Self* includes Michel Foucault's *Discipline and Punish* and Suren Lalvani's zealously Foucauldian study, *Photography, Vision, and the Production of Modern Bodies*. For Lalvani, camera work as such contributes to "the disciplinary apparatus of capitalist production" that Foucault saw, in microcosm, in modern prisons. In nineteenth-century portraits, Lalvani suggests, "lurks the discursive regime of the dominant culture they inhabit; power emanates from a unified, determinate space—the privileged site in front of the camera." Prisons are like photographs, and photographers are like wardens: "prison architecture is . . . first and foremost a luminous form, a place of visibility that distributes the visible and invisible."

One Big Self acknowledges the classifying, disciplinary work done by much photographic depiction: "My mug shot totally turned me against being photographed," an inmate says. Yet for Wright, as for Luster, the photograph need not discipline, nor need it serve bourgeois privilege. In these photographs, prisoners can imagine what it would be like to control their own bodies, to choose what face they show the world. Luster depicts the prisoners, never the prison; portraits have no backdrops or settings, just costumes and props. Inmates wear Carnival hats, step back from the camera, pose in pairs, hold boards or signs ("missing you"), scowl, smile, or flaunt tattoos. Some wear masks, turn their backs, or show arms and hands rather than heads. Pamela Winfield poses in her full-body Easter Bunny costume, worn for Children's Visiting Day. Johnny "Ray Boy" Madison had Luster photograph a model ship he built from matchsticks rather than photograph the man himself.

"I chose to photograph each person as they presented their very own selves before my camera," Luster writes; "I wanted this to be as collaborative an enterprise as possible." Wright describes watching prisoners prepare to be photographed, recording Luster's (at least partial) success: "The women pass around a handmirror and a tube of lipstick . . . They pass a stuffed bunny from hand to hand / for their turn in front of the camera." When Luster sets up her equipment, Wright notes elsewhere, "the inmates . . . swarm the improvised studio as if she were bringing ice to Macondo." Wright sets these largely welcome portraits beside the other images of themselves to which prisoners commonly have access: "Your only mirror is one of stainless steel. The image it affords will not tell whether you are young still or even real." "The act of photographing and returning prints to these incarcerated persons" became, Luster says, "as important to this project . . . as any formal exhibition or publication." Yet Luster also kept other viewers in mind: "I wanted the portraits to be as direct a telling as possible—to hold up a mirror for the viewer as well as for the subject."

One Big Self, in other words, tries to assemble a sort of antipanopticon, with many views of many people, but no center, and no way to see them all at once. Wright's verbal choices serve that end as much as Luster's visual ones do: both sets of choices rely in turn on other choices (visual and verbal, in speech and appearance) that appear as the prisoners' own. Even more than Wright's other books, *One Big Self* relies on the play of diction, on contrasts among registers of language, to provide its verbal music. These contrasts also keep at the forefront of the poem the questions about portrayer and portrayed, about subjects and subjection, which come up in documentary photography: Can the poem speak for, rather than just about, its prisoners? How can it let the prisoners speak for themselves? Frequently curt or jarring, in lists or short fragments, Wright's juxtapositions amplify the loneliness and the energy the quotations evince to begin with: "I miss the moon. /

I miss silverware, with a knife. / and maybe even something to cut with it." This inmate seems so hungry for freedom that he or she feels ready to eat the night sky.

As much as she tries to find rhythms for such feelings, Wright also tugs at the limits of identification, asking how much readers who have never been incarcerated can really know or understand how an inmate feels: "If I were you: / Screw up today, and it's solitary, Sister woman, the padded dress with the food log to gnaw upon . . . I don't have a clue, do I." Wright finds the prisoners' Big Selves, their revealed characters (as against their marked and damaged bodies), sometimes hard to see:

Difficult to look at the woman

much less photograph   and not ask
about a scar that runs from one ear
        to the opposing breast

        whose babies died of smoke inhalation

Or the gasoline-wrecked face
of the green-eyed black man

Wright's dislocated grammar, and her jarring metonym ("breast / whose babies"), imply the difficulty a photographer might have in shifting from subject to subject, portrait to portrait, when each brings his or her own disturbing story.

One Big Self also uses all Wright learned from Agee. Her poem, like his prose, finds bitter irony and high lyricism in long catalogs or *catenas* (chains of nouns). One list from *Let Us Now Praise Famous Men* gives the contents of a smokehouse:

four hoes; a set of sweeps; a broken plow-frame; pieces of an ice-cream freezer; a can of rusty nails; a number of mule shoes; the strap of a white slipper; a pair of greenly eaten, crumpled work-shoes, the uppers broken away, the soles worn broadly through, still carrying the odor of feet; a blue coil of soft iron wire; a few yards of rusted barbed wire; a rotted mule-collar; pieces of wire at random.

Wright has used such authenticating lists in her shorter poems (for example, in the page-long middle stanza from "King's Daughters, Home for Unwed Mothers, 1948"). *One Big Self* rises to new heights of listing, finds new ways to list, and even turns lists into mantras:

> in lockdown, you will relinquish your things:
> plastic soapdish, jar of vaseline, comb or hairpick, paperback
> Upon return to your unit the inventory officer
> will return your things:
> soapdish, vaseline, comb, hairpick, paperback
> Upon release you may have your possessions:
> soapdish, vaseline, comb, pick, book
> Whereupon your True Happiness can begin

Longer lists reflect prisoners' need to fill time (as well as their medical troubles):

> Count your grey hairs
>
> Count your chigger bites
>
> Count your pills
>
> Count the times the phone rings
>
> Count your T cells
>
> Count your mosquito bites . . .
>
> Count the flies you killed before noon

Others lists try to document emotions, much as sets of photographs document things: "the perpetually pissed-off ones who just wanted to hurt somebody, the incipiently pissed who had to be roused with a broom, the well-meaners who tried to help, the feckless risks, the nearly helpful teacher, the failures that can be achieved without trying, the sick bosses, the wrong beds with the wrong ones." Wright also lists types of fingerprints, as if to reclaim this particular human variation from the police and detectives who first made use of it: "you've got your plain loops, plain arches, tented arches, twin loops, lateral pocket loops, central pocket loops, whorls and your accidentals."

Still more important than fingers, costumes, props, or numbers, for Wright, as for Luster, are the prisoners' faces. *One Big Self* plays repeatedly on the word "face"; inmates' faces, like any faces, command human respect, and Luster as a photographer seeks to offer it. "Face" in prison lingo, however, also means a hardened attitude, one appropriate to life inside: "Drawn on a wall in solitary by a young one / MOM LOVE GOD / *before he had a face on him.*" "They keep the young ones in Eagle" (one wing of the maximum-security prison Angola) *"until they get a face on them."* To "get a face" in prison is to acclimate oneself to its rigidities, but it is also to learn the rules of a community, to become visible as a participant (rather than simply as an object of concern): "Got a face on you. / Not a part of, apart from. / Cropped out of the picture." "She was only 28 / cropped out of the picture / I know Nolan's daddy died of rabbit fever / *before he had a face on him.*" Wright herself adds that "get a face" means "until they grew into manhood and so were less vulnerable-looking," "looking mature enough . . . to stand on their own." Such claims even call to mind the philosopher Emmanuel Levinas, for whom "the meaningfulness of the face is the command to responsibility": "Seeing the face of the other," Levinas explains, "means that I approach the other so that his face acquires meaning for me." If Luster's pictures let inmates make and show faces, or even save face, Wright's poetic responses to those faces attribute voices to them, and match or respect those voices with her own speech.

"The peculiar boon of photography," Geoff Dyer writes, "is that the model is directly involved in the finished work of art—rather than in the process of its creation" in a way that painters' models (for example) are not. In this view photographers are not so much stealing souls or auras as making them evident, giving them back to their subjects, registering that even in death the soul cannot quite be taken away. Dyer even writes of "the simple message that is also there in all photographs," or at least all photographs of people: "'You are alive.'" Dyer expounds the optimistic view (it might be better to say the aspiration) about portrait photography that *One Big Self* appears to endorse—in its construction as a finished book and in the working methods Wright and Luster used; it is also the aspiration, or asymptote, to which *One Big Self* as a piece of writing aspires. Skeptics such as Lalvani still imply that photographic portraiture (whatever the photographer intends) finally numbs or regulates subjects and viewers. More optimistic viewers and practitioners believe that the right sort of portrait photography can (still) attest to subjects' indivisible human claims. "Good photography," Lucy Lippard avers, "can *embody* what has been seen. As I scrutinize it," she continues, a particularly generous image "becomes the people photographed—not 'flat death' as Roland Barthes would have it but flat life."

Such hopes go back to the origins of photography. The novelist and photographer Wright Morris described the cultural meaning of daguerreotypes: "The enthusiasm to take pictures was surpassed by the desire to be taken," and the resulting images still attest to human uniqueness and to human dignity: "There is no common or trivial portrait in this vast gallery. Nothing known to man spoke so eloquently of the equality of men and women. Nor has anything replaced it." Not only the portraits, but also the language Wright accords them, seek to reinstate such experiences of equality, such claims on behalf of all or any selves. "Every portrait could be titled *you*," Wright says. "The countenance directs the attention. . . . There is no negligible face, no negligible place." Luster places her subjects "in their finer, inner selves, where we are all enthroned." By printing the pictures on metal plates, Luster evokes not just the spirit but the physical feel of these earliest photographic portraits.

These ideals also bring us back to documentarians, to Agee and Evans and their 1930s colleagues. The "true meaning" of an Evans portrait, Agee writes, "is that [its subject] *exists,* in actual being, as you do and as I do, and as no character of the imagination can possibly exist. [The subject's] great weight mystery and dignity are in this fact." Agee and Evans thus announced their "effort to recognize the stature of a portion of unimagined existence," of "individual, anti-authoritative human consciousness," even of "human divinity." Susan Sontag considered Evans "the last great photographer to work seriously and assuredly in a mood deriving from Whitman's euphoric humanism"; his "message of identification with other Americans," she wrote in the mid-1970s, "is foreign to our temperament now." Both Luster and Wright strive to prove her wrong.

Barthes, Evans, Morris, Luster, and Wright all imagine as a goal for photography (or for one sort of photography) just what other thinkers posit as a goal for poetry (or for particular kinds of poetry). Allen Grossman (drawing on Levinas) writes that "poetic reading is a case of the inscription of the value of the person, a case of the construction of the countenance, the willing of the presence of a person": in poetry, "what is said is first of all the portrait of the other person present because of his or her speaking." Writing in 1957, Robert Langbaum gave almost the same mission not to poetry generally but to the dramatic monologue and to its modern descendants: "it is to establish the speaker's existence, not his moral worth but his sheer existence, as the one incontrovertible fact upon which the poem can rest . . . so that the speaker . . . *is* the poem." Even Lyn Hejinian—who rejects the idea of "an inner, fundamental, sincere, essential, irreducible, consistent self"—argues that "the idea of the person enters poetics where art and reality, or intentionality and circumstance, meet": "on the improvised boundary between art and reality . . . the person (or my person) in writing exists."

In other words: the goals some poets and critics attribute to poetry, to the dramatic monologue and its descendants, or to post-Romantic lyric, coincide with the goals some photographers, and some writers on photography, claim for photography. Wright not only calls to mind that coincidence but incorporates it into her poetic techniques. Her invocations of aperture, exposure, light levels; her compositions with mirrors and windows and doors; her descriptions of herself as a photographer's "factotum"; her Agee-esque lists; her vernacular quotations; her lines that double as captions, "details," and reflections; and her focus on faces, all try to make the experience of reading her poems resemble the experience of taking, and of viewing, photographs, especially portraits.

These resemblances help her poems manifest, and ask how those poems *can* manifest, the idiosyncrasies, the ethical claims, and the "faces" of individual persons. Wright's poems wish to be, to *persons in language,* as photographs are to *persons seen.* We might more simply say that Wright wants her poems to operate as she believes photographs ought to. The poems thus work toward the terms and conditions of life that Wright names near the end of *Cooling Time:* "We need to lower the veneration around the terms of communication . . . and aim to see better"; "the faces," she adds, "are . . . looking back at everyone out there, daring the viewer to see them now," to see in "no one a means," in "every one an end."

Wright's newest poems can find new ways to pursue this goal—and new ways in which photography can help her do so. The titular poem from Wright's most recent collection, "Rising Falling Hovering," responds to her recent travels in Mexico and to the current war in Iraq. The poem takes up the interest in portrait photography as a means of acknowledging human persons that we saw at the core of *One Big Self,* and the fragmentary documentary-travelogue mode Wright used in *Deepstep.* One structural aspect in "Rising" involves alternating depictions of young men who have died by violence (organized crime in Mexico, war in Iraq) with depictions of Wright's then-teenage son: both the dead young men and the poet's child appear as if in a series of photographs. In the homemade memorial to a dead man in Mexico City, we see "The slow open vulgar mouth drawing on a cigarette // In a face once called Forever Young // Now to be known as Never-a-Man." On Wright's return from Mexico to Rhode Island, she discovers—happily, but guiltily (since other mothers are losing their sons, their property, and their lives as the United States invades Iraq)—that "The glorious photographs of their [own] son were not stolen / from their second-hand frames."

Photography is both the method and the signal that all lives—especially, here, the lives of sons—ought to be cherished, and are cherished, whether or not their mothers can save them. And the likeness between poor Mexicans' image cherishing and bourgeois Americans' image cherishing, between the ways in which these different people treat similar (but never the same) photographs, helps Wright imagine how the "different world" of developing nations (whom Americans tend to ignore or to bomb) might be "rejoined" to ours. Late in "Rising" we return to the interest in blindness, in not-seeing, from *Deepstep,* and to

Wright's focus on the human face. The climactic scene in the poem depicts illegal immigrants, in pitch-dark night, trying to cross the U.S.–Mexico border. The literal darkness through which the immigrants must move, and the other tactics by which they must make themselves hard to see (and even harder to photograph), stand for the ways in which U.S. citizens find it almost impossible to "see," to acknowledge them, as full human persons. "Mira" (Spanish for "look"), Wright's poem, declares: "you will never see faces like this again."

Donald Revell

Dream Sermons

How much, in just twenty years, Donald Revell has changed! *From the Abandoned Cities* (1983) included a villanelle, a sestina, rhymed sonnets, and meditative terza rima, addressing bleak cityscapes from the Bronx to Belfast, where "sadness clings to the ground / like fog"; the book's grim descriptions both depicted and feared "the collapse of life / into signs and tokens." By *New Dark Ages* (1990) that collapse had taken place; Revell's landscapes had become wistful allegories or bitter, near-solipsistic dreamscapes. "All are private and seek even more privacy," Revell decided, writing elsewhere: "The stores will never open again. For the rest of our lives / we shall make constellations and gods / out of the guts of buildings and the stale damp."

Erasures (1992) and *Beautiful Shirt* (1994) moved even further from referential specifics; their sequences described erotic, political, and intellectual frustration, mingling plangency, difficulty, and self-pity:

Why have I chosen privacy over fullness?
Why have I chosen the strait, unmutual
loving of a small man whose heart is secrecy
and whose citizenship only that of the

reformed transient in the waste places
he fills from himself alone?

There Are Three (1998) showed Revell at his most austere—in poems like "Elegy," even syntax became a human connection Revell refused:

> myself the other
> winter even more
> myself the other
> still as obscure
> a milk white one
> a coal black one
> winter even more

For all his stylistic shifts, however, Revell's moods and properties had not altered, nor had his limited palette of diction, all gray and restrained blue gray. When regions or landscapes appeared, they evoked, as one title put it, "The Memory of New England"; when the poetic "I" acted, it acted alone.

Arcady (2000) grew entirely (its preface said) from Revell's grief for his lately dead sister: it comprised a book-length pastoral elegy, achingly conscious of Renaissance precedents. The volume made the terseness and the brief nonstatements Revell tried out in *Three* into visionary vehicles, clearing out spaces where Revell could demonstrate, haltingly, just how he felt: "In the country in dream in Arcady / One sentenced to death was given wings / I do not want to die." *Arcady* pursued attempts at otherworldliness, some of them bordering on religious faith: the book hoped, or tried, to believe in another world, one in which his late sister might remain:

> To dream like this
> Was worth the trouble
> Getting here
>
> My other ideas
> Seem premature
> Like ghosts now

The most beautiful star
Is crossing me

These thin lines and cryptic inscriptions owed something, perhaps, to Revell's translations of Apollinaire, and something to the younger poets he encountered as an editor and a teacher at the universities of Denver and of Utah (he has since moved to the University of Nevada at Las Vegas). Interviewed about *Arcady,* Revell said disarmingly that in his "earlier work I wanted to win an audience and an audience's approval, its admiration. And I did my circus tricks accordingly"; his pastoral elegy, by contrast, tried to "go alone to the alone." Yet *Arcady* resembled his first books in that it depicted a difficult solitude: the pastoral postmodern swain, exploring his American visions, remained bereft in a limited landscape of symbolic nouns—wind, river, grass, shadow, ax, grave.

By contrast with *Arcady, My Mojave* (2003) appears expansive, welcoming, easily grasped. By contrast with *There Are Three* or *Erasures,* it sounds, at first, like the work of an entirely different man. Revell now seeks a poetry appropriate not only to loneliness but to anger and happiness, not only to freighted symbols but to facts, not only to doubt but to faith: what's more, he appears to have found what he seeks. For the first time since the 1980s, Revell organizes poems around named people, dates, places, and proper nouns—Andrew Marvell, Christmas, the Fourth of July, his wife (the poet Claudia Keelan), his playful young son, their new Nevada home, "the 900 block of Fairchild," and even the 2000 presidential election. Here, entire, is "To the Destroyers of Ballots," perhaps the first good poem about that bad day:

For his cancer
My dog drinks
A wild tea
Of fallen leaves
In standing water

But this morning
We found ice
And underneath it

Nothing to drink
Only brittle leaves

No birds today
Except hawks keeping
A brown watch
Over no prey
Man and dog

Revell has not lost his attraction to modes of austerity, of meaning as much and stating as little as possible. Yet readers of Revell's past books may notice first not this political lyric's anxiety, nor its careful allegory (dog = body politic, "tea" = imperfect democracy, no tea = stolen election), but instead its stark lucidity, its openness to purely observed detail.

My Mojave presents itself as a book about that new openness, its clarity as a new, hopeful state of mind. "Pandemonium" opens by quoting Milton, thus painting two parents (perhaps Revell and Keelan, perhaps Keelan's parents) as Adam and Eve:

Some natural tears they dropped,
Especially on the 900 block of Fairchild
Where a bicycle leans against a broken Aphrodite
On porch-steps.

Behind them it was a jumble
Coming into flower and brown fences
Breaking like waves at all angles
And rooftops at all angles.

A sustained applause, and heartfelt,
Began only when they had gone.

Revell depicts people and dwellings, but withholds their stories: do the parents enjoy their departure, or the neighbors applaud their going? He leaves us instead with a very broad range of language, from the Miltonic to the American-demotic; with a characteristic Revellian music (six of ten lines concluding on unstressed syllables, none enjambed, all except the last hesitant); and especially with a sense of mystery, one these departing parents might themselves feel.

In Revell's new world, any experience—even at 900 Fairchild—could become hieratic at any time. "Pandemonium" therefore seems to him a surprisingly friendly place, inhabited by who knows how many spirits: the neighbors, or "a postman," or "Reverend Fate, / Interim pastor of Main Street Congregational," whose "sermons / Are shirts for my pillow, my dream sermons." Any stone, shirt, or scrap in Revell's field of vision can prompt a laconic sermon of its own: in "My Trip," for example, "A silver fish head glistens beside a bottlecap. / Plenty remains." Here Revell sounds like James Wright, or like other poets from the 1960s and 1970s who told (or still tell) us to trust the luminous details that prove to us that "This is really the world." When Revell's 1990s poems failed, they didn't make sense; when his new poems fail, they make too much sense, or rather avoid sense in overfamiliar ways: "Sometimes books / Are true because of rain."

Mostly, though, Revell achieves all the originality, and all the obliquity, his lines need. He generalizes wherever he can, then decants in, slowly, more information, taking (as he says) "instruction from accident"; poems interrupt themselves to give sights and dates ("October 20, 2000 Iowa City"), which then dissolve into Revell's abstracting and attenuating temperament, like sugar into hot water. That temperament prompts, in his descriptive poems, an enticingly diffident self-subtraction: Revell attempts to describe, and to accept, a changeable world by never asking more from it than it can give. The attractively brief "Counsel" sketches a Buddha that "Floats in marigolds / Until the August heat / Kills them," then decides that "True grief is endless / As happiness / Is unforgettable." The much longer title poem also mixes description with abstraction, resignation with metaphysical delight:

> I could say
> Shadows and mirage
> Compensate the world,
> Completing its changes with no change.

Without caesurae, sometimes without punctuation, Revell's lines (like W. S. Merwin's, like Michael Palmer's) now try to sound effortless, and to leave readers breathless; Revell's desire for open-endedness, and his attraction to grammar that works several ways, play productively against his desire for poems with beautifully quotable parts. "Harvest" makes a good example; it ends:

> Aversion then compulsion then
> Children exchange childish blood
> For coronets grown with God
> It is cool enough to breathe now
> It is autumn for the taking

Are the coronets (signs of martyrdom) grown with God, or does God make it cool enough to breathe? Who feels averse, then compelled— the children? Their parents? Revell wants to be sure we do not know, just as he wants (more generally) to demonstrate that propositional knowledge and logic, for him, will never suffice.

What will suffice? Apparently, Christian belief. "This is the miracle of Christmas," Revell wrote in *New Dark Ages:* "for one day, everyone in the world is a puppet." That bitter ambivalence, and that remove, give way now to ingenuous declarations of faith: "I'm not needed / Like wings in a storm / And God is the storm"; "It's no effort / To sing the hymns ourselves, and we do that." "In Christmas" opens with a vision of socioeconomic apocalypse: "I saw the mountains burning up and the rubbish / And the people trampling over their own food." Where his most political earlier poetry attempted vaguely Adornian critiques, Revell now writes what we might call (in praise or blame) a poetry of mystical Christian socialism, in which even the least specific political statements find transcendental sanction if and only if they prove unselfishly "accurate" as art:

> Start right now
> If you are a twig
> Start now
> Protest

Skins and skins of death
Offer you
Our life is what we fight for
With sun
The only stain in it
Taking out pain which was not accurate

. . . .
We are a protest
Raised against ourselves
And God comes now
And God is alone in a leaf
And we are snow in the desert
Making a new sound

Revell's early books rewarded source hunting in Ashbery; these passages send us instead to Psalms, to Isaiah 42 ("Sing unto the Lord a new song"), and to Romans 7: "Who shall deliver me from the body of this death?"

It may be that much of *My Mojave* reacts covertly to September 11, though the book as a whole seems more informed by the political deadlock that preceded it, and by Revell's much changed, much happier family life. Revell reacts to 9/11 explicitly in the verse diary "Given Days," which deflects or displaces the statements we might expect:

The attacks were tall, and then they burned.
I'd been reading, and then it was time
To take my son to school before the mustangs,
As they do every day, fled
The schoolyard for quieter fields up high.

"Attacks . . . burned" (not buildings), mustangs fled (not shocked New Yorkers); implied, or deleted, prose senses haunt these words, much as low-grade survivor guilt may haunt Revell's everyday acts. Yet this guilt seems to him only a special case of the guilt he experiences, all the time, anyway: "I go out and I feel that every step of mine / Spoils the rime across the grass." Revell believes (as he always has) that to be merely one person, in one place at one historical moment, is to be deeply unsatisfied, but he can now imagine, as he has not before, sources of satisfaction—some domestic, others explicitly religious—by which we become more than individual, isolated persons, by which we stand in a place outside time:

Lord dear Governor God
The elections come very near now
And still in the heavy leaf fall
And on all the pretty young people
Walking avenues of the deep color
I conjure more precise obscenities
Cruelties really sad as all liberty
Is sad without worship

Such lines face—even celebrate—the apparent conflict between Revell's new interest in things he can see, and his longtime drive toward subjects abstract, transcendental, or invisible. In "Halfway to Jehovah," Revell wants to convince us, or to convince himself, that "reality" (his word) is neither inherently cruel, nor hard to understand, nor socially molded, but capable of direct apprehension, if we only open our eyes. Yet that apprehension requires us to reject some other (more ambitious, more worldly, or more sociable) way of life. "The beauties of the world advertise its poisons," and any beauty becomes, for Revell, a poison if we subject it too closely to reason: "Telling is selling, / Even just two letters, / Very different from two birds." But if Revell now dislikes discursive explanations, he also dislikes poems that ignore the problems human beings have tried to explain—especially the problem of evil:

Who am I to be seen without shouting?
What use is knowledge disappearing down a hole?
Come out and be killed, poem says.
You'll find company. Three ash trees
I saw beside a lake in late October.
One was bare. One was flame-red. The third
Smoldered still in summer green, and it was screaming.

The trio of trees gives Revell a Nevada Golgotha: for all their moments of confidence, the strongest of these new poems come not to send peace but a sword.

"Jesus Christ is the next thing," the last line in *My Mojave* (2003) said: that volume's sometimes joyful immanence, its neat xeric-landscape details, and its work toward a religious calm, carry over into the fifteen new poems in *Pennyweight Windows,* a career-spanning *Selected Poems* with treasures from all of Revell's periods. "Lords, resound like a cornet band / Right across this mayhem," "Clematis" asks: "Lords, assort the live from the dead shades, / And move the flowers near." Several new poems are elegies, or prophecies, or both. One of the most personable (occasioned, like Robert Burns's once-famous ode, by the death of a mouse) sums up the journey this wonderful poet has made: "I spoke aloud, softly but out loud," Revell recalls: "'Who made the iris to stand upright and walk with me / All my life from house to house, from New York to Las Vegas, / Could recreate a mouse a good swimmer and he would live.'" The one book he has published since that selection, *A Thief of Strings* (2007), has enough formal invention (especially in its array of reinvented sonnets) to keep a reader like me coming back, but its interests, its tones, and its underlying faith remain as they were in *My Mojave*. Again Revell's odes and records of religious visions are also testimonies of love (for his son, for Christ, and for old movies), communions with an endangered natural environment (in Nevada, in "Eden Cemetery," in the middle of a baseball game), and messages from heaven. A watery "Landscape Near Biloxi, Mississippi" becomes, in Revell's eyes, both a welcome memorial to civil rights martyrs and a glowing record of the bloody instincts in every human heart. An unrhymed sonnet makes vivid, without apology, what has to be called an eco-friendly epiphany: "I am the grass I dreamed I was," Revell begins, and concludes: "I lay my head beside the broken animal. / Our eyes meet. The world belongs to him."

Readers who miss Revell's earlier, slippery work—or who object to Revell's forays against intellect—remain free to take up their own swords against his new style. They might do better to ask what states of mind its vaunting transparencies, and those alone, can describe. Revell wrote in *New Dark Ages:* "How badly I would like to sleep now / in the shadows beside real things or beside / things that were real once."

Such stark, post-Stevensian, ontological loneliness prompted the desolate tones of Revell's early work, and impelled the thin, resolutely inward language of his 1990s books, each of which sought new forms for almost the same feelings. Now, however, the feelings themselves have changed: the solipsism has gone, replaced by a confidence in domestic life, in "real things" outdoors, and, sometimes, in a Christian God. America looks, to Revell, far worse, and Revell's own private life far better, than either did when he began to write; his new poetry of prophetic statement sounds just as strange, just as rich in implication, as anything he—or almost any other poet of his generation—has done.

Laura Kasischke

The One I Love Needs Sunblock

When that genius of bluster, Ezra Pound, declared that no good poems had ever been written in a style twenty years old, he was right in this one sense: good poets make the templates they adopt seem brand-new, even if those same templates would otherwise appear overfamiliar or used up. So it is with the template we still call "confessional": the poem that presents itself as part cri de coeur and part diary, implying that the stories it uses are autobiographical; the poem that draws contrasts between past and present self; the poem whose lack of obvious structural constraints connotes speech from the heart; the poem that takes post-Freudian claims about generational succession, sexual attraction, or gender identity (or some mix of all three) as central to what and how we feel and know. So important to the generation of Robert Lowell, Adrienne Rich, and Sylvia Plath, so predictable in the hands of their epigones, the confessional model has become something many sophisticated poets and critics avoid or even disparage. But if you read the right books by Laura Kasischke—and *Lilies Without* (2007) is one of the right ones—you will find the aims we call confessional inseparable from an exciting, important, and smart body of work.

It seems to me that Kasischke has invented a new way for verse to sound. Her poems are like roller coasters, full of gradual rises and emphatic drops; they set the wildly variable forward motion of her lines (sometimes a few syllables, sometimes a lengthy mouthful) against the kinds of closure produced by sentence endings, echoes, and full rhymes. Here are the first lines from "Miss Congeniality," the third poem in *Lilies:*

> There's a name given
> after your death
> and a name you must answer to while you're alive.

And here is another passage from that same poem:

> They praised my feet, the shoes
> on my feet, my feet
> on the floor, the floor—
> and then
>
> the sense of despair
> I evoked with my smile, the song
>
> I sang. The speech
> I gave
>
> about peace, in praise of the war.

Such unstable free verse would fall apart, would feel random, if not secured in all the ways that Kasischke secures it—by intricate patterns of near and full rhymes, by closely repeated sounds, terms, and ideas. The poem presents no norm of line length, no predictable pattern of rhyme, and no plot, no sequence of cause and effect. It does, though, offer reasons for its varying line length, for the lines' extension (patience, anxiety, as in a green room) and their compression (as when it is time to perform). Kasischke's art requires, and displays, the utmost attention to pace, to the tempi—from adagio to velocissimo—at which a poem can move, and to the variable speed at which we regard our lives (it is one of her great subjects), zooming from second grade to second marriages within seconds, or saying to one moment, "Stay, thou art so fair." It might be a terrible "punishment," she says, to "Spend a lifetime trying to trace / the veins of a maple leaf," a punishment—we realize lines afterward—that she imagined, at age thirteen, standing by her parents' garage, having just been told "Go / out there and think about what you've done."

Kasischke's subjects are so consistent from poem to poem, and so oblique at times within poems, as to be worth listing: the bad fit between the responsibilities of a parent and the desires for independent glory that parents recall from their teen years; the sometimes very poor, sometimes hauntingly close correspondence between past and present desires; the uncomfortable and contradictory expectations imposed on teens, and the gender-specific expectations imposed on adult women, by consumer culture and by male and female age-mates; the ways that we realize what harm (and otherwise) our parents have done to us, and what we might do to, or for, our children in turn. Kasischke is at once "the mother, the one / with a bag of groceries, fumbling / with her keys at her car's trunk" in a poem called "Tuesday" (with a nod to Randall Jarrell's "Next Day"), and the woman, so recently a girl, familiar with scofflaw demigods of glamour and allure, if not of *Glamour* and *Allure*. The poetry includes, and its variable speeds acknowledge, the mix of ephemera and eschatology, of mortal peril and playground play, that runs through the consciousness of many parents. That mix leads those parents' inner lives to dreamy heights and sudden drops:

It's June. That boy
brought up blue
last summer from the bottom of the pool, he's

chasing a girl
this afternoon
with a black balloon. The earth

trembles beneath his tennis shoes. His mother

in the kitchen hums
a familiar tune, *Boatman*
rowing. Rowing. Boat

full of plans, but he keeps going

Notice how dense with full rhyme, then with repetition, the otherwise irregular verse becomes; notice, too, how Kasischke gets effects, not from one story unfolded at length, but from several (sometimes melodramatic) incidents juxtaposed.

When Kasischke does not juxtapose fragments of stories, she usually makes lists. Here, she evokes the force of all the memories that give her, and give poets like her, their powers: they come back to her, she says, in a rush, like

> the tangible, divine just-loosened
> hair of nuns
> spiraling toward you, and all
> the uncontrolled laughter of twelve year-olds, all
> the hydroelectric power of the Atlantic seacoast
> in you, all
> the songs written on envelopes
> accidentally tossed
> onto raging fires.
>
> And the winning
> lottery tickets. And the flippant
> remarks of sorority sisters. And
>
> the wedding dresses stuffed into dumpsters.

It would be silly to deny that Kasischke depicts specifically female— at times, specifically feminine—experience: she has done so since her first published poems. *Lilies,* however, shows an increased interest in the lives of boys and men. Kasischke's son—a newborn and a toddler in the poems of *Fire & Flower* (1998)—has grown old enough to take part in such manly pursuits as Civil War reenactments: "The one I love leans up against a fence, and then / pretends to be shot." His masculine goals evoke pathos when set beside hers, which speak not to world-historical heroism but to pedestrian, undeniable needs: "O, // the one I love needs sunblock, I think, too late, and, / perhaps a bottle of water, but now // I have no idea where we are."

Kasischke's previous books almost always compared a past (youthful) to a present (adult) self. *Lilies* also looks ahead to old age. She imagines her future as a "Hag," a frightening and bedraggled bearer of omens, showing up "to say to her younger self, It's me." An uncharacteristically long, uncharacteristically diffuse, but often haunting series of fifty-nine lyrical fragments titled "Warehouse of Prayers" assembles brief takes on the end of life, from Orpheus's pursuit of the dead Eurydice to the poet's own father's demise to "a woman sobbing in a hospital gown, Not fair. / Just this one body, and not even the body I wanted." So used to looking at women's secrets and guises, Kasischke, in another new poem, "My Father's Closet," sorts her parent's belongings after his demise. In the eponymous closet, she finds "The birdlessness of a winter night" and "The phantom lover writing letters on the wind," the blankness and bafflement of male old age.

More interested in death and dying than most of Kasischke's books, *Lilies* also takes more interest in allegory: the sometimes superb poems about representatives of qualities ("Miss Congeniality," "Miss Post-Apocalypse," "Miss Consolation for Emotional Damages") are her answers, I think, to the allegorical countries that poets such as Seamus Heaney ("From the Canton of Expectation," "From the Republic of Conscience") conjured during the 1980s. "Miss Estrogen," who incarnates a specifically feminine life course, was once a wild bird, and is now a tree; she remembers the day when a coworker said of her, "'She's // the temporary girl'"—all girls are temporary, and cease to be girls, given time. "Miss Weariness," one of Kasischke's best creations, has tired of the icons that comprise (alas) the world as Kasischke sees it— its pathos, its sleaze, its futility, its fun. "O, enough," she says,

> even, of the simple stuff:

The will-'o-the-wisp, the rain on a lake, all
those goldfish in their plastic
baggies at the fair. To them

it must have been
as if the world were divided
into small warped dreams, nowhere

to get to, and nothing to do but swim.

I suspect that in Kasischke's Michigan accent (though I have never heard her read) "them" and "swim" come close to a full rhyme.

Kasischke has been writing the same kinds of poems, with the same kinds of lines and the same set of ideas—about autobiography, about sexuality, about family life—for over a decade. The best new ones are as good as ever. *Lilies Without,* by my count the fifth book in her wholly recognizable style, suggests that she might be tiring of the devices she has made her own. For whatever reason, she interleaves those devices, here, with new ones that work less well—with paragraph-long prose poems, with the beads-on-a-long-string structure of "Warehouse," with regular rhyming stanzas, always italicized, dropped uneasily into her otherwise irregular verse. Without "Warehouse," *Lilies* would be her shortest book, which is to say that it left me wanting more. (More of the same, perhaps, but more.)

Kasischke has also become a prominent novelist, a success nobody should mind: her young adult novel *Boy Heaven* makes a near-perfect contribution to that restrictive genre, the summer-camp book. One of her novels for grown-ups, *The Life Before Her Eyes* (which begins with a Columbine-like high school shooting), was made into a film starring Uma Thurman and Evan Rachel Wood. Kasischke's powers as a poet do not depend on the merits of her sometimes melodramatic prose fiction, nor do they depend on her potential popularity as a writer of verse. Yet the ways in which her poems succeed aesthetically make them ripe for popular success of a kind rare now, but familiar in the 1960s and 1970s, when many readers turned to Lowell or Plath, to Adrienne Rich or to James Wright, to help understand their own lives, just as they might turn (for example) to Lorrie Moore now.

If Kasischke's poems get half the attention they deserve, they will be praised (as Rich's verse was once praised, as Moore's prose fiction is now praised), both for their music, and for their demographically representative qualities: for the way they capture the excitements and the anxieties of a generation just after that generation realizes that it, too, has entered adulthood, that its teens are a memory and its mortgages a burden. Kasischke is—should be celebrated as—the poet of high school cliques remembered and of terminal wards observed, of "the cigarette lighter's dangerous eye," of "a dead mouse / under the kitchen

counter" with "a postcard of the cosmos in its eye." She is the poet of
the prom in the past, the cocktail party next week, and the nursing
home in the future, the poet of strollers in driveways and the "Credit
Card in My Hand" (the title of a poem from her 2002 collection, *Dance
and Disappear*). She is the poet of walking out of a walk-in closet certain that the wrong choice will ruin your evening (see "Black Dress,"
from 2004's *Gardening in the Dark,* and then see "Fashion Victim" in
Lilies Without); the poet of realizing that you hired the wrong babysitter, of realizing that you were once the wrong babysitter; of teens
who tell their mothers "You ruined my life," of the mothers who hear
them; of the life that you have to revisit, decades later, in order to know
whether it was ruined after all. When denizens of the twenty-second
century, if we get there, look back on our era and ask how we lived,
they will take an interest both in the strangest personalities who gave
their concerns verbal form, and in the most representative. The future
will not—should not—see us by one poet alone. But if there is any justice in that future, Kasischke is one of the poets it will choose.

Liz Waldner

How I Got From Dictionary to Here

"Gusto in art is power or passion defining any object," wrote William Hazlitt in 1816; no contemporary poet shows more wild individuality, more gusto ("truth of character . . . in the highest degree of which the subject is capable"—Hazlitt) than Liz Waldner. Waldner's loquacious and rapidly mutating poems quest after, and long for, not just forms adequate to her desires, forms that enable other people to fulfill them, but forms as odd as those desires; they are satisfied with no stable, single form at all.

"I always want the words out faster," Waldner writes, "because I can feel the press of more to say." Her poems seem to have been written fast, but demand that we read them slowly: their verbal speed implies years of thought and experience (though few conclusions) propelling each sentence (or nonsentence) or line. That experience includes her frustrations and her Romantic (big "R") and romantic (small "r") ambitions: "So she set herself to win Omnity / From Nullity in her sublunary estate-and-sleeping-bag"; "Everything / Under the skin is deep and the skin is also deep. O, // Someone be the one for me." Waldner's departures from ordinary grammar, her "amateurish" tricks of spelling and layout, her insistently personal quality, all add to her poetry's general and appealing unmannerliness, its quality of not caring what strangers think. Much of it is like the friend you defend against offended acquaintances, the friend you like more because few of your other friends appreciate her, the friend who breaks their rules.

Waldner grew up in rural Mississippi, "there in the South where we Sir and Ma'am each other and I, a girl, was being Sir'd." On the evidence of her work, she struggled in her teens with needle drugs and has made most of her erotic commitments to women; she attended Saint John's College (the one where everyone learns at least some ancient Greek), and, later, the Iowa Writers' Workshop, where she may well have been older (or lived more in the "real," nonacademic world) than the students around her. *Homing Devices* (1998) and *Etym(bi)ology* (2002), the first books she wrote (though *Etym(bi)ology* appeared only much later), contained most of this autobiographical material; Waldner managed to present it while avoiding predictable patterns of confession, victimology, or simplified advocacy.

Instead she offers bizarre, nonnarrative patterns of her own devising. The parts of Waldner's technique most likely to alienate new readers are also the parts that show most clearly her continuing goals. You're not reading Waldner if you don't come across passages like this one: "Noise is like nuts in French; hence Bedlam as a name that spread, that left, that leaves. I think it's *l* but it's *s*. I think it isn't but it is—ok. Sieve, sieve, sieves." Or this one: "Little Jack Horner, his corner. Thumb, plum, sex in a nutshell, plumb line, heart line, throw out the live line (phone sex) I mean life line, Jesus is coming for me." Such barely controlled associative thinking, whose links range from obvious puns to recondite allusion, help Waldner escape what she sees as the trap of the rational. The speed bumps and gear switches her writing moves through (as with Stein, as with Bernadette Mayer) give us the illusion that she is writing the poem even as we are reading it: "O small sunlight on the bark which faded before I could finish my sentence / and so changed my sentence in its course, / so change me." Because Waldner mixes her phenomenological and metapoetic interests with others—locality, memory, sex—her writing-about-writing-while-she-is-writing is not (usually) abstruse or overintellectual, nor (like Stein) insistent on particular cognitive demands, but (instead) splendidly scattered, every which way:

> She asks herself.
> The disruption of writing instead
> 'asked' herself almost
> undid me. Let us have none of the implications
> of the past in our future. Please. Suh.
>
> Mississippi, *mon lecteur.*

Waldner's extravagant originality, her drive to exceed or break out of all received forms, is as obvious as her purposefully awkward, lengthy titles: "The Unmourning Water of the Writing Pen," "Cleave vs. Cleave, occasion for a little play." Another Waldner trademark is the portmanteau word, created to show how her thoughts outrun standard English and its artificial divisions: "Did you call them typologisms?" "Melizalphabet," "Shrimpy Girl Talk TypoParenthetical)." She sees those inherited patterns that she does *not* reject as methods of movement, rather than as kinds of fixity: Waldner defines syntax, for example, as "that ride in the cab / from an 'I' to a 'thou' / on a map made of need for a map": "how much I want to ride your grammar, / how good it costs to hire my car."

These techniques tend to fragment her works, to move them further from older poetry as well as further from prose sense. Waldner's near-manic and masterful interest in rhyme, on the other hand, does the reverse: euphonies both help hold the poems together and remind us that they are, indeed, kinds of lyric—for example, scenic meditation:

> Two crows above the marsh: sew.
> Stitch the seventeen sleek shades of blue
> to the shadow-patterned greens below.
> See fit to make me a suitable view who
> having nowhere else to go
> might as well wear this world well.

Waldner's rhymes also help her poems sound, when she wants them to sound, flirtatious:

> I hear
> High heels
> On concrete far below.
> High heels. Furbelow.
> My poem for Lauren
> With high heels in it.
> Lauren who does not wear high heels Hello.

Here is (part of) a rhyme-driven love lament:

> I think of you
>   all the day and in the night
> and they are long. I long
>   to believe most
> of my thoughts are wrong.

And here is Waldner's shortest good poem, "Wood (First Daughter)"; its euphonies accrete her characteristic strangeness, though its "meaning" is thousands of years old, expressed in semantically (but not aurally) similar ways by Cole Porter, Sappho, and the Rolling Stones:

> The bugs plug in. So do some frogs.
> And we—of your hipbone, your shoulderbone, soon.
> I would like to do it with you so the look of you is the breeze:
> *I would be content that we might procreate like trees.*

Who are "we"? Waldner won't tell; if she insists that poems make her emotions visible, the events that prompted those emotions (from regret to longing, from anger to ecstasy) appear only on occasion. "The Franklin's Tale," one of the longer poems in *Homing Devices*, is one such occasion; it is a sort of queer-positive, U.S. version of Basil Bunting's great lyric autobiography, *Briggflatts*, draping its dreambook notes and *ars poetica* speculations around a moving, formative, long-ago sexual encounter, perhaps the poet's first:

> *She gets out of bed, invites me in, then somehow they're dancing*
> *to the Talking Heads, then somehow we are making love and then*
> *somehow I ask if we shouldn't invite her friend, a thing which has*
> *somehow irked her all these almost 20 years.*
> *
>
> *

boris, natasha

the border a product of Englishmen, the comma
of (juris)prudence
(dear)

here's the heart, the white bone of despair: people who were
witnesses to what life means for me are not there any more. yes,
chance, lord, bread 2 loaves.

Such nearly naked longings return in the later poem "Washed Clean
by the Blood" (a newer poem in the old tradition of Christ-as-beloved,
beloved-as-Christ), and in "The Nonne Priest's Tale," a heterosexual
answer to the earlier poem, and one that nearly (if perhaps uninten-
tionally) quotes Bunting verbatim: "If I say it right (Lust suggests with
its own reasons) / he'll come out of the rain and we'll head for my bed /
again and undo it for sixteen years." How can you "undo" anything
"for sixteen years"? You can't, as Waldner knows—though you can aspire to do so; she specializes in verbal manifestations of impossible demands. Her wishes defy all paraphrase and all measure, as she shows
in this prose love lyric, which doubles as prayer: "undo number; make
leaves of the wings of the calendar; evergreen, let them stay, these days.
or make going go away. or as a yearned wave into your inner ear, let
me go and gone, stay."

Waldner has written of her "usual curiosity about the construction of the concept of selfhood"; her poems do not so much decon-
struct that concept—or, worse, "interrogate" it—as show how slippery

and compounded, how founded on desire, it must be. (Lacan fans take note.) Each work "arises as desire / does: oblique, out of something else." "I look in the mirror so I am there. / I sing so I make a noise." In the long-lasting debate between organicists (who see language, emotion, and poetry as living things that follow only their own rules) and constructivists (who see all three as comprehensibly heteronomous), Waldner sides decisively with the former: a seed, she writes, "grows and develops / by powers of its own / and so I love it"; her poetry emulates botany in promising to "study the way / a living being lives," though it also wants a life of its own, since "an explanation is / only a likeness / only like another Thing." (Waldner's vitalist suspicion of normal science, her apparent preference for Lamarck over Darwin, does not hurt her as a poet, though I wouldn't want her teaching my biology class.)

I called Waldner's longings romantic, and Romantic, but it might be better to call her goals baroque: for Waldner—as for Gongora, as for Donne—the heart's great drives require great, and continually changing, artifices, and larger-than-usual ranges of references, to do their scope and their energies justice. To quote the *Princeton Encyclopedia of Poetry and Poetics:* "baroque poetry exhibits not only explicit awareness of the nature and passage of time but also a tendency to manipulate time and exploit its paradoxes"; "Baroque poetry often attempts to span the entire range between . . . beauty and ugliness, egocentricity and impersonality, temporality and eternity." Although certain things cannot come out of a Waldner poem (step-by-step arguments, pragmatic rationality), almost anything can go in: epistles to apostles, maps, linguistics, pet names, technology, hymns, chart hits, mineralogy, verb tenses and moods ("Transitive, Intransitive, Extemporary Measures"), even "monolithic Home Depot" and its problematic credit lines. Pop music references (the B-52s, Lloyd Cole, John Cale, Bowie, Judy Nylon, Talking Heads, "Elvis and Mimphis [as it is sayed in the South]") give Waldner landmarks, but classicists and their editions give her models. Since the poem is a text in a world of texts, but also an incomplete one (because it is still in progress), Waldner can take for herself all the typographical marks, and the argot, classicists use in their reconstructions: ". . . heart . . . altogether. . . . [if]. . . . I can." These effects can seem contrived (and aren't hers alone; cf. Anne Carson), but they did help her learn what to do with a line, how to break the habit of representing her run-on thoughts only in run-on prose. (No coincidence that the only pop musician who gives her structural models, the one to whom her work alludes most often, favors empty space, many-layered surfaces, and self-conscious technique: the Brian Eno of *Here Come the Warm Jets* and *Another Green World*.)

As for the English and American literary past, Waldner views it as bowerbirds view sticks and pebbles: she finds whatever she can detach and incorporate into her own constructions. *Homing Devices* complains (and here it says what many creative-writing students must sometimes feel) that Waldner's verbal capacities exceed those of her peers: "I find in myself the desire to quote myself. I won't, and so you won't know how I got from dictionary to here. I can't, it doesn't work, because no one's read what I'm quoting from." (Let poets who have never felt this way cast the first stone.) Yet (she goes on) "it's the same problem if I try to use what used to be canonical and thus kosher for quoting, because nobody's read that either." In practice, she quotes whatever she wants—Thomas Browne, the New Testament, whole characters from Shakespeare:

Hamlet's birthday's late this year.
The candles on his cake are bare.
Their warm breath in colder air
spells out *Ophelia* and then spells *Where?*

Although Waldner learned techniques from Stein (and from her own peers), the poet she names, and quotes, most often is Berryman, whose vertiginous, fiery psychology seems (despite his sexism) close to her own. She also uses Berryman's self-dramatizing, alcoholic misadventures to help us understand, without sentimentalizing, her past: "When I was fifteen I could have said with Mr. Berryman: *It's not a good position I am in.* I melted drugs in spoons and shot them into my veins by the railroad tracks when the train came by with a roar."

Yet it is Emily Dickinson who stands behind (if far behind) almost everything Waldner has done, from her fascicle-like organization of sequences to her off-balance grammar to her metaphysical interrogations of ordinary words. "Wd you be surprised," *Etym(bi)ology* asks, "to know I know many portions of many Emily Dickinson poems by heart?" *Dark Would (the missing person)* (2002) emulates Dickinson more directly. Sometimes these emulations seems untransformed, a simple appeal to Amherst authority: "Not to choose is all— / is every Thing (in thrall)." Elsewhere in *Dark Would* Waldner finally masters Dickinson not just as spiritual model but as formal resource. Waldner's "Interpretation" interprets (a) Waldner's apology (to a friend, to a lover) and (b) Dickinson's poem no. 1755. Here is Dickinson:

> To make a prairie it takes a clover and one bee,
> One clover, and a bee.
> And revery.
> The revery alone will do,
> If bees are few.

And here is the end of Waldner's poem "Interpretation":

> Only a certain kind of flower
> for a certain kind of bee.
>
> Here's one favors rosemary;
> I favor impossibility
>
> and the fragrance of might
> but couldn't be.
>
> I am sick of being
> this bee.

Always dissatisfied with the world, this prolific poet has learned (as any poet who wants to get better must learn) to become dissatisfied with her style. Starting with *Self & Simulacra* (2001), and especially in *Dark Would,* she has complicated her tendency to expand, to go on and on, by repeatedly cutting herself off: her decision to write more lineated poems, and fewer prose works, amounted to one step in this direction. (When she takes several steps more, as in "Tyler," she resembles Lorine Niedecker, whose cautious sensibility one would have thought entirely alien to Waldner's own.) *Dark Would* also marked Waldner's independence from the modes of journal-like prose, and collage-like imitation of source texts, which dominated (respectively) *Homing Devices* and *Self & Simulacra*. Not coincidentally, *Dark Would* shows the greatest variety, and the greatest successes, with individual lineated poems. Here is the ending to "A/ppeal A/pple A/dam A/dream," the second poem in *Dark Would*, and the one that convinced me to listen to her work in general. Waldner addresses a lover, or former lover, and describes a dream:

I unpinned pins until I saw the wrapper bore pictures of pins
In the places they'd been.

When I put them back in, I woke. When I woke I wore that coat
You knew how to fit instead of my skin.

Friend, come button me in.

Waldner punned on her name (*Wald* is the German for "wood" or "forest") and mentioned Dante's "dark wood" in previous books; as a title, *Dark Would (the missing person)* brings in the forest where Dante lost his way, a secret or shameful wish ("would"), and a "missing person": an incoherent identity, an absent beloved, or the lover who misses him or her. *Dark Would* is for most of its length (and for all the best parts) a surprisingly traditional book of poems about erotic love, its satisfactions, and the loneliness its departure leaves. Here is the start of "A History of Divinity":

What did I do one day?
I tried to be loved.

I have still the mask I used.
Are you very pleased about it?

Yes, let us stay here.

Part of the darkness in *Dark Would* comes from the suspicions that follow from any idea of value based on desire: if nobody wants me, or sees me, what am I worth? Or, as Waldner puts it:

Undress, what's life? . . .
An empty place at the table
when they've already eaten
and all gone away.
. . . .
I'm all shadow.
Bird song bleeds out of me as substance
therefore. I go
away.

Waldner now finds the Rilkean, Orphic idea that poetry validates souls alone in space implausible (even if its proponents might offer her own work as proof):

Alone with the Alone, like Guadalajara,
won't do. What's the point of no
one knows it's you?
. . . .
What's the point of Long Long Long and yearn and
Name That Tomb? The rock is all
that's left of you.

Lest we take ourselves too seriously, lest we forget that human be-ings are distractable, and that our distractions give us reasons to live, Waldner leavens these queries with Steely Dan (the song quoted is "My Old School"), and with grammatical oddities (verbs used as nouns; "of" for "if").

In proving that Waldner has something to say and capacious ways of saying it, and in concentrating on poems about gender, love, desire, I am perhaps neglecting her lighter virtues. She is regularly *funny*, not in the slapdash postsurrealist way so many recent first-book prizewinners display, but in a humor derived from pain, as when she has Abednego say, "Pass the marshmallows, please." I have also skimped on Waldner's large-scale imitations of source texts—of nineteenth-century botanists, of seventeenth-century essayists, of Greek geometers. I have skimped in describing Waldner's commitment to theology as a subject, preferring her Christian symbols and allusions when they are vehicles rather than tenors. And I have mostly left alone the Southernness that seems to have become more important, especially in *Saving the Appearances* (2006), within the language of her poems.

Waldner's poems submit to no decorum, only to her own goals for each of them. Some of their virtues will stand out for any reader: great range and rapid intellectual motions; delight in wordplay and in unusual single words; sexiness, both in the sense that she uses sex, and flirtation, as subjects, and in the sense that her poems seem to flirt with their readers. Waldner goes as far as anyone recently has to put into words a frustration with the preconditions of material existence and of social life: "If all we have is our choices, what kind of having do we have?" Such frustrations have, of course, no solution—they are what we learn to live with, when we must, and what we challenge, where we can, even if those challenges may sound ill-mannered, out of bounds, immature: "What am / I doing here where did I go where should I be? We / were all perhaps nineteen." Because reading all of Waldner—once you get used to her quirks—becomes a passionately strange experience, one I'm happy to recommend, it seems less needful than usual to name her single best poems: in the earlier books it seems impossible. In *Dark Would*, though, it can surely be done: to future anthologists, I recommend "A/ppeal," "Washed Clean," "Interpretation," "Memorandum of Understanding and Plea," "Ho, the Isle of Lesbos," "The Gift of Time," "Role Call," "A History of Divinity," and "Wood." To everyone else, I recommend the whole of Waldner, with *Dark Would* as the best place to start.

Juan Felipe Herrera

Undocumentary

Most of Juan Felipe Herrera's many books evoke at once the hardships that Mexican Americans have undergone and the exhilarating space for self-reinvention that a New World art offers. The child of migrant workers, now a professor at the University of California–Riverside, Herrera began to publish and perform verse in the late 1960s, amid the Chicano cultural ferment of Los Angeles and San Diego; he has been, and should be, admired for his portrayals of Chicano life. Yet he is no mere recorder of social conditions: Herrera is, instead, a sometimes hermetic, wildly inventive, always unpredictable poet, whose work commands attention for its style alone.

If there is one earlier writer Herrera resembles, that writer is Allen Ginsberg, whose volatile temperament he shares. In a poem dedicated to Ginsberg (and to "Oloberto & Magritta"), Herrera calls himself a "Punk Half Panther": his slangy enthusiasms make him at home among "Toyota gangsta' / monsters, surf of new world colony definitions / & quasars & culture prostars going blam." Like the young Ginsberg, Herrera is at once idiosyncratic visionary and antiestablishment advocate; like Ginsberg, Herrera manifests glee in extremes, in paeans and in jeremiads. "Blood on the Wheel"—part blues, part doggerel, part litany—denounces a pathologically American nexus of sex, commerce, and violence by drawing on the border and on the biblical Ezekiel: "Blood of the painted donkey forced into prostitute zebra, / Blood of the Tijuana tourist finally awake & forced into pimp sleep again."

Like Ginsberg, Herrera presents not stories but simultaneities, in which everything takes place at once. Such crowded worlds find adequate praise, or damnation, only in rapid-fire lists: "the dawn-eyed village alley, / the intrepid nets of hushed camps, you // with your embarcation, gypsy-Indian hair, and me / without a hat, did you love me." He delves insistently "Into the tilted factories, the smeared taxis, / the stunted universities, into the parlor of bank notes, / in the cramped cookhouse where the dark-skinned / humans still stoop and pitch the daily lettuce bags": such an art of accelerated inclusion uses its fast pace and its adjectival surprises to propel into view scenes we may otherwise avoid.

Herrera had energy from the beginning: he needed to find forms that would let him use it. Like Ginsberg in, for example, his poem "America"—like Pablo Neruda, like Walt Whitman—Herrera found such forms in long lists, long lines, long poems made out of short parts, and in the literary device called anaphora, where many lines begin with the same words. No poet alive, perhaps, uses anaphora better; none relies on it more. The title poem in *187 Reasons Mexicanos Can't Cross the Border* is also the first in the book. Each of its 187 lines begins with "Because": "Because multiplication is our favorite sport," "Because someone made our IDs out of corn," "Because we're still running from La Migra / Because we're still kissing the Pope's hand." Herrera's anaphora pivots, over and over, between ironies directed at Mexican Americans, and anger over California's Proposition 187, designed to keep illegal immigrants out.

"Performance & text-in-the-community work," Herrera claims, "is at the core of all Chican@ poetry": it certainly lies at the core of his own. Arranged with the most recent (and best) poems first, *187 Reasons* gathers, from throughout Herrera's career, verse and prose especially fit for oral performance. Herrera calls these works "undocuments" because they solicit the voice, rather than lying flat (like "documents") on the page, and because they often concern undocumented immigrants.

They are "undocuments," too, because they are works of imagination, rather than pieces of evidence. The title "Autobiography of a Chicano Teen Poet" (1987) may promise the literal record of a life, but delivers, instead, such lines as these: "My brother died in the ring, / stabbed 14 times by the King of Desire. / All the electric guitars moaned in the pawnshops / and my mother grew smaller with memory."

Herrera's vaulting confidence, and his concessions to the demands of a live audience (where subtlety may be no asset), can raise poems above the page, or sink them. "Señorita X: Song for the Yellow-Robed Girl from Juárez" can soar: "This is the song of mumbling fathers with harmonicas conjuring the winds / This is the song of tiny lost brothers and sisters hiding under mercado glass." Yet other parts of the same elegy sound clumsy, or naive: "The mothers push the blood ocean & cradle close the blood crib cry . . . They are the black center where you dwell." Elsewhere vigor and naïveté prove inseparable, as in these lines about children dying of thirst: "hey moony moon they said / give me a flask of your water white fresh / hey moonmoonymoon." That poem ("One By One"), like others throughout his books, appears in English and in Spanish (where the corresponding lines read "oye lunitalunera dijeron / dame un vase de tu agua blanca fresca / oye luna lunita lunera"): Herrera does not say which is "original," which translation.

Herrera titled one of his best books (in 1999) *Border-Crosser with a Lamborghini Dream*. Each border or barrier in Herrera's work seems meant to be denied, crossed, overcome: oral and written, Spanish and English, oneiric and public, lyric and oratory. He also unites two kinds of Mexicanness, which might (without him) seem forever at odds: one urban, youthful, tough, fast-paced, and secular (as in "Punk Half Panther"), the other older, bound up with folk religion and with agricultural life. This second version comes out in the chants and spells that punctuate many poems, but takes center stage in the sequence "Thunderweavers," spoken by ethnic Mayans in Chiapas: "This womb is another willow, little moon leaf / branch of green winds and raw combat. It is of drum, / flute cane and day-break corn."

Trying to break down old borders and orders, Herrera risks making his poetry, simply, a mess. A suite about Frida Kahlo declares: "There are no frames / It goes against the nation of love." "Style, Genre &

Craft" seem to him in one mood maleficent "interests of Master-power." No artist could believe such a claim all the time, and Herrera does not: he may say, in a 1999 prose poem, "I hate sonnets. Sestinas are for pigs," but the same year saw him publish fine unrhymed sonnets, one of which ("La Victima") warns, "Don't believe anything I've said." Herrera's best work seems, not formless, but endlessly fertile, open-ended, "full of beginnings": "Stop resisting the rupture. / Stop grasping the form," he advises. "Recognize the rubble. My mother's rubble sky."

Half the World in Light draws on all of Herrera's thirteen books of verse for adults (though not on his writings for children): it contains all the kinds of poems he writes—verse orations and evocative monologues, but also imitations of imaginary paintings, travel poems about the Middle East, and visual-typographic verse in the manner of e. e. cummings. Herrera's talent invites such amplitude, though *Half the World* may overdo it; it seems too various, too generous, and simply too long to make an ideal introduction.

Along with *187 Reasons,* however, it is the introduction we have. Herrera's worst poems seem disorganized, excessive, frantic; his best seem disheveled, excited, uncommonly free. "A poem," he promises, "brings . . . a way to attain a life without boundaries." All life, all art, involves boundaries, if only those of birth and death. Some poets keep us conscious of those boundaries; others, such as Herrera, discover their powers by defying them. Many poets since the 1960s have dreamed of a new, hybrid art, part oral, part written, part English, part something else: an art grounded in ethnic identity, fueled by collective pride, yet irreducibly individual, too. Many poets have tried to create such an art: Herrera is one of the first to succeed.

August Kleinzahler

Cool among Shadows and Cellophane

Raised in Fort Lee, New Jersey, long based in San Francisco, and drawn by wanderlust or employment to Montreal, Lisbon, Auckland, Austin, Dubai, and Berlin, August Kleinzahler is as much a travel writer as he is a poet: his sometimes bitter, sometimes astonished poems (several even titled "Traveler's Tales") seek the distinctive qualities of each place, repellent or beautiful or (in places he loves best) both at once. In Vancouver, "the neon mermaid over the fish place / looks best that way, in the rain." At Coney Island, "a cluster of hip-hop Lubavitch punks" watch Neil Diamond (yes, it's really him) amble past on the sand; in the American South, the poet imagines "pecans suffering / their convoluted slumber in the heat." The poet's interest in places spans the globe now, but it began with his native New Jersey, where (an early poem called "Poetics" says) "I have loved the air outside Shop-Rite Liquor / on summer evenings / better than the Marin hills at dusk." Few poets since William Carlos Williams have done more for the Garden State, or rendered with such mixed feelings what they saw there.

North Jersey also gives Kleinzahler his other great subject: American masculinity, the qualities we attribute to tough guys and men. Kleinzahler's sole book of prose, *Cutty, One Rock: Low Characters*

and Strange Places, Gently Explained (2004), begins and ends in the
Fort Lee of his youth, a gruff, if upscale, Mafia stronghold. "Boys are
formed by the playgrounds they come from," he wrote there. "Ours
was violent, noisy, and profane." That book ends with a memoir of
the poet's adored older brother, "a tough guy, a jock," a "hard-living,
hard-loving, haunted, hounded kid" who killed himself in the early
1970s. The poems (unlike the prose) rarely discuss masculinity outright: instead, they take on, and render aesthetically interesting, the
qualities that tough guys are supposed to have. They can be, for example, caustic, even sarcastic; interested in baseball, in airplanes, in
old-fashioned bars; attracted to sharp, rough, or grating textures and
sounds; and unlikely to examine in detail the reasons behind their
emotions. Instead, especially if they name those emotions, they turn
laconic and stop short.

Laconic guys (as in the early Hemingway) may be trying not to lie,
or trying not to let themselves believe lies. Kleinzahler organizes many
poems by simple accretion, detail following detail, as if any argument
or story would imply an attempt to deceive: he therefore makes most
points through juxtapositions. The title poem depicts "Cretaceous
pink sandstone," "the Black Hills School of Beauty" and the "campaign headquarters of one Jack Billion" (a real person, as of 2008 the
head of South Dakota's Democratic Party). The same block that holds
"the exact center of the Oglala known universe" contains the incon-
gruously opulent hotel where the poet wakes up to a freight train "rat-
tling through this sleeping town." "Here, at the exact dead center of
America," white tourists can admire the landscapes sacred to the same
Indians their ancestors killed. One topic here is American (male) hy-
pocrisy, but the other (set against the sandstone's permanence) is the
traveling poet's transience: he cannot belong to this "sacred place,"
cannot find more than temporary "surcease here from all my cares."

Kleinzahler's poems stumble and lope with a technique on the far
side of fluency, one that can no more be approximated by naive writers than a beginner can play fluent free jazz. Most pages use long lines
along with an intricate syntax, diving into metrical regularity for just a
phrase or two: when Kleinzahler asks himself, in a poem about dreams,
"who were they all in your sleep last night?" the triple rhythm ren-

ders ironic the quiet "big room" where he wakes up alone. Kleinzahler sometimes deploys another kind of line, always end stopped and nearly unpunctuated, whose slow progress mimics perception itself: "There goes another plane / Its engines reverberating in the clouds / Now sirens too / Very like the sirens we heard only yesterday." Unpromising subjects, apparently ugly scenes, attract Kleinzahler in part thanks to his temperament, so averse to conventional prettiness, and in part because they offer a challenge: "two snails" crawling along "the inside of a Granny Goose / Hawaiian-style potato chips," "cool among shadows and cellophane," require all of his skills before we, too, can find them interesting. Though the poems offer easy visual analogies—to Ashcan School scenes, say, or film noir establishing shots—they also compare themselves to music. Kleinzahler worked for years as a record reviewer; his eclectic tastes let him bring into his poems show tunes, Mozart, jazz from Dixieland to Mingus and Monk, even a gamelan orchestra, whose "shimmering arabesques. . . . ring in the treble as though beaten out / on a thousand wee anvils, xylophones clicking like hail."

Like all selected-and-new volumes, Kleinzahler's *Sleeping It Off in Rapid City* shows continuities along with the ways in which the poet has changed. Kleinzahler's first alter egos were derelicts: "Jimmy the Lush," and a drunk named Johnny who wandered through Montreal "burning off all the stillborn Johnnys / that hatched in his head in the night." Now his doppelgängers are weary professionals: frequent fliers who stay "at the Hotel Oblivion" and say to themselves, "I cannot yet recall what city this is"; a great architect; and a "famous travel writer" with no "home / except that of airports / and a perpetual predawn realm." Kleinzahler never speaks from a height, much less from a lectern. On the other hand he is no populist and never pretends to know less than he does. He seems, instead, to write the poems that he wants to read. Those poems describe aversions and attractions, things discovered and overheard, friends met in adulthood and, on rare occasions, the poet's own youth, served up with a compression that approximates (but never becomes) self-mockery: "What a lot of erections, voidings, pretzels, / bouncing the ball against the stoop. / She really did love you, all along."

Kleinzahler's first books (published in the 1970s in Canada) started and ended in melancholy solitude: one compact poem began with

"Loneliness," another recorded "sadness coming on in waves." The poet seems happier now. He has written about sex, and about difficult breakups, since his twenties, but only now can he write well about romantic love. The wonderfully counterintuitive "Anniversary" finds an emblem of marriage in a hawk whose cry ("kee-eeee-arrr, kee-eeee-arrr, / a harsh, descending sound") seems threatening, even "terrible," to human ears, yet summons, for the hawk, the companion it seeks: "off they flew . . . / enraptured by all they were, were able to do, / not as separate beings, but as two." The tough poet, like the hawk, has found—however unlikely—a suitable mate.

Kleinzahler's poems of guyhood, like his poems of travel (they are often the same poems), make fun of the very qualities they admire: when they praise Shop-Rite Liquor, or envy the raw sex drive of a tomcat "grooving to a limbic tomtom," they are kidding and they are not kidding at once. Many poets try to sound tough, or masculine, or self-conscious about manhood, and fail miserably: what qualities let Kleinzahler succeed? His eye, and his ear—he is, first and last, a craftsman, a maker of lines—but also his range of tones, and his self-restraint: he never says more than he should, rarely repeats himself, and keeps his focus not on the man who speaks the poems (and whose personality comes across anyway) but on what that man sees and on what he can hear.

Allan Peterson and Terrance Hayes

Believe Your Naysayers

What makes poets, or their poems, seem important, worthy of public notice? Should poets, or readers, care? In the decades of Byron or of Longfellow, when poets could write best sellers, such questions might have sounded reasonable; now they often seem beside the point. "In the history of large behaviors I am not mentioned," Allan Peterson writes; "In the small I am equally left out." Peterson does not think himself important—he knows, though, that he is exceptionally articulate about the apparently unimportant events that make up most of any life. The diffidently elaborate poems of Peterson's *All the Lavish in Common,* with their involuted syntax and their rococo associative armatures, stand for the proposition that such events can be made important if we write well enough about them. The capacity of art to make otherwise dull things fascinate us becomes, for Peterson, one reason it is bearable, even enjoyable, to live:

> I remember being made
> to stand in the corner for punishment
> because it would be dull and empty
> and I would be sorry.

But instead it was a museum of small wonders,
a place of three walls
with a weather my breath influenced,
an archaeology of layers, of painted molding,
a meadow as we called them then
of repeatable pale roses,
an eight-eyed spider in a tear of wallpaper
turning my corner.
The texture. The soft echo if I talked,
if I said I am not bad if this is the world.

Peterson aspires to make the world as attractive to us as it is to well-treated, smart dogs: "People are interesting, the black lab thinks / who comes earnestly to visit with her ball." (If you think this aspiration trivial, you haven't spent time with well-treated dogs.) One way to make things interesting is to make them difficult—not impenetrable, but resistant to our first guesses. Peterson takes to heart Wallace Stevens's prescription that a poem should "resist the intelligence / Almost successfully," so much so that many passages look at first like programmatic bafflement or mere verbal meanders; many such passages resolve, on rereading, into transparent, calm, even wise analyses of consistent situations. At home among his own memories, in his own backyard, or amid terms from scientific ecology, Peterson refuses to designate his topics as either ordinary or exotic, since, viewed rightly, anything is both: "Nothing is simple but what we choose to ignore / like the ciliated tufts in the oviducts of a mouse waving like grass." Because nothing is simple, nothing is banal, and nothing unfit for Peterson's sometimes whimsical, never cynical verse: when "a man in Elvis glasses plays on TV," a chain of associations leads the poet to conclude that "spirit is . . . subject to gravity as when the ghostly mylar balloons / in Safeway after only a few days start descending to the floor, / earth is so compelling."

Peterson has recently retired from teaching art at Pensacola (Florida) Junior College. (He has one previous book, also outstanding, from the otherwise-unknown-to-me Defined Providence Press.) Like any good art teacher, he looks hard at things, but he also seems determined not to settle for merely visual comparisons: everything he says about how something looks also says what it could mean, or how it may feel. On a clear night, in Peterson's Florida panhandle, "The moon is on. Lights are, at home, / down deep in the wires." His subtropical landscapes suffuse their residents with humidity and unbelonging, with fecundity beyond use: "When the rain grows up the cyclones spin / like roses on radar. We name them. They answer . . . We had thought they were atmospheres, not friends." His Gulf Coast seashore emulates, and inspires, some of his admirably sudden transitions. It also tropes human indecision:

> In the heart of the water, the tide re-decides every few hours
> to run in the other direction,
> the earth and the moon fighting over it.
>
> Look at your money. No one is smiling.

By tradition, and by virtue of their brevity, lyric poems encapsulate one moment. Yet moments, as we live them, pull us in many directions: outward toward other people and events, inward to our memories, forward to the future. Peterson's (always) long sentences and (usually) long lines mimic those unpredictable, competing pulls. "Under Oath" ends with Peterson as a child, saying to himself, "I promise not to misuse the past or the future / if I should have one." He has (to quote Stevens again) not only "studied the nostalgias" but also learned how to make the oldest ones sound fresh. A poem about species extinction (and also, I think, about a breakup) begins: "Things we love best have backbones / but leave us." Another warns: "We are becoming something else at all times."

That term "becoming" should help us see what Peterson wants his reticulated, shifting sentences to do. In his favorite rhetorical figure, metalepsis, the vehicle in one comparison becomes the tenor for the next:

> we think ourselves unique, heirs to almost nothing
> but blue eyes and hair, dim skin
> on which we have pinpricked symbols as reasons, reminders,
> like seeing sky twice, one birdless and empty,
> one almost metrically alive.

Here the skin, with its tattoos or scratches, becomes sky, and the sky, with its birdlessness and then its birds, represents the whole potential space of human perception, in which we seek reasons and find only details. In another metalepsis, waves on the sea become archaic soldiers, which become us, dismayed: "silver in breastplates and greaves, shingles for shins, / horizon to horizon, lost relatives among them. / They are learning, but too late."

Peterson shares John Ashbery's nose for disjunction, his sense that the search for one right word is self-defeating, "that whatever we suggest, there is always something / behind it, or beside it, or many at the same time." He shares, too, the Ashberian feeling that pathos is everywhere, that behind every specific lies a melancholy universal: "As it is in Arkansas, so it is in English, / but the outcomes are more complicated." Yet Peterson looks less like Ashbery the more one reads him, and the more the individual topics for his poems emerge. Perhaps because his best, most idiosyncratic poems can (like Ashbery's) confuse inexperienced readers, Peterson writes easier, chattier, more clearly narrative ones as well: these recall David Kirby (who blurbs his book, and who shares his panhandle location). "One Day in Texas History," for example, describes the schoolday when "Mike McCoy, who came in his pants when Missy kissed him, / tried to get most of the people" (that is, the students) "in the row along the window / to faint" by exhorting them to take deep breaths, then hold their own noses closed. (They fainted en masse: the prank worked.)

"One Day" notwithstanding, Peterson's verse can require patience; with its distance from trends, its quiet oxbows and verbal doublings-back, its busily inventive reworkings of initially quiet, unpromising topics, the work falls closer to (say) Cézanne than to (say) Van Gogh, Caravaggio, or Pollock. Like Cézanne's landscapes, Peterson's poetry gets better, and reveals more thinking, the harder you look. Very few books of poetry feel richer, stranger, more thoughtful the fourth time through than they do at first reading. *All the Lavish in Common* is one of those few.

Importance is not only a matter of temperament but also a matter of expectations: of what a poem expects its readers to want. American readers, black and white and neither, often want black poets to write about race. Terrance Hayes handles that expectation with an approach partly vaunting, and partly satirical, trying to show, as his poems proceed, how race matters without having to say just what it means. Hayes's third book, *Wind in a Box* (2006), collects both formally subdued, first-person poems, from which race is never absent for long, and bravura experiments with outlandish personae, in which race, when it turns up, appears flagrantly artificial, and comically overdetermined, even if it also furnishes a source of pride.

We might say that this mixed approach allows Hayes to satisfy normally incommensurate tastes; we might also say simply that it lets Hayes write all the kinds of poems he wants to write. Quite a lot of *Wind* has to do with performance, with which performances satisfy which audiences (the poet himself being one of those audiences): Is blackness performed? For whom? If so, is whiteness? Is the self (whatever that means) a performance? What makes for a good performance, or an authentic one (whatever *that* means)? Such questions have generated enough recent scholarly books to weigh down an ocean liner, but they have proved hard to make into good poems.

Hayes makes them into good poems. "Black History," for example, describes Hayes's failed turn in a school talent show, "cursed by the ghosts // of Black History Month Decency for going barebacked" as he crooned "Lift Ev'ry Voice and Sing" with his shirt off. That's one of his quiet, serious poems. For his outrageous jeux d'esprit, start with "A Few Rumors Concerning Mr. Potato Head": the big-headed toy with removable limbs is for Hayes one more brown-skinned public figure, a minor celebrity often dissected, reinterpreted, or reassembled by irreverent, fidgety children, like a black poet in a school anthology, or a black actor on TV. "Doctors say latex is ageless. *Doctors say the body is nothing but money.* Bet his tongue quivers in a pillbox. *Bet his tongue is shy, in debt, and depressed.*"

Hayes's panoply of incompatible styles implies a range of apparently incompatible attitudes toward language. Sometimes he sounds nearly diffident, conversationally flat; sometimes he accumulates consonance and syncopation until the poem approximates scat singing, as in "The Blue Kool" (about Kool Keith, a chameleonic, prolific, sometimes self-parodic hip-hop star):

You need to say your prayers
You need to believe your naysayers.

Those parachute pants you wear
are baffling. There's hot air

in your bread basket. You penny-loafer.
I got a chauffeur.

"The Blue Strom"—Strom Thurmond, he of the secret black daughter—
resonates with slightly slower consonances: "Master the filibuster, / for
it will wear out the sentries / of heaven. Cultivate horticulture." It is a
nice, and nicely measured, revenge for a modern black poet to put his
words in a segregationist's mouth.

Hayes's anecdotal, autobiographical mode offers simpler pleasures.
In its treatment of remembered violence, of memory and complicity,
and in its slow tercets, Hayes's "A Girl in the Woods" recalls (this is
a compliment) Allen Tate's "The Swimmers." Another poem in full-
fledged terza rima morphs effectively into a blues at the end. Hayes
also revivifies old subgenres—the palinode, for example, and the verse
testament: "To the boy with no news of my bound and bountiful kind /
I offer twelve loaves of bread." Another poem in tercets, "The Whale,"
uses its hints of terza rima to highlight careful extended similes: beside
a beached "young whale," Hayes hears

> the sound of saltwater sweet-talking the shore
> As if sweet-talking the earth from her prom dress. . . .
> . . . .
> The sound of the silk passing over her body
> Like the sound of the tide uncovering
> And then covering the hard news of the day,
>
> The news returning each time it's washed away.

Affecting enough with its susurrus-based sound effects, "The Whale"
grows stronger and more disturbing once we remember that the whole

poem addresses a friend whose father has just died: the doomed ceta-
cean suggests the father's corpse.

Hayes's "Blue" poems, with their distorted ventriloquism and his
sincere reminiscences—two modes apparently so far apart—prepare
us for several poems called "The Blue Terrance," in which the poet
represents himself as a distorted, synthetic, uncomfortable celebrity.
These poems also emulate the unpredictable, extreme emotions of
Hayes's youth:

> There was a girl in a black training bra
> and a mother in silk pajamas. That was the year
> Baybay held me out a window by my ankles. . . .
> There was a deep inarticulate grief
> for David Banner and a high frothing euphoria
> for the Hulk.

Superheroes, shape-shifters, and secret identities (David Banner became the Incredible Hulk when enraged) offer a neat analogy for
Hayes, a poet never content to be one thing at once. The Hulk analogy
also suggests Hayes's undercurrent of anger; most of the lives he envi-
sions exhibit persistent aggression, resentment, or anxiety, even when
they attempt tenderness, too.

Beyond anger, beyond tenderness, the poems aspire simply to represent, fully enough to do them justice, the many sides and the mixed
feelings of the personality behind them. We might say that all lyric
poets want to do this, or even that no lyric poet wants more. We might
also say that all black poets interested in what it means to be black (and
no law requires that black poets pursue that interest) must ask how the
socially given idea of race informs more personal representations.

It is a question too big for any one answer. "Wherever there is a
mention of solitude or desire," Hayes writes (in a poem about Langston
Hughes), "I think, without wanting to, of Race." Elsewhere he asks
"if outrunning your captors is not the real meaning of Race," and,
in a pun, whether "parallel worlds . . . race at each ear of the universe," where "It was / not always as it was." Hayes's poems of autobiography, mockery, and memory, of alternate universes and alternate

selves, repeat and revise both the Hughesian commitment to speak of (if not, quite, for) a people, and the Horatian promise that this individual poet will not wholly die. For this wary proponent of black history, such promises about personal survival also trope the Great Migration, in which a generation of black Americans trekked up from the rural South: "I come from the hot season / gathering its things and leaving," Hayes declares; "I come from the dirt road / leading to the paved one. I will not return to the earth / as if I had never been born."

Mary Leader and H. L. Hix

Envisioning Pain

Most of the poems in Mary Leader's outlandishly elaborate second book, *The Penultimate Suitor,* concern visual art in some way, and she addresses it in almost every way a poet now can: Leader imitates actual or notional pictures with typographical form ("Heavy Roses," with its rows of @s); pursues the physiology of perception; makes sculptures talk ("Poesia"); uses a couple of pictures to tell a story ("Orange Rose and Blue Reader"); and juxtaposes art with instrumental music ("Series as Opposed to Sequence"). "Man in Top Half of Dutch Door" gives Leader a perfect instance of *ut pictura poesis*—by the end, it's a *moving* picture, too; the whole poem reads:

> He stays inside for indiscernibility
> Like tears beneath closed lids. Closed lids describe
>
> A shallow scalloped border. The kitten's mews describe
> A shallow scalloped border. Dusk erases chances, moots
>
> A day, invites a second widening, of sight and sound and of
> His need to convey himself: *expanding broad rotations.*

"Snow on the Skylight All Afternoon," a monologue in jumpy Sapphics, follows the thoughts of a nude model in an art class:

> I expect I'd hate the
> Muck of actually being a sculptress, but
> After all, it washes off. But I see that—
>   Who's-it, Norwegian-
>
> Sounding—Birta, I think it might be—watch her
> Work, she'll pause, and squint at her figure, run her
> Hands—wet clay and all—back through her hair, fingers
>   Spread out like men do.

Leader wants to engage all the senses at once, vision to texture, moisture and proprioception; at its best her verse (as she says of music for "electric organ") "Sets up a kind of rhythmic energy / It's as if you're in the desert and you're running as fast as you can." Her awareness of poems both as actions in time and as objects in a visual field comes across in "Rowboat on the Seine":

>   you realize—
> Right—you're way ahead of me—if we see the—yeah—
> Rower from behind, of course: the boat's approaching.
>
> This, then, is what she is to be given: a growing
> Of the dark coat-back, the boat's dark hull, its banded
> Rim: narrow red / broad blue / narrow red: coming,
> Reflection breaking up . . . oar-splash, loudening, close!
>
> And what she is not to be given: his face, his body,
>   His mind, mating hers, that blurring, when apertures flare.

Here Leader joins her obsession with sight to the disappointed love affair that (along with her visual modes) unifies her book: Irving Penn's photo tells Leader, and Leader tells us, that vision can bring us as close as we like to external forms, but not to emotional truth.

For Leader, every poem is a new formal project, one that requires some formal invention—this even though the poems can rehash the same failed romance over and over. (Her faithless man resembles Hitchcock's MacGuffin: she has to care about him, but we don't.) The love poems, or breakup poems, can be disarmingly flat. They can also yield disquieting, accurate analyses of how we read, or how we read poems, in general:

> I say to myself, Don't read his poem if
> It hurts you so. Don't sit, emporched, rocking,
> Reading a young man's poem as if
> It were yours, or, as if it were *to* you.

"Album of Eight Landscapes & Eight Poems" (the landscapes are American and autumnal, the poems perhaps addressed to that young man again) answers the long-standing question of whether any contemporary poet can do anything with William Carlos Williams's three-step lines. Patterns borrowed from Williams's late verse let Leader depict big psychological swerves in small spaces, balancing her emotive unguardedness against confining, yet still irregular, measure:

> If I can't have you coming, then
>   I want you gone. I'm Grown—*I don't*
>   *want this—*
> HUGE LOVE
>   scaled
>   down.

These three-step lines also accommodate sight and touch. As she sweeps broken glass into a paper bag, the bag offers her eye

> A brown not unlike *these oak-leaves.*
>   Big deal. I hate all mirrors,
>   like myself in you.
> Brown paper bags,
>   candles set inside them
>   in sand at Christmastime:
> *Luminarias.*

Leader has an imagination so intensely visual, and a psyche so attracted to artless extremes, that she can neither stop finding symbols for her shattered romance nor accept any symbol at all (not candles, not glass) as adequate to what she feels.

Even more than she likes these three-step lines, Leader likes sonnets, couplets, syllabics, and Sapphic stanzas; she views them, however, as species of visual form, as much as or more than she hears their aural patterns. Her insistence that poems are seen as much as they are heard can produce flimsy concrete poems, or silly parts of poems (such as a stanza of Zapf dingbats). Yet that same insistence on visual form frees Leader (as in "Snow on the Skylight . . .") to explore with great fidelity broken speech rhythms (since she feels no attachment to any *particular* way of hearing the line). Impelled by erotic letdowns, crowded sight lines, and extreme self-consciousness about the poem as artifact, Leader can turn almost anything into (a) a richly descriptive, post-Keatsian bit of an ode, (b) a meditation on photography or painting, or (c) a letter in verse. Sometimes she does all three at once:

> Dear Water, How I wish you would gather yourself together and rise,
> Gather yourself together with thunder and together
> Overpower my sole lover, the air,
> Commanding him,
> *"Send this woman this hour no barrier,*
> *Rain on slurry-gray waves."*

The high diction, and the consciously baroque grammar, suit the way Leader sees the world. Her desperately elaborate celebrations of framing devices and singled-out details postpone the grown-up disappointment that awaits her after the end of each poem. Yet if Leader expects to lose out in love, she also feels that her desires are stronger than other people's and that her works of art should depict those desires. And depict them she does, not least in the erotic, lofty "Spider Mums," which also examines a photograph:

> it's the
> Innermost petals that intrigue me, those in the formative stages:
> Something in

The way they minutely
Grip, curl, they're preparing for something later,
They're enduring the tension, the desire to do something,
    somehow make
The part that

Feels the desire obtrude:
A young girl in her skirts squats to pet the cat
Who lies on his side for her, a kind of girl: lonely, adult.

That's not just descriptively accurate, it's *sexy,* in a way I wouldn't associate with the few writers (Anne Carson, May Swenson) who strike
me as Leader's overt influences. For all her interest in passionate extremes, however, Leader can also shine in much calmer meditative poetry. "Poesia" (modeled, I think, on Stevens's "Angel Surrounded by
Paysans") "imagine[s] . . . / 'The Canto of the Terra-Cotta Angel'":

I'm glad I'm no inhabitant of the other heaven,
That paneless, shutterless, shadowless place.
Glad, yes glad day and night,
Even when I learn how the drunken boy has broken
The window below. This way I have knowledge
At least of something, something of the human,
Something in addition to the permanent ache
Between my immutable shoulders.

Although Leader offers plenty of verbal beauty, she is not always
verbally reliable—her poems can sound amateurish in both the good
and the bad senses of that word. Her worst lines can pull up alongside
her best, ruining whole poems with their proximity: "Don't you see
that I long to fill you with // Erections . . . ?" Too often her poems seem
programmed, top-down, by her sentiments, rather than built from the
bottom up, language first: they can sound willed or willful, unart-
ful or artificial, especially when they lean hard on snazzy typogra-
phy. In some sense, though, almost none of these flaws should matter.
Leader has more ideas than she knows what to do with, and each of
her poems offers something new: together they adumbrate an enticing

and insistently personal way of *looking*—both at the sights the world offers, and at the people with whom she hopes to share them.

Leader assumes (with reason) that her own sights, feelings, and odd, bold forms will hold our attention in and of themselves: she feels no need to give her elaborate structures moral or social rationales, nor to link her phenomenological inquiries to any philosophical framework. H. L. Hix generates equally striking poetry out of an almost exactly opposite temperament: as good as he is in recording sights and sounds, he designs his very ambitious sequences (almost never freestanding short poems) as inquiries into large problems of ontology, morality, and human knowledge—inquiries that he can neither conclude to his own satisfaction nor willingly break off. Hix produced three books of theory and criticism (including a study of W. S. Merwin) before the first book of his own verse appeared; *Surely as Birds Fly,* his third, remains his most original, his clearest, and his most violent. It consists of three novella-length verse sequences about theodicy, bodies, and pain, titled—somewhat misleadingly—"A Study of Thermodynamics"; "Thistle, Clover, Rape"; and "A Manual of Happiness." "More pathetic situations and sentiments," Wordsworth opined, "that is, those which have a greater proportion of pain . . . may be endured in metrical composition . . . than in prose." Hix's sequences seem designed to test that proposition, stretching both our sympathies and the poems' crowded lines to their limits.

"Thermodynamics" comprises eleven "Laments" for parts of the body (lungs, blood, etc.), each focused on a scene of distress or death: their range of speech and speakers includes the demotically limited, the journalistically flat, the sermonistically abstract, and the hauteur of deliberately antiquarian lyric à la Geoffrey Hill. "Lament for the Feet" shows almost all of Hix's range, from moral philosophy to animal cruelty, and from dense argument to wincing rhyme. The poem concerns a house full of maltreated dogs:

> The problem of human freedom one might couch
> in other terms than Kant's. *It's nasty in there.*
> *Dog shit everywhere. I don't see how she could breathe.*
> The woman, nearly ninety, wept and pleaded
> with the workers. *I've been raising dogs right here*

in this very house since before your mothers were born.
If I'm treating these dogs as bad as you say,
how come you need those chokers to drag them away?

Most of Hix's people are poor or near poor, implicitly Caucasian, small-town midwesterners, people whose scars (economic, emotional, physical) leave them barely able to care for themselves. Their dilemmas can seem found rather than made: "A baby is born into a high school toilet every day." When Hix frames them rightly, however, the same dilemmas might stop any reader cold. Here is the middle of "Lament for the Hands," one of the few poems whose rhythms seem learned from Merwin, though Hix puts them to excruciatingly un-Merwinesque effect. In that poem's troubled household:

Someone has to feed the dogs and let them outside
so they don't piss on the floor and put the diaper
on whichever one is in heat and run the sweeper
once a month or so while she's out dancing because
it takes her mind off not dancing which she prefers to avoid
and he's out following her to prove to himself he knows
what she's doing and to make sure he knows who she's
doing it with . . .

Such tasks pile up for a dozen more lines, until Hix finds one task his speaker (presumably "his" and "her" child) will not undertake:

                    someone has to tell them
that if they had been as happy then as they insist they were
they could not be as unhappy now as they tell each other
they are not and someone has to remind them I can
watch tv as well with them gone as I can with them home
and somebody has to learn to be like somebody besides them
because they won't do it themselves and soon it will be too late.

"Thermodynamics" juxtaposes stories like this one to create moods and clinch arguments about human suffering; "A Manual of Happiness" instead weaves one painful narrative out of many. It tells the story, or stories, of a middle-aged welder repeatedly struck by lightning, of his wife, and of their ten unfortunate children; all are named for parts of Alaska, and all but one die or vanish in improbable or frightening ways. (Hix writes in the voices of all ten children, with interpolated quotations from mother and father.) Each child's fate comes with heavy dramatic ironies. "He has a gift. He can be somebody. / Don't stop him," the mother says of Kodiak, who plays the piano: a railway spike severs his finger at age ten. Aurora's anorexia "started with learning to make desserts, / ever richer and more extravagant, / but eating smaller and smaller servings": "I who feared god's wrath," she concludes, "died from his embrace." Hamilton dies from a commonplace playground beating, or (put another way) from their small-town locale: "The ambulance took / half an hour to arrive; the hospital / was out of his blood type . . ." As for the youngest brother,

> Elias was hydranencephalic.
> Our mother called him her little angel:
> the halated, empty globe of his skull
> shone, a paper lantern, lit from the back.
> It was not our world that made him smile,
> but some other that transformed his pupils
> into searchlights scanning a blank black lake.

Each day (especially each day with young children) contains *in potentia* thousands of frightening accidents, and this family seems to have realized them all; by the end of the poem one believes Hix's claim that its calamities each derive from "some 'real' event." Hix even renders credible the father's strange relations with electricity: young Kenai (who dies in a tornado) describes that biophysical problem in one of its less hazardous manifestations:

> In winter, my brothers and I would ski
> in our house shoes across the red shag carpet.
> The tiny spark when we touched each other
> made our fingers tingle; touching father
> hurt. It sounded loud, like a small cap gun,

and left a residue of smoke like the streak
on a finger passed through a candle flame.

Hix's lightning-charred set of private disasters consciously adapts
the book of Job, and reverses its ostensible moral: "Heavens so charged
imply a pantheon / of adversaries but no advocates." In another place,
or an earlier time, Hix's insistent and near-airtight case against God
might land him in jail, or at least get his name in the news: here and
now it looks almost anachronistic (though no less powerful for that).
Its hyperarticulate, shocked, and shocking incidents put me in mind of
Robert Penn Warren's *Brother to Dragons,* or of Thomas Hardy's *Jude
the Obscure* as it might be directed by Peter Jackson. Hix's strange
set of verbal registers, however, has no close counterparts at all. Here
and in much of his earlier work he seems to ask whether any kind
of language can suffice in explaining such painful events. "Since" (he
writes) "god never speaks when spoken to," no one sort of language
(no prayer) will do, and so Hix tries unheard-of combinations—the
slangy and the lawyerlike, for example, or the elegiac and the medical:
"the Lichtenberg's flowers that mark my father's skin."

Almost as grim but less shocking, and slower paced, "Thistle,
Clover, Rape" is of these three sequences the least narrative, comprising short poems set in (and named for) Baltic and ex-Soviet locales.
Instead of wounded bodies and their fates, Hix here depicts wounded
places and cultural space: without the obligation to tell a story, he can
pay full attention to how his lines sound, and how they chime or grind
against one another. Here we are, at the sequence's outset, in "Riga":

Stones remember. Their scars never heal.

Souls fall like leaves from a linden. Souls mimic cottonwood seeds
    in the breeze.

Birds part for the passing of purpose.
In a world so badly blurred, who would not laugh at such
    scattering?

Suffering passes from hand to hand and kiss to kiss.

Notes from a phone call to parliament pattern a woman's dress.

Such sentences fling themselves out across their long-broken cities as if to seek restitution from richer nations, or from the rocks, or from God. In "Moscow," Hix finds poverty and homelessness inseparable from hospitality: "For every toast, a single swallow. Name a joy, drink a sorrow. // Contorted sleep on the subway. Sleep on the sidewalk. Sleep in the snow." And in the much quieter "Tartu," an inlet encapsulates romantic love, genealogy, and the bleak arc of East European history, whose ironies may or may not be closing in:

Confinement erases what liberty writes.

Here is where my father's fall broke my mother's ribs.

What separates us flows to the sea.

The next world broken through into this one.
Side by side, staring across the river.

On a bright morning after a long sleep, one person's hand on
    another.

Hix does not write poetry because he wants to but because he must: though he appropriates (and cites) all sorts of sources, he is less a magpie than an uncommonly serious bowerbird, compulsively collecting and arranging phrases meant to catch our eye. His characters talk and talk, sometimes too much; he and his people can have so much to say that they step on each other's words. In "Thistle," where most of the poems have just one speaker, Hix's additive temperament can hurt individual poems' shapes (I preferred the sonnet-sized "Novosibirsk" I found in a journal three years ago to the longer version here). The Baltic sequence's narrow range of tempo (slow) and tone (grave) can also hinder its cumulative effect (a problem Hix ameliorates by mixing in three translations). But all this means simply that Hix is still figuring out what he can, and what he wants to, do. I have been waiting for him to write a book of reliably sounded, profound lyric sequences since his imperfect debut, *Perfect Hell* (1996): if that perfect sequel remains to be written, this triptych is more than enough for now.

"Here Is the Door Marked *Heaven*"

D. A. Powell

In five and a half years, D. A. Powell has achieved durable acclaim for three books whose topics, though not their techniques, permit quick summary. *Tea* (1998) used long lines and striking extended metaphors to describe Powell's own experience of gay America, including his own very early sexual encounters; his long, troubled romance with Scott Gulvas; and the loss of friends and lovers to HIV and AIDS. *Lunch* (2000) gathered the short poems that prefigure his *Tea* style, including a sequence about his childhood in blue-collar, exurban California, along with a suite of poems about his own HIV-positive diagnosis. *Cocktails* (2004), the genuine sequel to *Tea*, returned to its settings and methods in the first of its three sections; the second rewrote Powell's sexual history through a series of films, most of them with queer plots or subtexts. The third and most original section of *Cocktails* took on biblical themes, finding versions of queer life, erotic devotion, and suffering in the Gospels and other early Christian writings. Powell has received, and surely deserved, attention as a voice of the HIV/AIDS crisis, and as a chronicler of gay life for his generation. He is hardly the only such voice. What has made Powell stand out in other poets' eyes is not his set of affecting subjects, but his invention of a style.

Powell writes in the foreword to *Tea* that his work is "not about being queer and dying. It is about being human and living." His style makes continuities and progressions, ongoing poems that represent ongoing lives, out of verbal and structural elements that look like termini, obstacles, premature closures. Powell's poems also flaunt, and sometimes quote, works of art and cultural codes created by gay American men; he likens his project to that of a DJ, who collects, sorts, mixes, and makes available for a community existing songs. Powell's extended metaphors and double or triple entendres frequently link alluring, or highly esteemed, experiences to things and actions rejected, degraded, debased. These figures, combining the stigmatized with the sacred, make his biblical sequence consonant with the rest of his poems: these songs of St. John and Simon the Cyrene, like his earlier poems of hospitals, discos, and curious Boy Scouts, turn the abject into the exalted, keeping the Christian promise that the last shall be first, the rejected stone the cornerstone.

Powell says he began writing *Tea* when he "turned my notebook sideways, pushing into what would traditionally be the margins of the page." The long lines of *Tea*—replicated for most of *Cocktails*—remain Powell's most recognizable formal feature. These lines (and even the shorter lines in most of *Lunch*) make room for multiple caesurae, indicated by multiple em-spaces midline; often these caesurae separate nouns or noun phrases with no corresponding verb: "the new seed germing: gifting in the storehouse.   comb of honey / a jar of fragrant oil. physique rid from its abscess: robed in saffronia." Powell's defiance of prose syntax also includes abrupt changes of verb tense and mood. He may shift from first-person, past-tense indicative to first-person present, or from indicative to imperative, several times within one poem: "I saw this movie twice. . . . now I wander into someone else's story . . . take my hand and lead me stranger."

What do these devices let Powell do? "The long lines of *Tea*," Powell has said, "are made up of short bits, of fragments. I felt like my life at that time was putting together the broken bits. Making a whole out of something that had been shattered." Paul Monette opened *Borrowed Time*, billed in 1988 as the first "AIDS memoir," with a far gloomier statement: "the world around me is defined now by its endings and its closures, the date on the grave that follows the hyphen." Powell's style begins by acknowledging such closures, many—though not all—due to HIV. The grammatical stutters and emphatic metaphors mean that almost any line in a typical poem of Powell's could be its last—and that most are not. Changes in verb tense, person, and mood make the poems seem immediate, unsettled, while also describing the way the poem coheres: "the ends I took up and selvaged. This veil shall not fray." In "[remembering the taste of skin . . .]" (from *Lunch*), any of its five lines could work as an ending:

remembering the taste of skin: dim prehistory of dives

secretions of the body: spume and seawater
cells of the voluble tongue welcome old chums

rapture of the deep: lungs fill with oceania
rubber suit flops into the skiff.   fins in the water

This effect of hyperclosure or repeated false closure gives Powell's poems the sense of insistent continuance through obstacles: extended metaphors (here equating evolution, diving, drinking in "dive" bars, and sex—with a condom) seem to hold the poem together, while collapsing syntax threatens to break it apart.

Repeated efforts to overcome potential endings, to move past a break, define not only the structure of individual lines and poems but the structure of *Tea* as well. Punning on one of Robert Duncan's titles, *Tea* promises "to end and to open with a field," both the field in which Powell's friend Andy is "buried under a hunter's moon" and the scene of a car wreck in which Powell, at age twenty, almost died: "20. the year I went through the windshield"; "the crash divides my life." Powell plays the resurrected survivor—"death puked me back out of its paunch"—committed to surveying the "field" of his friends' deaths. *Tea* not only begins with the crash but concludes with it, turning a symbol of auto safety into a symbol of sexual release: "the shiny buckle unfastens at last."

Powell's corpus, especially *Tea*, tries to work both as art and as record, "trying to archive that period" of his life: "somehow, if I don't put all this stuff in it'll be lost." No wonder collections, possessions, collectors—especially music collectors and DJs—play such a prominent role. Powell's collections show remarkable scope: Boy Scouts, John Waters, Air Supply, Häagen-Daz, Pushkin, Marvell, the disco producer Patrick Cowley. (The operas and the Continental modernists who gave high-culture touchstones to a previous generation of white gay poets, such as Richard Howard and James Merrill, play little to no role in Powell's work.) Powell finds many uses for what he collects: song lyrics and song tunes (here, "The Girl from Ipanema") can substitute for the metrical substructure his lines reject: *tall and thin and young and lovely the* Michael with kaposi's sarcoma *goes walking.*" More often Powell leans on proper nouns and song titles for their metaphors: "Eleven Disco Songs That Equate Sex and Death Through an Elaborate Metaphor Called 'Heaven.'" Powell's world is full of figuration already; he shows himself not just collecting but documenting, advocating, demonstrating, bringing out figures already available in American culture (especially in its queer subcultures). Such collecting and demonstrating can take whole poems. "[first fugue]," the last poem in *Tea,* uses three-part lines: the first part of each line quotes a gay male poet, the second a Sylvester track.

As late as 1979 (when Powell was entering high school), Robert K. Martin required a whole book to argue (what now seems beyond question) that "the sense of a shared sexuality had led many gay writers to develop a particular tradition, involving references to earlier gay writers," especially Walt Whitman and Hart Crane. Poems like "[first fugue]" do not only place Powell in Martin's (and Crane's) "homosexual tradition"; they also expand that tradition far outside high culture, placing Whitman, Crane, Essex Hemphill, Merrill, and Sylvester in the same celebrated company. "The culture of disco," Powell explains, "wasn't just Gay culture, it was African American and Hispanic culture, too; it was a hybridization, but it was definitely distrusted and abused by the dominant white, heterosexual culture. And so disco went underground, and transformed and transmuted into all sorts of other musics. It survived. Queer people survived."

Like the disco scene he describes, Powell's verse not only celebrates an identity but works to pluralize it. Movie protagonists, biblical characters, glimpsed counterparts in grocery stores, could all (for a few lines of poetry) *be him*. (Whitman's poems boast similar effects.) Powell's project of representing *many* people—friends, dead and living; relatives; strangers; characters from literature, music, film—comes as a deliberate alternative to clearer autobiographical (not to say confessional) modes. Powell has been alternately laconic and explicit in describing his early years in Yuba City, California: that life includes time at Yuba College and at Sonoma State University (where he began to write seriously). "There were times when I was younger," he has said, "when I had limited options and had to prostitute myself"; "believe me, I've had times in my life where I truly hungered and had nothing." Such hints (combined with those embedded in his poems) suggest that his life story, told straightforwardly, could capture many readers.

Powell avoids such telling. Instead, the poems sketch and merge their episodes, often deflecting attention onto the other characters with whom he identifies (or whom he grieves). Rather than one life, or one life story, the poems offer sets of roles, all of which Powell inhabits, all of which are "real" and become part of him: he is not, so to speak, the dancer but the dance floor, and the DJ who keeps it alive. The DJ set, the one-time-only live mix for a particular place and occasion (rather than the rock album of discrete songs), also gives Powell a model. "He must have been a deejay this one" (in *Tea*) imagines "[the mix as a product of survival] pushing up to 144 bpm." Matching beats, controlling tempi, turning separate and preexisting units into continuous (and communal) experience, a club DJ constructs a set out of records very much in the way that Powell constructs lines, poems, sequences, and indeed books out of events, references, found pieces.

Where did he learn to write those fragments, those books? Powell remembers his "first foray into the genre of poetry" by way of Dudley Randall's anthology *The Black Poets;* he describes his earliest creative efforts as work "from the time when I was Black" and recalls, "It took me a long time to learn how to read white people's poetry. But I do now." Other early models included T. S. Eliot, Gertrude Stein, and Powell's teacher at Sonoma State, David Bromige. What about Frank O'Hara—is *Lunch Poems* a source for *Lunch*? "As soon as I started reading Frank O'Hara," Powell told the *Harvard Crimson*, "I thought, this guy's ripping me off. Except he died when I was three." The same interview suggests that the long lines of *Tea* owe something to hip-hop: "Sugarhill Gang and Grandmaster Flash were as important to me as Gertrude Stein and John Keats." Powell's comments elsewhere suggest a self-conscious San Francisco tradition—Spicer, Duncan, Gunn—in which he situates his own efforts. None of these writers except Gunn has any use for English meters and closed rhyming forms; Powell belongs, in fact, to the first generation of American poets who may have grown up without even a vestigial connection to the accentual-syllabic, rhyming English tradition—his inventive lines have this absence at their back.

"Before I wrote *Tea* I had written a collection entitled *Lunch*," Powell explained in 1998. Interviews suggest that the earlier *Lunch* became most, but not all, of Powell's 2000 book; in it, we can see his style take shape. "[sonnet]" looks like a prospectus for *Tea;* the poem offers "morsels of my lifeswork: the story of a professional party hostess," comparing itself to the music of the Eurhythmics and offering "newamericanwriting" its "nice mix of plights and music. boomerang boy and disco dollies . . . written in an enjoyable present: continuous. an unresolved work." The poem gathers parts and characters in intimate earnestness; it assembles, too, a set of extended metaphors anchored by puns. ("Boomerang" and "dollies," for example, are microphones used in film work, as well as labels for dance club habitués.)

Such extended metaphors and double entendres seem even more fundamental to Powell's aesthetic than are his fragmented, extra-long lines. "A song of Sal Mineo" depicts, simultaneously, for six long lines, the poet receiving anal sex, scenes from the last reel of *Rebel without a Cause,* and Persephone's abduction by Hades: "in the restroom at the probe I welcomed a sweet thrust. pomegranate droplets dotted the commode // he was the disembodied voice of the planetarium. I want to pretend it did not happen in the dark." Jonathan Dollimore writes that "gay fiction from Radclyffe Hall onwards" presents "the gay underworld as a place where the hero or heroine suffers into truth, and, by dissociating himself or herself from the tormented inhabitants of the place, writes of its tragedy." Powell's double exposure creates a "gay underworld" but does not dissociate the poet from it at all: he "want[s] to pretend," not "that it did not happen," but that "it did not happen in the dark." (He is both a Persephone who enjoys her time in Hades, and a Sal Mineo who survives.)

One might object that such a passage wants to have gay sex (or a sex club) both ways, celebrating a descent that it nevertheless views *as* descent, as shame or sin. Yet "having it both ways" is just what Powell's metaphors do—often they make it hard to sort tenor from vehicle. One of the densest (and most anthology-friendly) poems in *Tea* carries a triple entendre through six lines, describing (a) a feigned tea service enacted by (b) boys camping in the woods (apparently Boy Scouts) who (c) engage in erotic play. (All three situations become ceremonies of queer initiation.) With its "floating" noun phrases, midline breaks, abrupt endings, and changes of verb person, tense, and mood, the poem makes the best brief example of Powell's *Tea* style:

> the merit of reading tea: gunpowder variety unfurls puptent
>   green.   sleeping bags zipped together
> all summer our mouths wore the parfum of shattered blossoms.
>   see: you like butter your chin says
>
> in a clearing in the wood we were made to play nice & dainty:
>   petite cookies amid elegant service
> were we taught to rub two sticks together?   proper steeping.
>   poise and balancing upon the knee
>
> our leaftips turn silver.   one would wander in search of cress:
>   strangling in the creekbed
> each discovery triggered by a broken cup.   using a trusty
>   fieldguide to earn badges: we identify

Some of the visual puns are obviously sexual ("rub two sticks together"), some less obvious ("leaftips turn silver" with semen or pre-cum), and some faint indeed: Is the "broken cup" a teacup? A buttercup? The Grail, as parodied in Robert Frost's "Directive"?

If "[the merit of reading tea . . .]" relies on visual analogies, other poems instead depend on puns: "kenny lost in *the mineshaft* among silver stalactites. his irises bloom in darkness / the night is an open 'o.'   he caverns and groans engulfing: largerbonessoulsweddingrings // leaking from the socket of his anus: cocytus. he stands apart involuntary. pooped himself." The club's name already suggests the anus, but Powell goes further: almost every noun and verb here holds a pun. "Irises bloom," for example, means that Kenny's eyes widen in dim light, that he "flowers" sexually, and that other sphincters prepare to assume their receptive role.

Such extended figures (*Mineshaft* club = anus = actual mineshaft = classical underworld; tea party = Scout camp = sexual initiation) serve as principles of unity, and as principles of entertainment, even comedy; they balance, perhaps, the fragmentation of Powell's grammar, and the seriousness of his subjects. In parts of *Tea* and especially in *Cocktails,* the figures take on a grander goal: they redeem Powell's own, and his friends', suffering by linking stigmatized, even conventionally disgusting, experiences to elevated or even holy states. One of the shortest and strangest poems in *Tea* appears to remember a pedophile uncle:

> when did the darkness climb on with its muscular legs pinning me
>   under: goodnight uncle boo
>
> giant teeth grazed me: he descended from the clouds.   wanting
>   to explore the downthere of me
>
> the biggest thumb.   I had to go bathroom but vines held me
>   fast.   beanstalk sprouting my pyjamas
>
> at the foot of my trundle: magic beans could conjure him.   say
>   it again: "I'll eat you up"

Most of Powell's poems place their first lines in brackets to create their titles: he calls this one "[untitled]" instead, since the child had no name for this confusing, exciting experience, which seemed both to endanger him and to open a magical alternate realm. (This child may not even have a name for the penis, which he calls "the biggest thumb.") Again, the repellent (what is usually called molestation) is compared to the exalted, and the remembered experience partakes of both.

Perhaps overwhelmed himself, the critic and poet Cal Bedient called

Tea "a book of abject self-discoveries," comparing its sentence fragments to "seeds spat out in disgust." Yet Powell often invites us to link
disgust with joy. "[college roommate gone . . .]" shows Powell sorting the roommate's laundry: "piggish delight the rooting after truffles.
Whiff and snout." "[dogs and boys can treat you like trash . . .]" seems
to relish sexual self-abasement: "when a boy goes away: to another
boy's arms. what else can you do / but lie down with the dogs. with the
hounds with the curs. with the mutts." In "[untitled]" and "[college
roommate gone . . .]," the joyful side of the poem remains secular—
the otherworld of fairy tales; intimate knowledge of a beloved (or at
least of his laundry). Elsewhere Powell's paired opposites draw on
Christian belief. "Once I had really thought about it, I have all of the
Christian values that I was imbued with through my reading of the
Bible," Powell says; "it's more radical for me to go back into the church
and to say, 'I am a Christian,' than to just turn my back." *Cocktails*—
the whole book, but especially its last section—uses extended metaphors to redeem (from homophobia, from physical pain, from early
trauma) experience we have been taught to view with disgust; its sexy
tableaux and broken taboos try to free (from its modern fundamental-
ist shell) what Powell sees as the core of Christian faith.

Christianity already has at least one ceremony whereby the prohib-
ited (the eating of flesh) becomes holy (the Eucharist). Powell's metaphors extend the ideal of communion. "Rather than drawing clear
metaphorical equations," Powell has said, "I've mixed up the sexual
eating, the medical eating, the corrosive eating and the ecclesiastical
eating into a big, amorphous stew. Let god sort it all out." "[because as
lives are aching . . .]" (from *Lunch*) introduces the poet as both saved
and damned, his blood both poison and communion wine: "doing
all the poisoning myself // myself. need no wine to sanctify. as of the
right now I am lucky: / need no litter bearer. children undigested I am
able to throw back up." (The last line, interviews make clear, refers to
Powell's first months of taking anti-AIDS drug "cocktails," when he
found himself vomiting pills he had to reingest.) Circumcision, communion, winemaking (the communal trampling of grapes), sex, astrology
(observation of Mars) and blood tests all represent one another: "un-
sheathed the sword and cut the veil. visible the planet red / he wrapped in

cloth: a loaf in offering. stained: they crushed his grape / now wine trickles from the vats and the barnfloor aches its charge." Christ's foreskin—the only part of the Son that remained on Earth after His Ascension—stands for the interpenetration of transcendental with earthly concerns (as well as for penetration of other kinds).

Although Powell compares himself to Christ on occasion, much more often he sees himself among the marginal figures whom Christ redeemed—"Lazarus the leper," the Magdalene, "Lazarus of Bethany." He also emphasizes Lazarus's indignities: "we was a beautiful lad once: not putrefactive nor foul / not blistering in the lips or nose." Near the head of Powell's parade of New Testament surrogates stands Simon the Cyrene, by some traditions a black-skinned African man, who carried the cross to Golgotha (Mark 15:21, Matthew 27:32). Like Simon, Powell has become a "carrier": "'the carrier' I was called. so did I carry: my hand did not defect. my sores / who can tell us all about love: a flaying." Gnostic Christians such as Basilides believed that this Simon was crucified in Christ's stead. "In modern times," adds the *Oxford Dictionary of the Christian Church,* "Simon the Cyrene has been claimed as patron by groups of people working among outcasts." His blackness, his outsider status, his role as "carrier"—sharing the *physical* pain of the cross—and his relative obscurity all make him an especially appropriate mask for Powell.

Nor do the resemblances stop there. "I am writing the spiritual self through sexuality," Powell says of the last part of *Cocktails;* "There's a long tradition of that going back to the Song of Solomon, and the odes that are attributed to Simon of Cyrene." More often called the Odes of Solomon, these poems are early Christian (Jewish-Christian) lyric works modeled on the Song of Songs and on the psalms; the most remarkable among them express a homoerotic devotion to the crucified, resurrected Savior. In the Sixteenth Ode (in Willis Barnstone's translation), "His love feeds my heart, / his sweet food reaches my lips"; in the Nineteenth, "The Son is the cup / and he who was milked is the Father / and he who milked him is the Holy Ghost." These odes recall in their blend of erotic and sacred the odic ambitions in both *Cocktails* and *Tea.*

They also suggest a serious aim toward which almost all of Powell's techniques point. Club nights, backroom sex, church services, even hospital visits all become in *Tea*—as cinemas, bars, supermarkets, and Christian rituals become in *Cocktails*—*communal, ritual experiences where performative language exalts a vulnerable (gay) male body,* confirming rather than countering its erotic charge, and rendering desirable, or honorable, its experience of disgust and pain. Rather than offer a safe, clean description of gay male desire, one designed to dissociate it from dirt, mortal danger, corruption, and infection, Powell's double meanings, and his willingness to describe taboo topics (child molestation, feces, sores, nausea), offer gay persistence and gay pleasure as a triumph over the corruption they appear to incorporate.

If these books retain serious purposes (mourning, celebrating, promising), they also flaunt comedy. *Tea* calls the now-deceased "nicholas the ridiculous," "nick at night. tricky nick. nicholas at halloween a giant tampon." "We toy in earnest," a later poem insists. Powell's forms make room for excess, for frivolity, too, boasting mordantly comic sound effects: "we slip and slop and spill our soup—we pop our rocks—droop and droplet / flung over the back of the sofa: limp as a cashmere coverlet. damp as a bloodclot." Powell works hard to reject any kind of decorum: neither light humor nor repellent detail nor the conventionally beautiful will be left out. He rejects, instead, ironic distance, balance, "maturity": "don't make me mature by myself."

To sound fun, sexy, flirtatious, voluble, is not, for Powell, to reject memorial or sacral purposes: indeed, to repudiate one of those ways of being is to dishonor them all. "[coda & discography]"—which closes *Cocktails* as "[first fugue]" closed out *Tea*—suggests that Powell's antinomian, redemptive project has at last been accomplished, the strands of queer heritage, personal experience, elegy, blessing, and purgation all complete—"the garment that tore: mended. the body that failed: reclaimed." Echoing Whitman (and Lorca) he invites "voyeurs, passion flowers, trolls, twinks, dancers, cruisers, lovers without lovers // here is the door marked HEAVEN: someone on the dancefloor, waiting just for you." What follows is not more language of Powell's invention but a list of important disco tracks, including Patrick Cowley and Sylvester (the tutelary artists of *Tea*) but also many other singers and groups: the "HEAVEN" that comes together in Powell's verse is not, cannot be, Powell's alone.

My Name Is Henri

Contemporary Poets Discover John Berryman

When John Berryman's 77 *Dream Songs* appeared in 1963, discerning readers recognized it not just as the fulfillment of talents promised in Berryman's *Homage to Mistress Bradstreet*—nor as simply a brilliant response to Robert Lowell's *Life Studies*—but as something so new it was hard to describe. Elizabeth Bishop wrote to Lowell, "One has the feeling 100 years from now [Berryman] may be all the rage—or a 'discovery'—*hasn't one?*" Berryman achieved increasing recognition from his peers, winning the Pulitzer Prize for 77 *Dream Songs* and the Bollingen and National Book Award for *His Toy, His Dream, His Rest* (1968); interest in Berryman later prompted two biographies.

Yet after his death in 1972 Berryman's influence on younger poets (other than those who had known him personally) seemed almost non-existent. His unpredictable blend of erudition and comedy made him harder to imitate than his so-called confessional peers, while his use of African American dialect, and his sometime sexism, made him less attractive as an imagined poetic forebear. The poet's sometimes flaunted learnedness, his self-mythologizing, the frequently topical or occasional nature of the later Dream Songs, and their formal debts to Berryman's early master Yeats, might seem to make him even less usable now than he would have seemed in the 1980s.

In the past decade, however, a number of American poets have made new claims on Berryman's legacy. "My course is rotten," writes Liz Waldner in *Self and Simulacra* (2001); "I channel Mr. Berryman who am not such a man." Her more autobiographical volume *Homing Devices* explains, "When I was fifteen I could have said with Mr. Berryman: *It's not a good position I'm in*." Jeremy Glazier's "Berryman's Bones," a direct pastiche of the form and grammar of *77 Dream Songs,* graced a 2002 issue of the *Boston Review;* an even more recent poem by Joanna Fuhrman (in *Dream Songs*–like stanzas and diction, though unrhymed) imagines "Glimpsing John Berryman Reborn as a Hasid."

Recent poets who may not name Berryman in their poems make more extended use of his work. In sequences based on personae, in investigations of linguistic extremes, and attempts to merge difficulty with comedy, or in long poems about mourning, grief, and guilt, American poets have recently "channeled" Berryman's style in general, and *77 Dream Songs* in particular, to create their own work. Influential first and second books from the past ten years—from Mark Levine, Lucie Brock-Broido, Kevin Young, Susan Wheeler, and Mary Jo Bang—draw on Berryman's style to meet their widely shared goals. Another acclaimed poet whose career dates from the seventies, Frank Bidart, uses not the stylistic surface but the psychological substructure of *The Dream Songs* in his own oeuvre.

Levine and other poets indebted to Berryman may trace those debts to broader American trends. Many poets now distrust a unified lyric "I," and find in Berryman usable models for plural or unstable selves. Berryman's work also speaks to a widespread interest in liberal guilt (intensified as poets have sought shelter in the academy) and to a fascination with fame and celebrity (which present-day American poets often view as beyond their reach). Bidart's debt to Berryman has no such correlates in broader literary or cultural history: that debt stems instead from the two poets' shared beliefs.

I begin with Levine's widely praised—and widely imitated—*Debt* (1992), whose debts to *77 Dream Songs* can hardly be overstated. Levine's signature poem, "Work Song," features a voraciously self-destructive character rather like Berryman's Henry; lest we mistake his source, Levine begins:

> My name is Henri. Listen. It's morning.
> I pull my head from my scissors, I pull
> the light bulb from my mouth—Boss comes at me
> while I'm still blinking.
> Pastes the pink slip on my collarbone.

Levine's Henri can behave much like Henry, converting his sense of discomfort with middle-aged male adulthood into anecdotes designed to provoke comic outrage. Like Henry, he displays a discomfiting, almost prurient interest in anti-Semitism and the Holocaust. Like Henry, he loves to complain, and likes to remind us that he is not quite a real person, only a literary representation in a world of representations:

> I am Henri, mouth full of soda crackers.
> I live in Toulouse, which is a piece of cardboard.
> Summers the Mayor paints it blue, we fish in it.
> Winters we skate on it. Children are always
> drowning or falling through cracks. Parents are distraught
> but get over it. It's easy to replace a child.
> Like my parents' child, Henri.

Readers of *77 Dream Songs* sometimes take Henry's volatile tone, his desire to expose his least attractive sides, as a desire above all to hold and keep a reader's attention: Henri's outrageous, physically impossible adventures take to new extremes the logic behind Henry's travails. Both poets use suicide, or the threat of suicide, as an attention-getting device, and both tell us exactly what they are doing: "Come on, man, / put yourself together!" Henri/Levine tells himself: "You want so much to die / that you don't want to die." Henri (like Henry) takes refuge in a riot of alternate symbols for his speaking voice:

> My name is Henri. I am Toulouse. I am scraps
> of bleached parchment, I am the standing militia,
> a quill, the Red Cross, I am the feather
> in my cap, the Hebrew Testament, I am the World Court. . . .

I am an ice machine.
I am an alp.
I stuff myself in the refrigerator
wrapped in newsprint. With salt in my heart
I stay good for days.

Not only the attitude of seriocomic extravagance here but the distinctively iterated phrases that project this attitude seem learned from the Berryman who declared in "Formal Elegy," "I am four feet long . . . I am an automobile," and who wrote in Dream Song 22:

I am the little man who smokes & smokes.
I am the girl who does know better but.
I am the king of the pool. . . .

I am the enemy of the mind.
I am the auto salesman and lóve you.
I am a teenage cancer, with a plan.

Levine repeats this rhetorical figure throughout *Debt:* "I am a TV. I buzz. I receive everything"; "I am, at bare minimum, a two-headed monster."

Both Levine's self-presentations and his allegorical scenes—often courtrooms or battlefields—replicate the confusions in which the Berryman of *The Dream Songs* situates himself. Berryman: "I am, outside. Incredible panic rules. / People are blowing and beating each other without mercy"; Levine: "I watch them come at me from all directions. / The traffic is not about to swerve around me tonight." Berryman's division of the lyric "I" among Henry and his interlocutors turned some of the early Dream Songs into mock trials, with Henry defending his actions before his "friend." Helen Vendler has described Henry's "perpetual and unidentifiable free-floating anxiety and sense of homicidal guilt." Berryman invites us to judge him, comparing his readers to judges, his page to a court, and his poems to evidence of crime, not only in the famous Dream Song 29 (to which I'll return), but elsewhere throughout *The Dream Songs:* "'Oyez, oyez!' The Man

Who Did Not Deliver / is before you for his deliverance my lords. / *He stands, as charged.*" Levine, too, pursues the idea of poetry as self-indictment, as confession in the juridical sense: "I've been identified. It's him," the title poem decides. Levine, like Berryman, plays both felon and detective: "I'm looking for remains. A body. I'm looking for bodies."

Accuser and accused, Henry and friend, or superego and id, emerge throughout *The Dream Songs* as special cases of the divided psyche the sequence always imagines. Berryman explicitly contemplates the possibility that he might not have a unified self, that the parts of him represented as (for example) lust, shame, tenderness, and ambition, or as different speakers with different dialects, might fit together into no whole: "I am—I should be held together by— / but I am breaking up"; "Henry's parts were fleeing." "'Underneath,' / (they called in iron voices) 'understand, / is nothing. So there.'" Levine's poems of self-interrogation go even further than Berryman's in portraying unresolvable self-division, since Levine's personae cannot even manage to remain in evidence as consistent parts, nor to reassemble into an episodic diary such as the later Dream Songs comprise. Levine's voices simply divide, and are conquered: "I am bought and divided and placed on the hearth."

Unstable, violent self-division forms something of a leitmotif in Levine: the poems sometimes look like angry or puzzled responses to Levine's inability to see himself as one person. Like Berryman, Levine even finds outrageous metaphors for his psychic division in the history of U.S. race relations: "Once I was white and then I was black. / It happened overnight." And, as with Berryman, parts of Levine strike other parts as repulsive, abject, deserving moral or aesthetic dismissal. One example from *Debt:* "The me on the bed they avoid / he makes a gurgling noise with each breath / he stinks very bad. I am not the man he used to be." Another: "What little control I have / over my lost parts!" And a third: "I have been speaking someone else's lines. / Someone small. Someone perfectly dangerous." Similar images of compulsion, ventriloquism, and dismemberment animate the first poem (or "song") in Levine's second book, *Enola Gay* (2000):

He hadn't meant to go on so long. He hadn't meant
it. But the song would not go.
And the words no longer sounded like words.
Though he sang with his tongue behind his teeth.
Though he struggled to remove his hands from his shirt.

Levine sounds so often like Berryman because he shares so many of
Berryman's projects, hoping to find a lyric form as unstable, guilty, and
anxious as the American life he depicts. A list of devices Levine picked
up from Berryman might include named or otherwise distinguished,
but never realistically detailed, personae; very divergent voices for dis-
junct parts of the self; off-kilter or uneven stanzaic form; historical erudition; clashing, unstable, or nonnaturalistic diction, including both
colloquial and erudite extremes; and the pretense that a poem is at
once a theatrical performance and a trial for a crime. All these devices
appear throughout *The Dream Songs,* though they seem most evident
in the earlier, more difficult installments, which in turn sound most
like Berryman's heirs in the 1990s. Berryman's "I am X, I am Y" rhetorical figure, in particular, has become (partly thanks to Levine's example) an almost predictable feature of first and second books: "I am
a service / revolver in a swimming pool . . . I am a love letter" (Joshua
Clover); "I was that season, the little ends I made" (Amy England); "I
am spring I am not spring / I am Voltaire he said" (Ange Mlinko). Nor
do the debts stop at this now-familiar device. I will survey briefly a few
recent books that draw on Berryman more extensively, then dwell at
some length on one more (by Mary Jo Bang), before moving on to consider a deeper, less obvious kinship between Berryman and Bidart.
   A quick, partial list of recent books that follow Berryman's linguistic lead might include Lucie Brock-Broido's *The Master Letters*
(1995), Susan Wheeler's *Smokes* (1996), *Lawrence Booth's Book of
Visions* by Maurice Manning (2001), Kevin Young's *Jelly Roll* (2003),
and Brenda Shaughnessy's *Interior with Sudden Joy* (1999). Brock-
Broido's "I" subdivides herself as Berryman's did, taking on historical
and even zoological roles. "At Lissadell," one poem begins, "I am the
red she / Fox in habitat." "I am a shoemaker's apprentice," declares another; a third, "I am angel, addict, catherine wheel." Brock-Broido, in

an interview, credits Berryman, despite "all his hysteria," for some of her distinctive tones. Promising to "be pristine in excess Rhetoric" and giving "a mummer's wave to Media, the angst of evening news," Brock-Broido also explores the American "celebrity culture" and "fascination with fame" that, as the scholar David Haven Blake says, "shaped the public dimensions of" Berryman's verse.

Other poets take up what might seem the most recalcitrant, least usable aspect of *The Dream Songs* style: a white poet's ostensibly playful use of dated Afro-American stage dialect. Susan Wheeler not only seeks figures for shock and self-division ("The cavities in my mouth / play harmonics, they do it without me") but uses a Berrymanesque synthetic dialect to do it: "Manman got a special s'rup t'cures the lonelies. / All the night, up the tree'f the pickling shed / Ise drinking from it elixir." Maurice Manning (the Yale Younger Poet for 2001) goes even further to resurrect Berryman's blackface, deploying multiple pseudo-nyms and baroque syntax along with a mix of standard and dialect voices: "*Mad Daddy* is the man with the shotgun full of history"; "Why come Mad Daddy make Law play dat game / a tremble-hearted Twenty-One all night . . . ?" W. S. Merwin's foreword understandably finds in Manning's verse "the disturbing ghost of Berryman's Mr. Bones."

Berryman also remains available as a midcentury precursor (neither premodern nor High Modern) for the contemporary lyric sequence, with (as Berryman put it) "parts . . . more independent than parts usually are." Kevin Young, who has edited a selection from Berryman, writes that Berryman's "engagement with voice and invective and ultimately humor" allows his "influence on postmodern . . . or experimental traditions." With dozens of short poems named after musical forms, Young's *Jelly Roll* perhaps attempts to merge the principles of *The Dream Songs* with the principles of other kinds of "songs": "In the calamitous city / in the songs & sinners / among the thousand throngs," Young concludes, "I barter & belong." Berryman (he might imply) belongs to him, too. And while the ampersand alone hardly counts as sufficient evidence, ampersands, rhyming stanzas with pentameter norms, rapid high- and low-culture allusion, distorted syntax, and flirtatiously plural personae (in poems focused on sex and metaphysical guilt) together might be enough: if so, we might hear traces of

Berryman's music (perhaps by way of Brock-Broido) in the sequences of Brenda Shaughnessy's *Interior with Sudden Joy* (1999). "Your voice & eye are muscle & they hurt / like prodigy too soft or quick in class," one poem promises a would-be lover; "Vampiring I would have killed / all I loved & kept all our lives // for centuries, crypt-crock" confesses another.

None of these poets goes as far as Levine in appropriating and renovating both Berryman's techniques and his concerns. Nor does Levine himself adopt one aspect crucial to *77 Dream Songs:* Berryman's volume functions not just as a set of poems but as a series with narrative components, loosely indebted to the sixteenth-century sonnet sequences that Berryman earlier imitated directly. To find such a book-length, quasi-narrative sequence in contemporary writing, we might turn to Mary Jo Bang's *Louise in Love* (2001), which puts Berrymanesque leaps, allusions, and jokes to new narrative use, chronicling whimsically named characters through their circuitous, bookish love affairs.

Bang opens by listing six "Dramatis Personae": the titular Louise, her sister Lydia, Ham (Louise's sometime lover), Charles (his brother), "Isabella, a child," and "The Other." Her first poem, "Eclipsed," promises "Nostradamic foretelling / of retinal damage written in novelese." She promises something like a novel, that is, but damaged, and hard to look at directly (like the sun, like the love affair itself). Individual poems gloss and describe, but avoid explaining, the events that shape Louise's feelings:

> Mother did say, Louise said, try to be popular,
> pretty, and charming. Try to make others
> feel clever. Without fear, what are we?
>
> the other asked. The will, said Louise. The mill moth
> and the lavish wick, breathless in the remnant
> of a fire.

The questions promise autobiographical incident, but the poem delivers something stranger, as Bang splits her voice up into question and answer; flaunts syntactic inversions as signs of artifice; and concludes with a series of incompatible metaphors.

Berryman, Bang wrote to me when I asked her about him, "was very much in my mind" when she wrote the majority of *Louise*, "especially after teaching *The Dream Songs*." "What I got from Berryman," she continues, "was this idea of letting a character stand for some aspect of one's own psyche . . . Louise would become a Huffy Henry and allow me to court disaster on paper," while "the more timid side of myself got jealous and I had to bring Louise's sister Lydia into the mix . . . Lydia might be the equivalent of a Mr. Bones." *Louise in Love* follows *77 Dream Songs* (and *Berryman's Sonnets*) in presenting itself as a modern *ars amatoria,* a manual explaining—with sometimes outrageous examples—how lovers behave. Louise both fears and celebrates her "excessive frivolity" (as the poems say), imagining "denizens of a splendid / language they spoke sotto voce." Tonal leaps and drops divide the sequence, arrest or control its moment, and hold our attention at all costs: "the boat could not be capsized / as long as someone listened." Bang's poetry thus identifies itself at once with artifice and with irrepressible instinct:

> The mind says no,
Louise admitted, but the heart, it loves repetition
and sport:

> cat's paw from under the bedskirt,
> dainty wile, frayed thing,
> fish hook.

Love—"love, love, love, love, love, love, love," as Bang also writes—animates these retrospective poems (poems about love, but by no means love poems) as a game and as a source of regret; the poems become examples of gamesmanship and attempts to discover what went wrong. Bang's disillusioned interrogation of lovers' behavior, her appalled deconstructions of men in pursuit, thus raise a feminist answer to the decidedly masculinist Berryman who had celebrated "my splendid getting / four ladies to write to Henry," or confided, "Them lady poets must not marry, pal."

It is Bang's insistence on the artifice that enables a love affair—on the self as something consciously, even lavishly, constructed for others' temporary consumption—that links her view of the self most securely to Berryman's, her story to the stories the Dream Songs tell. If syntactic inversion signaled that constructedness in lines already quoted, "The Ana of Bliss" offers the same signals through rhyme:

> His mouth was the yes that was wished on,
> feet angled in. He said, My but aren't we?
> Si, she said, aren't I
>
> a rampant array
> of negatives bashed and belittled?
> Come in, come in, my little passion flower, he would often say.

In its set of signs for inconsistency, for the self's failure to hold together as one thing, Bang's verse offers her own version of the "I am an X, I am a Y" device we saw in Levine and others: "She would be a blue new, the terrain of now, / a nice never waiting, one destined / for pleasure in that place."

Why should all these poets use Berryman now? Some possible answers have, I hope, already emerged. Berryman's off-balance array of competing voices dramatized an unstable and plural sense of self: "'The sovereign I,' called Henry yet again / in storm & weariness, and 'No' said she, / 'We are not that way made,'" says one of the Dream Songs collected in the posthumous book *Henry's Fate*. Helen Vendler found "no integrated Ego in *The Dream Songs*," only voices "talking to each other across the void." "When he found his voice," agreed Louise Glück, Berryman "found his voices." Suspicious of "voice," poets now find in Berryman a source for always-plural voices. And they want such plural voices, often, because they do not seek, cannot credit, or in some cases even lack sympathy with, conventions of lyric poems as poems of one voice, expressing one self at one time. In *Fence* magazine's "Symposium on Subjectivity and Style," the poet-critic Juliana Spahr says that her own "subjectivity bears little resemblance to grounded, coherent subjectivity," while the critic Jeffrey Jullich claims flatly that "the subject does not exist." In a similar symposium organized by the *Iowa Review*, Levine declares that "writers like me . . .

tend to need to hold in ambivalent high regard the set of metaphysical precepts"—among them "empathy, and self, and subjectivity"—that advanced critics and their allies "claim . . . to reject."

What about Berryman's sense of himself on trial, his recurrent focus on crime and guilt? The guilt Berryman expresses about his philandering, about his drinking, about his father's death, and (later) even about his success finds a distant echo in the guilt about privilege, and about the aesthetic as a category, that contemporary poets imbibe from their colleagues and friends in academia, and in the different but often related guilt about racial appropriation that today's white readers can feel in reading, enjoying, or advocating poems as dependent as the Dream Songs are on racially marked traditions. Berryman's interest in his own reputation—his self-consciousness about his own position as a poet—also looks forward (as the humility of Bishop or Jarrell, and the monumentality of Lowell or Olson, would not) to contemporary poets' anxieties about their art's apparent inconsequence, and to their heightened desire for even fleeting notice. Berryman's legacy thus helps poets describe what George W. S. Trow called in 1981 "the context of no context," the American cultural condition in which events and beliefs seem important (or real) only inasmuch as they affect famous people or represent collective grievances; in this situation, Trow felt, "the one freedom [white middle-class men can] make use of is the freedom carved out by certain adolescents to make an aesthetic out of complaint."

All these rationales speak not just to individual poets but to the temper of their times. And none of them accounts for the different debts to Berryman detectable within the poetry of Frank Bidart. Those debts also make implausible the concepts of poetic influence that seek to ground all such influence in cultural history. Berryman wrote that "the elementary thing required" of any poet is "to *sound as if he meant it*." Readers wary of, or even hostile to, some of the poets discussed earlier in this essay might complain that those poets take techniques invented for psychological or social truths and use those techniques for études or mere experiments.

No critic would say that about Bidart, whose life and stated influences link him not to Berryman but to Berryman's peers, especially to Lowell (with whom Bidart worked in the last decade of Lowell's career, and whose *Collected Poems* Bidart coedited). And yet Bidart's well-known dramatic monologues—among them that of the serial murderer "Herbert White" and the Freudian analysand "Ellen West"—feature, just as the Dream Songs do, deeply divided psyches with more than one voice; uncontrolled, or barely controlled, sexual passion; clashing registers of diction; and psychoanalytic meditations on juridical and existential guilt. Bidart's poems owe much to the Berryman who inhabited "Mistress Bradstreet," and who wrote in Dream Song 29:

> never did Henry, as he thought he did,
> end anyone and hacks her body up
> and hide the pieces, where they may be found.
> He knows: he went over everyone, & nobody's missing.
> Often he reckons, in the dawn, them up.
> Nobody is ever missing.

The gruesome crimes of Bidart's "Herbert White" are almost exactly those Berryman describes in this, perhaps the most admired and most often quoted of all the Dream Songs.

Glück finds that "more profoundly than any poet since Berryman (whom he in no other way resembles) Bidart explores individual guilt, the insoluble dilemma." Bidart's fascination with deep-rooted guilt may both generate, and occlude, further debts, for example, in his sundered personae. Bidart has written that the Borgesian "I" "asserts a disparity between its essential self and its worldly second self"; the principal dancer in *The Rite of Spring*, in Bidart's poem on Vaslav Nijinsky, "finds that there is a self // WITHIN herself / that is NOT HERSELF." "Herbert White" says of his first crime, "it was funny,—afterwards, / it was as if somebody else did it." These split psyches suit both poets' theatrical tropes. Henry and the friend who calls him "Mr. Bones" behave as stage minstrels, and the individual songs allow Henry to act (sometimes comically or hammishly) many parts. "Tomorrow be more shows; be special need / for rest & rehearse now." Bidart, too, compares his poems to theatrical spaces and performances, especially those that tolerate grotesque extremes: *"I saw,"* he writes, *"the parade of my loves // those PERFORMERS comics actors singers."* Asked which critical works inform his poetry, Bidart names Francis Fergusson's *The Idea of a Theater.*

For both poets, these imagined performances extend not only through individual poetic units but throughout a body of work. Berryman, who defined a long poem as including "the construction of a world," stretched out his Dream Songs into two books and many more later poems (some of which still sit, unpublished, in the University of Minnesota archives). Bidart, too, has been turning his separate poems and volumes into a unified work, reusing titles and invented forms ("The First Hour of the Night," "The Second Hour of the Night"), as well as key words. The early poem "The Arc" (in which arcs represent an amputee's abbreviated life cycle) informs both Bidart's later biblical lyric ("LET THE FIRMAMENT // ARC THE EARTH") and the recent "Advice to the Players," which evokes "the shape cut by the arc of our lives."

Finally, Bidart resembles Berryman—and appears to draw on Berryman—in his tendency to derive all the lyric kinds he uses from elegy (in the narrow sense of a formal lament for the dead). *77 Dream Songs* offered elegies for Faulkner, Frost, Roethke, Stevens, and the dead in Vietnam ("The war is real"); *His Toy, His Dream, His Rest* famously mourned Blackmur, Jarrell, Plath, W. C. Williams, and "the sacred memory of Delmore Schwartz." Yet the Dream Songs also present themselves as elegy in a more global sense. Early and late, the poems present themselves as meditations, not just on suicide or on Berryman's father (as some have claimed), but on the omnipresence of death, the fact that everyone dies. "The high ones die, die. They die," said one poem, and another:

Appalled: by all the dead: Henry brooded.
Without exception! All.
ALL.
The senior population   waits. Come down! come down!
A ghastly & flashing pause, clothed,
life called; us do.

In one of several Dream Songs that present Henry as the defendant in a criminal trial, Berryman hears "the grave ground-rhythm of a gone / . . . makar." He writes—here as in the *Op. posth.* Dream Songs—as if he were dead, in order to mourn the dead, and in order to hear them. No wonder, then, that Berryman cites the medieval Scots poet William Dunbar's "Lament for the Makars." And no wonder Bidart (standardizing the spelling) does the same, in his "Lament for the Makers," which includes (just as Berryman's laments do) both poets and family members: "What parents leave you / is their lives." No wonder, too, that Bidart has become the preeminent poet of his generation (as Berryman was of his) to write elegies for named (or otherwise specified) individuals; consider "For Bill Nestrick (1940–96)," "In Memory of Joe Brainard," "Lady Bird," "If I Could Mourn Like a Mourning Dove," "For Mary Ann Youngren," and Bidart's several poems to his father or mother, among them "Golden State": "It's in many ways / a relief to have you dead."

Bidart's poem on Lady Bird Johnson has special interest here, because its seemingly slight six lines end by describing Bidart's speakers in general, who teach us "that people look at / the living, and wish for the dead." Such wishes are something Berryman explored: we might even say that the Dream Songs derive from them. "It all centered in the end on the suicide / in which I am an expert, deep and wide," Dream Song 136 concludes. The Songs toward the end of *His Toy, His Dream, His Rest* sum up the volume's themes in funereal settings. In Dream Song 384, Henry/Berryman "stand[s] above my father's grave with rage," recalling previous visits (and previous graveside poems) before modulating to aggression: "I come back for more, / I spit upon this dreadful banker's grave." Placed after several Songs that warn us that the sequence will end soon ("I will not come again / or not come with this style"), Berryman's concluding gesture at once presages a suicide and recapitulates the inquiry into the death wish that the Dream Songs have conducted all along:

I'd like to scrabble till I got right down
away down under the grass

and ax the casket open ha to see
just how he's taking it, which he sought so hard

we'll tear apart
the mouldering grave clothes ha & then Henry
will heft the ax once more, his final card,
and fell it on the start.

This self-dramatizing and self-consuming violence—aimed both at the dead father and at death itself—looks forward to the self-punishments and self-annihilations Bidart's characters seek "within / that *broken mirror made // by all the things . . . inherited and remade.*" Bidart, like Henry and like Berryman, grieves and makes songs from grief as he investigates, through historical and fictive masks, the origins of his psyche, whose wounds sometimes represent existential dilemmas, and at other times his particular past. *"Release me somehow,"* Bidart's doomed, incestuous, mythological character Myrrha prays, *"from both / life and death."* Bidart says in an interview, as Berryman might have said, that he is "trying to figure out *why* the past was as it was, what patterns and powers kept me at its mercy (so I could change, and escape)." Dream Song 385 (the last in the one-volume book) in fact presents itself as tragic acceptance: "Fall comes to us as a prize / to rouse us toward our fate." Bidart's characters seek such acceptance, though they do not often find it (or else they go mad when they do); his long poem about Myrrha, "The Second Hour of the Night," becomes (as the poet and critic Dan Chiasson has argued) a poem of theatrical and tragic seeking, a poem about Bidart's "difficult necessity of playing himself."

Bidart and Berryman share not a style nor a surface but a set of strategies and intentions, each portraying his oeuvre as theatrical performances of extended mourning by a fractured and guilty self. Those shared strategies (rarely visible at the levels of sound or diction) broaden the contexts for the stylistic debts described earlier in this essay. Those debts mark Berryman's more visible influence on poets whose careers began much later, poets—Bang and Levine, certainly, but also Brock-Broido, Waldner, Young—who may still be developing their palettes. Where Bidart appears to adopt some of Berryman's obsessions into a style of his own, younger poets have found in Berryman a stylistic model (perhaps the only one of his "middle generation") fit for their own, up-to-the-minute concerns.

III

James K. Baxter

I Do Not Expect You to Like It

Published when he was only twenty-one, his first book got him noticed right away; soon he became his nation's leading poet, lecturing (and raising hackles) across the country. He changed his style drastically several times, becoming not just a celebrated literary man but the famous head of a scandalous commune and a public voice for the dispossessed. A worshipful Catholic, he enjoyed a reputation as a libertine; a noted drinker, he became an apostle of Alcoholics Anonymous. A master of academic technique, he considered himself an heir to Scottish bards; he also embraced non-European folkways, renaming himself in a local language. His last publications made him his country's closest answer at once to Dylan Thomas, to Robert Lowell, to Walt Whitman, and to Allen Ginsberg; his sudden death occasioned national mourning.

The poet is James K. Baxter (1926–72), of New Zealand, and most Americans—no, most Americans *who read modern poetry*—have never heard of him. Why? New Zealand is far away and small; Baxter never visited the United States; parts of his work sound defiantly local, keyed to New Zealand's social and political history, as Yeats keyed his work to Ireland's. Other parts of Baxter's work, though, belong to the international 1960s, with its embrace of intuition, its flight from institutions, its attention to the young. To read Baxter's best poems is to enter an English-speaking culture that bears surprisingly little relation to the contexts most American readers know. It is also to enter a passionate, tormented psyche, and to find an original verbal world.

As with many poets, the poems track the life. I've pulled details from Frank McKay's slightly hagiographic *Life of James K. Baxter;* if capsule bios irk you, skip six paragraphs down. Baxter's mother, Millicent, grew up in an academic, Anglophile family on New Zealand's South Island. His father, Archie—of Scottish descent, little formal education, and fierce pacifist beliefs—ran a successful farm before being drafted into the First World War, then found himself jailed and tortured (in New Zealand and in Europe) when he refused to fight. James and his older brother, Terence, (born 1921) spent semirural boyhoods on the South Island and part of their teens in a Quaker boarding school in England; back home, James's high school years (1940–43) coincided with the Second World War, when Terence, like his father, was imprisoned for refusing to serve. The contrast between uncaring institutions and the defiant men who oppose them fires many of James's poems:

> When I was only semen in a gland
> Or less than that, my father hung
> From a torture post at Mud Farm
> Because he would not kill. The guards
> Fried sausages, and as the snow came darkly
> I feared a death by cold in the cold groin
> And plotted revolution. His black and swollen thumbs
> Explained the brotherhood of man.

Coming in 1944 to the University of Otago in Dunedin, Baxter distinguished himself as a pub crawler and as the university's best young poet; by the end of that year his first volume was in press. That book, *Beyond the Palisade,* made Baxter a big fish in a small— but churning—pond; the New Zealand poet-critic Allen Curnow made him the youngest author in an influential 1945 anthology, calling him "strong in impulse and confident in invention, with qualities of youth in verse which we have lacked." Today the book, and the rest of Baxter's 1940s verse, seems less original than they did to Curnow, though they are stunning as student work, revealing a young man's quick assimilation of Thomas, Louis MacNeice, and W. B. Yeats. One of the best of the 1940s poems, "Wild Bees," remembers how Baxter and his boyhood friends torched a hive; its melodramatic, self-chastising announcements prefigure the acrid guilts of his adult life:

> O it was Carthage under the Roman torches,
> Or loud with flames and falling timber, Troy!
> A job well botched. Half of the honey melted
> And half the rest young grubs. Through earth-black
>   smouldering ashes
> And maimed bees groaning, we drew out our plunder.
> Little enough their gold, and slight our joy.

Baxter quit the university to work in an iron foundry, as a shepherd, and then at industrial jobs in Dunedin; there he met the university student Jacquie Sturm, and the pair fell in love. (Her Maori heritage would turn up in his later poems.) The new couple moved in late 1947 to Christchurch, the South Island's other university town; there Jacquie would finish her degree in psychology, and Baxter would resume his literary rise. (In the Christchurch university magazine, Baxter listed his address as "any pub.") James and Jacquie married in 1948, then moved to the capital, Wellington, where James began training to teach elementary school. He also began to give lectures and write reviews: *The Fallen House* (1953) turned him from a rising star into a recognized literary light. In 1954, he joined AA, the first of the dramatic spiritual commitments that enter his later poems; the second came in 1957, when the poet announced that he planned to enter the Catholic Church. Separated from Jacquie, and from their two children, in 1958, James wrote his first play, saw his first UK book *(In Fires of No Return),* and won a fellowship to Japan and India, ostensibly to research publications for teachers. (Jacquie rejoined him in Bombay, healing their split.) The poverty Baxter saw in India's cities seemed to him to indict international capitalism, while the religious life in the villages gave him examples of ascetic vocations: he had, he wrote, "become almost unawares, a member of a bigger, rougher family."

Back in Wellington, Baxter worked hard as a playwright, with national attention the result. The poem "To an Adult Education Audience" (1963) asks his public "which of my selves do you want to eat?" Fed up with what he viewed as white-collar compromises, he left his job writing educational bulletins in 1963 and became a letter carrier. His postal routes, and New Zealand's political climate (labor disputes and the nearby Vietnam War), inform the vigorous, cantankerous *Pig Island Letters*. A fellowship named for Robert Burns (one of his heroes) took him back to Dunedin's university in 1966; there this outspokenly antiacademic poet wrote prose for Catholic newspapers, charmed students, involved himself in antiwar protests, and finished his last set of stage and radio plays. Baxter could never forgive the English and Scottish "hangmen and educators" who had imported the mores, and the taboos, all over his collegiate "city of youth": he decided, in "On Possessing the Burns Fellowship 1966," that

> If there is any culture here
> It comes from the black south wind
> Howling above the factories
> A handsbreadth from Antartica,
>
> Whatever the architect and planner
> Least understand.

In April 1968 Baxter experienced a vision of Jerusalem—"not the city in Palestine, but the mission station on the Wanganui River" on New Zealand's North Island. He resolved to "go to Jerusalem without money or books," "learn the spoken Maori" language, and "form the nucleus of a community where the people, both Maori and pakeha [European-descended] would try to live without money or books, worship God and work on the land." In 1969 he did just that. First, however, he left Jacquie (and their new granddaughter) for Auckland, where he lived with junkies and hippies, seeing himself as their patron. Arriving at Jerusalem in September, he arranged with the local nunnery to use a cottage and build his commune, itself called Jerusalem ("Hiruharama" in Maori). The settlement crystallized the myth of his life, becoming a magnet for troubled youth and an unintended tourist attraction. Baxter's late poems describe his endeavors there: the first and most important batches appeared as *Jerusalem Sonnets* (1970), *Jerusalem Daybook* (1971), and *Autumn Testament* (1972). The poet built up the community he had imagined, but could not reconcile its antiestablishment ethos with the daily requirements of bookkeeping, maintenance, hygiene: he gave up in September 1970, traveling home to Wellington, but returned to Jerusalem in 1972 to try again with a smaller group of people. Again inspired, but physically exhausted, he finished a scary, resigned last set of poems ("The Tiredness of Me and Herakles," "Ode to Auckland") and died that October. Eight hundred people attended the funeral.

Baxter's New Zealand profile remains far larger than life, larger perhaps than that of any living poet in the United States. A CD called *Baxter,* released in 2000 by National Radio (New Zealand's equivalent of the BBC), presents twelve New Zealand artists singing the poet's verse (among them Martin Phillips of the Chills); the liner notes promise "it doesn't get more Kiwi than this." One of my students grew up in New Zealand; when I asked her what she thought of McKay's *Life,* she answered, "How can you write a biography of a myth?" New Zealand poets now try to get out from under his shadow. Yet for all the cross-cultural, historical, travel-broadens-the-mind reasons to read Baxter—reasons that emphasize the distance between his New Zealand in 1958 or '68 and America now—the best reasons have to do not with the politics or the history in the poetry but with the poetry in the poetry: Baxter found sound and form for limitless anger, moral judgment, immanent religious feeling, and dramatic self-abasement, inventing a new kind of sonnet, even a new kind of line.

Baxter is a poet of fireworks and hammer blows, of vaulting flights and searing wounds to pride, and of emphatic rhythmic effects to match. Poems rocket away from their first, sudden phrases: "I do not expect you to like it" ("The Millstones"). "An afternoon of spitting / rain, teaching nothing" ("House Painting"). "There was a message. I have forgotten it. / There was a journey to make. It did not come to anything" ("Letter from the Mountains"). These openings, like most of his best before Jerusalem, sound negative, aggressive; the Jerusalem poems begin no less rapidly, but invite a pastoral calm: "The circle of the hills contains my house; / The house contains the tribe"; "When the spokes fall out of the wagon one has to wait, / Unyoke the horse, hope for the kindness of heaven" ("How to Fly by Standing Still"). Sometimes Baxter will launch such opening phrases into sentences indefinitely prolonged, as if the poet's life might end at the first full stop. He learned to adapt the English pentameter into propulsive five- and six-beat lines designed for immediate force:

> This humid morning half the town is waking
> Like Jonah in the belly of the whale,
>
> Uncertain whether the light is light or else
> A delusion of the blood.

Even in more deliberate, slower forms, Baxter liked to depict Dionysian wildness: his pre-1968 specialties include violent seascapes, jeremiads, and drinking songs. One of his better, lighter self-portraits is "Tomcat" (1964):

> He has no
> dignity, thank God! has grown
> older, scruffier, the ash-
> black coat sporting one or two
>
> flowers like round stars, badges
> of bouts and fights.

Syllabics (each complete line has seven syllables) guide, but do not tame, the poem, which ends: "They said, / 'Get him doctored.' I think not." Few poets start out so skillful, and Baxter did not: his early writings borrowed the stanzas of Yeats, the heated sexual symbolisms of Thomas, the knowing pronouncements of Auden and MacNeice, and the clangorous aural shapes of the young Lowell. By the time of his return from India, Baxter had found clearer routes for his own thought and feeling, discovering (with help from Lowell's *Life Studies*) a less ornate way to map his anger and bitterness. Take "Fishermen" (1962):

I invent nothing.
> Those men in oilskins
Won't ever stagger up the beach
And drop their bundles. Those who believed
Only in the sea and themselves—
Norwegian Maoris—one was dragged down
When his gumboots filled;
> > another's boat
Struck the sandbar at low tide,
Drunk, with a load of fish and manuka.

(Manuka are leaves from which oil and honey are made; the dead sailors—themselves Lowellesque—are "Norwegian Maoris" because they are native New Zealanders who try to conquer the rough sea.)

For a while, the poems got harsher as they got better. Although Baxter enjoyed (and described) landscapes, travel, and sex, to flip through his most accomplished pre-1969 poems is to travel through often choppy waters of blame and gloom (if you want happier poems, skip down five paragraphs more). Existential outrage and political angst seem to merge, and people look worse the more we compare them to animals. The "tiny lizards" in "Election 1960" "dodge among the burnt broom stems // As if the earth belonged to them / Without condition," while "in the polling booths / A democratic people have elected / King Log, King Stork, King Log, King Stork again." Drawn to rebels and extremes, Baxter complained in 1967 that his Kiwi democracy would never see revolution:

We are not that kind of people;
We have learnt to weigh each word like an ounce of butter;
Our talent is for anger and monotony—

Therefore we will survive the singers,
The fighters, the so-called lovers—we will bury them
Regretfully, and spend a whole wet Sunday
Arguing whether the corpses were dressed in black or red.

From a life of frustrations death might seem a welcome escape. Though he seems never to have approached suicide (unless you count self-destructively heavy drinking), Baxter long believed, with Plathlike intensity, in the supremacy of the Freudian death wish: he remembered his adolescent self as a '"sad boy," "thoughts crusted with ice," "who having no / hope did not blow out his brains." "East Coast Journey" (1963) shows a pleasant-enough coastline until the "voice of the sea" arrives and explains:

> As a man

> Grows older he does not want beer, bread, or the prancing flesh,
> But the arms of the eater of life, Hine-nui-te-po,

> With teeth of obsidian and hair like kelp
> Flashing and glimmering at the edge of the horizon.

The nightmarish, motherly ocean looks startling enough; the lines stand out even more for their triple rhythms (*arms* of the *eat*-er of *life, teeth* of ob-*sid*-ian), into which the name of the Maori death goddess fits.

Baxter also attracted attention for rhyming political verse, modeled on Burns, Yeats, and eighteenth-century broadsheets. "A Rope for Harry Fat" (1956) denounced the death penalty; "Ballad of the Three Monkeys" (1963) took on unemployment:

> Down to the Wharf Commission I went
> *(A bag of nails and a union card)*
> For a regular job on the waterfront
> *(And the cash would have come in handy).*

These poems remain fun, and surprisingly few sound dated: they take place in separate styles, separate universes, from the more personal Baxter whose unrhymed stanzas followed "like salt and fresh inside me / The opposing currents of my life and death," and whose recurring characters were not prime ministers and union organizers, but his wife, close male friends, Jonah, the Virgin Mary, and Rhadamanthus, the classical judge of the dead.

"All / Knowledge, my son, is knowledge of the Fall," Baxter imagined his "inward guardian" announcing in a 1962 poem. Yet Baxter also gave voice to a kind of freedom, adapting Rimbaud and Catullus, or playing the Yeatsian wild old wicked man. A relatively calm poem of 1967 displays, instead, the Yeatsian anti-self—the calm, responsible grown-up whom this born prophet, established in his antiestablishment commune, would soon try to become:

To clean up after the party, emptying
Five ash-trays, washing the wooden plates,
Scouring the sink where someone has vomited,
Putting the screen up in front of the fire—

And afterwards to have a smoke, go out
And see the low grey shapeless clouds move
Above the Phys. Ed. building—I can only
Describe it as a form of prayer,

Because it is necessary. Without it I would not
Understand the joy that father Jonah had
In the whale's belly—all but ashamed
To be cut off from human sadness,

Brawls, hopes, and the sexual rigmarole,
So quietly carried in the belly of what is not
That I would wish, if it were possible,
No other light, no other heaven.

All this brings us to Jerusalem—that is, to the last four years of his life, which make up a quarter of his *Collected Poems* and represent his peak. *Jerusalem Sonnets,* and its several sequels, are documents of late-1960s communal life, of the back-to-Eden attitude that distinguished those years from our own. They show Baxter digging and planting, kneeling and praying, running interference with priests and nuns, trying to learn from Maori elders and to incorporate spoken Maori into his own written work. They show his habitual self-confidence and his learned (or not quite learned) humility: "when the wind flutters round my chest / It seems to say, 'Now, now don't be proud that you are poor!'" And they show his often generous, occasionally erotic, frequently comic dealings with the young men and women who organized themselves around him, the group he called "Ngati-Hiruharama" ("Jerusalem tribe") and "nga mokai" ("the fatherless"). Given the personality and the life they record, the writings from those years would be worth reading even if they were not works of great verbal power.

Fortunately they are. Here is the nineteenth sonnet of *Autumn Testament*—not the single best, but a good introduction to the whole:

> The bodies of the young are not the flower,
> As some may imagine—it is the soul
>
> Struggling in an iron net of terror
> To become itself, to learn to love well,
>
> To nourish the Other—when Mumma came from the bin
> With scars from the wrist to the shoulder,
>
> They combed her hair and put their arms around her
> Till she began to blossom. The bread she baked for us
>
> Was better kai than you'd get in a restaurant
> Because her soul was in it. The bread we share in the churches
>
> Contains a Christ nailed up in solitude,
> And all our pain is to be crystal vases,
>
> As if the mice were afraid of God the cat
> Who'd plunge them into Hell for touching one another.

("Kai": food, meal; "Bin": loony bin, asylum.) The poem typifies late Baxter in recording the commune's daily life, praising Christ, attacking social divisions, and placing stark declarations of purpose—announcements about God, love, and the soul—right beside unpredictable metaphor. Those announcements may raise the hackles of urbane readers, fans of Merrill or Ashbery; yet this confident, unguarded manner, risking preachiness to make clear each thought, seems to me an original, achieved style, as suited to Baxter's charismatic sensibility as Ashbery's involutions are suited to his.

Baxter's new life at Jerusalem gave him what many 1960s poets sought: some way to stand outside the Western, urban, industrial systems he denounced. Yet Baxter never repudiated syntax, allusion, or other Western techniques as he chronicled his new life: instead he made them work for him. The sonnets' interdependence of concentration and abandon, of self-abnegation and conscious control, describes not only Baxter's Jerusalem style, but the attitude he had to adopt as the commune's de facto leader, the man who kept it—or tried to keep it— welcoming and minimally sanitary. On the one hand, he wished to abandon secular life, even to give up his own will: "Let the Maker of rainbows and mountains do what He wishes / With this poor idiot, this crab in His beard." On the other hand, he had new obligations:

The kids here don't shout out, "Jesus!"
Or "Hullo, Moses!" as they did in Auckland

When they saw my hair—these ones are too polite—
They call me Mr Baxter when they bring the milk;

I almost wish they didn't; but Sister has them well trained—
And soon she wants me to give them a talk about drugs . . .

The dual roles of penitent and authority figure, of recluse and superstar, exhausted, even destroyed, him, and Baxter's verse could welcome the destruction. He saw himself not as a fisher of men but as rod, reel, and bait, using himself up in a self-denying joy for which he gathered homely figures: "They say it is best // To break a rotten egg in the creek / To get eels—I think I am that egg."

You don't have to be religious (much less Catholic) to appreciate the later Baxter, but you do have to appreciate Baxter's commitment to his idea of religion—half would-be asceticism, half service to those in need, with a tinge of antinomianism, too. On the one hand, his Christ is "the only Master"; on the other, He is "incurably domestic," "An only son with a difficult mother" who "has saddled me again / With the cares of a household," a "Joker who won't let me shuffle my own pack." Often Baxter pushes guilt over First World citizenship, over the privilege of leisure and literacy, over his half-abandoned hopes for distinction (as artist or righteous man or saint) until it becomes guilt about being alive at all: "The wish to climb a ladder to the loft / Of God dies hard in us"; "Some lightness will come later / When the heart has lost its unjust hope // For special treatment." Baxter even referred to himself in Maori, as Hemi (James) or "te tutua" ("nobody"), as if to give up the privilege of English names.

If you hear Baxter's contrition as slightly stagy, his humility as forced, you may be right: his poems acknowledge it. Baxter enjoyed—nobody has captured it better—the gesture of giving up, or of refusing, distinctions and powers one used to command, and of demonstrating those powers even while doing so. (Think of Prospero drowning his books.) These renunciations, as his poems track them, sometimes look like generous gifts to other people, sometimes like sacrifices before Christ, and sometimes like signs of despair. Written after the failure of his first settlement, before the start of the second, "He Waiata mo Tana" ("Song for Tana") presents itself as a poem of repudiation, giving up on all Baxter's vocations in a concussive lament derived from Psalm 137:

Grey and muddy the waters of Babylon
Flowing out of the broken hills,

The river serpent swollen with proud silt
Pushed down his gullet by our fires and our machines,

But the willow branches, green for the tangi,
Delicately flourish on the banks—

I have hung my harp there, the harp I made
Long ago, in a different time—

The wind can pluck the strings, and I
Am a stranger to myself, e Tana,

No longer a man of words, no longer
The master of the rostrum, but a man without a name

Lamenting for the fallen village of Zion
Into whose doors and windows the knuckles of bramble are
    growing.

("Tangi": funeral, or funereal cry.) Baxter did not remain long in such unrelieved moods. More frequently he presents his exhaustion as healing, even holy, and tries to make jokes of it: "The little flies that rustle on my collar / Mistake me, no doubt, for a parcel of dead meat. // They like my stringy hair."

If Baxter's drama lay in abasing himself, it lay also in elevating the fallen—appreciating people, places, even animals and vegetables, elsewhere overlooked or disparaged, from Mumma to "the small grey cloudy louse that nests in my beard" (crab lice are recurrent figures in *Jerusalem Sonnets*) to a more appetizing "sprig of wet wild mint / That should go well tomorrow with the potatoes." Sonnet 27 from *Autumn Testament* remembers his time in Auckland. Here it is, whole, from the journalistic first eight lines to the thunder-and-lightning final phrase:

When I stayed those three months at Macdonald Crescent
In the house of Lazarus, three tribes were living

In each of the storeys—on the ground floor, the drunks
Who came there when the White Lodge burnt down;

Above them, the boobheads; and scattered between the first
And second storey, the students who hoped to crack

The rock of education. The drunks are my own tribe.
One Sunday, the pubs being shut, they held a parliament

In the big front room—Lofty with his walking stick,
Phil the weeper, Taffy who never spoke much,

And one or two others—in conclave they sat, like granite columns
Their necks, like Tritons their faces,

Like tree-roots their bodies. Sober as Rhadamanthus
They judged the town and found it had already been judged.

You can admire the poem for its sincere praise of the drunks' circle, a serious parody of the AA meetings on which Baxter earlier relied. ("Boobheads," writes the lexicographer Tony Deverson, in New Zealand are "chronic recidivists," especially those who want to return to jail.) You can also admire—once you notice them—the interplay of long and short sentences, or the hammering hexameters, with their grim resolution in the last two lines (stress falls on "judged" twice).

The casual feel of the late verse, with its stretched-out lines and associative movement, reflects Baxter's (impossible) desire to write poems that were both less (because less finished, less premeditated) and more (because more consequential, or more sincere) than works of art. Nor did he confine that desire to sonnets—take, for example, his 1972 sestinas. With six six-line stanzas, each with the same six end words, the sestina form normally connotes frustration, rigidity, circular motion: Baxter made it suggest ease instead. "Sestina to Frank McKay" begins:

> The winds of spring are starting
> Even in June to blow
> From a wild sky, and round this house
> Where a cat sleeps on a bed
> And my friends bring me in some kai,
> Goat chops roasted a bit too much
>
> In our family oven. But that's not much
> To gripe about. When we were starting
> Here we often had no kai
> Except onions, and the rain would blow
> Through broken windows. Now I lie on a bed
> In what the cops would call my house
>
> Though it is in fact a Maori house
> Under the wing of the marae too much
> For many to like it.

("Marae": meeting ground of a tribe; tribal council.) The alternating guilt and pride, the self-accusation and the sense of freedom, that animate the sonnets work almost as well here.

I do not expect you to like all of Baxter, nor even all the poems from the Jerusalem years (though his sets of sonnets make beautiful wholes). The 1988 paperback *Collected Poems,* edited by John Weir, tops 650 pages—longer than the standard edition of Yeats's verse, if not for the latter's long notes. (Baxter's *Collected Plays* is a separate book; *Collected Prose* would be hefty if it existed.) Baxter rarely stopped writing, and he composed far more than he chose to publish: seven full books of previously uncollected verse saw print in New Zealand after Baxter died, with more new poems revealed in the *Collected.* Baxter offers the pleasures peculiar to prolific talents (you can read him for years and still find overlooked gems) along with the disadvantages (some poems repeat others; some are just bad). The sheer amplitude of his work (and the often derivative nature of its first half) means that though we should be glad the *Collected Poems* has reappeared in America (thanks, Oxford University Press!), that mountain of a book makes a hard place to start. Better to begin, if you can, with *New Selected Poems* (published by Oxford Australia-New Zealand, edited by Paul Millar), or even with Weir's slim *Essential Baxter.*

If Baxter poses barriers for non-Kiwis, his work also holds special pleasures for Americans. The fight for an original national voice, founded in part on local landscapes and seasons; tragic midcentury tapestries of Catholic symbols; "confessional" self-abasement; poems as tools for late-sixties radicalism; and the open-ended process poem, meant to end when the poet's life does—these in the United States come in separate packages, and usually in separate generations, from Whitman and Hawthorne to Flannery O'Connor to Charles Olson and Adrienne Rich. Baxter moved through them all within twenty-five years. (You could argue that Lowell undertook a similar journey, but no other comparison comes to mind.) Baxter's sense of original sin, and his self-dramatizing drive toward self-abasement—derived, if you like, from AA, or from Catholicism, or from his defiant life history— set his poetry above almost all the others that took up, during the 1960s, one or another utopian program: the way we behave and the way we ought to behave, our bad track record and our lofty hopes, remain simultaneously visible. (By contrast, American poets most associated with the late 1960s—Ginsberg, Snyder, Merwin, Bly—often ascribed only the best intentions to themselves and their allies: it is, perhaps, a deeply American fault.) American readers might find themselves ambivalent about Baxter's late identification with native ways ("Maoritanga," as they are collectively called); and yet I can't think of a white American poet who has done or thought half as much, within his or her poetry, about any of our racial issues as Baxter tried to do with New Zealand's.

"Poems and stories," Baxter wrote in 1956, "are not pills, manifestos, or blueprints of Utopia, but ways of coming at life, as private as a kiss and as public as a morgue." By the Jerusalem years he had become at once humbler and more ambitious: the poems warm themselves at "the flame of non-possession // That burns now and always in the heart of the tribe." Baxter believed—as Americans like to say—that his poetry could "make a difference" and that he as a poet could save at least a bit of his nation; he grew increasingly ambitious, and increasingly rueful, about the part he played. Late poems addressed, and apologized to, the Father; the Son; Baxter's wife, children, friends, country; even the Maori source of life and death, "the dark unknowable breast / Of Te Whaea, the One who bears us and bears with us." The last word on how to hear Baxter might come instead from a sonnet addressed to Satan ("Hatana" in Maori), which also speaks to Baxter's posthumous readers: "you sift and riddle my mind, / On the rack of the middle world, and from my grave at length / A muddy spring of poems will gush out."

Les Murray

From the Planet Dungog

Prodigious and frustrating, welcoming and cantankerous, full of Australian history, places, and names, Les Murray's poetry also displays more abstract qualities Murray likes to call Australian. Chief among these is "sprawl," defined as ease, cheerful excess, unbuttonedness, and unsnobbish self-confidence: "Sprawl is really classless . . . Sprawl is loose-limbed in its mind." Murray's verse really does sprawl, and there's a lot of it: readers who come to the wrong poems first find them blustery, sloppy, or unlistenable. Murray's work flaunts its roughness, its male friendliness, its "defiance of taste," its provincial or "Boeotian" identifications, its ethical doctrines and its Catholic ideals. If his attitudes can be hard to take, his accomplishments ought to be hard to ignore. Among them are spectacular feats of description; character studies with real moral force; sharp storytelling; and, now, the best long narrative poem in English (as far as I know) by any writer alive now.

Murray was born in 1938 and grew up on his grandfather's farm in Bunyah, New South Wales: by his own telling, he seems to have been an isolated child, and then an exceptionally unhappy adolescent: "all my names were fat-names at my new town school." Murray attended university in Sydney, married in 1962, entered the Roman Catholic Church the following year, and published his first book of poems (a split volume with Geoff Lehmann) in 1965. In 1975 Murray purchased the farm in Bunyah, which his father could never afford to buy; he, his wife, and their children made it their full-time residence in 1986. Murray's early and recent involvements with farm life have made him a master of poetry about it; his youthful exclusion ("I was never a teen-ager") now fuels his anger against in-crowds, elites, and urban centers. A recent reference work quotes Murray declaring: "I hate people being left out. Of course, that I suppose has been the main drama of my life—coming from the left-out people into the accepted people and being worried about the relegated who are still relegated. I don't want there to be any pockets of relegation left."

Murray's often-defensive rhetoric champions the unsexy and the inarticulate: more than most poets who claim these goals, Murray has developed a real (and articulate) style in which to do such things. "Ill Music," one of Murray's most memorable early poems, begins with slashing, deliberate unsubtlety:

My cousin loved the violin
and played it gracefully in tune
except when, touching certain chords
he fell down, shrieked and bit at boards
till blood and froth stood on his chin.

The froth stands when the cousin falls, and even the laws of gravity seem upset. "Jim said little when his kin / found a place to place him in": the original horror of witnessing seizures compounds Murray's horror at a family that could simply institutionalize Jim, that fell down where it should have stood up for him.

Solidarity with people like Jim requires that Murray's poems make "ill music" too, that they not sound well made nor pretend all is well. Murray makes a point of extending his solidarity to those whose disadvantages are not only social or physical but cognitive. The volume *Dog Fox Field* (1990) took its title from a Nazi test for mental function; the title poem is an angry elegy for the so-called feebleminded:

These were no leaders but they were first
into the dark on Dog Fox Field:

Anna who rocked her head, and Paul
who grew big and yet giggled small,

Irma who looked Chinese, and Hans
who knew his world as a fox knows a field.

(Although autism is not mental retardation, it helps to remember that Murray has an autistic son.) Insisting that the dignity of persons is not based on intellect or achievement, Murray can be astonishingly good at expressing bodily feelings—physical disgust or hunger or jocular satiety: "Pie spiced like islands, dissolving in cream, is now / dissolving in us. We've reached the teapot of calm." His "quality of sprawl" carries goals at once political and simply sensual: against other people's exclusive hierarchies, Murray's verse stretches out to let everything in.

Bad Murray poems mostly seem ungainly and formless; the good ones tend to justify their forms by analogy with the deeds of persons, with artisanal work, or with shapes and events in the nonhuman world. Murray especially enjoys mimesis of action—lines emulate "motoring down the main roads," riding a horse, wielding a hammer, lying in bed. He relishes onomatopoeia: "The channel-billed cuckoo / shouts, flying, and the drug-squad helicopter / comes singing *I'll spot it, your pot plot.*" Murray avoids a consistent level of diction as he avoids regular iambics, riding with tractor treads over the contours of individual words. His jaunty or angry rhymed poems can recall Kipling's: an accordion "can conjure Paris up, or home, unclench a chinstrap jaw / but it never sang for a nob's baton, or lured the boys to war."

Murray believes in principle that people have souls and that poems describe them, but in practice his work consistently makes clear its roots and references in the material and social worlds: he remains deeply uncomfortable with lyric's tendencies toward abstraction, its drive to represent not men and women in particular places but (as Rilke has it) a "soul in space." All of Murray's characteristic effects suit the nonlyric genres in which he excels—narrative, travelogue, topical ballad, verse letter, scenic description, moralized anecdote, and georgic, the genre of poems explaining farming. In one early sequence "The Georgic furrow lengthens"; a few books later, "Laconics" contemplates the purchase of a farm: "Where we burn the heaps / we'll plant ki-kuyu grass. // Ecology? Sure. But also husbandry." "Unsecured farm boors, open / verandahs, separate houses," some comfortable trimeters conclude, are Murray's "emblems of a good society." The wrenching "Cowyard Gates" contemplates (on the evidence of the poem) the house from which his cousin evicted his father: that cousin

> didn't want an untidy widower aging
> on his new farm.
> I'll want the timber for cowyard gates, he said.
>
> The floor joists will persist awhile
> and the fireplace, that pack-ice of concrete, stained
> with the last spilt fat.
> I didn't go look.

Shame and its inverse, comfort, which these curt lines remember and contrast, together make one of Murray's central subjects. One harsh recent poem describes a young Murray desperately embarrassed in Sydney, "feeling abashed by proper people": the feeling, like the poem, Murray calls "the Big Shame." Sometimes I wish Murray were more easily embarrassed by his own phrases: all his books include clumsiness and redundancy, masses of lines it's hard to take seriously: "the is-ful ah!-nesses of things"; "the human gamut / leaping cheerfully or in heavy earnest"; "Love never gave up rhyme: / its utter re-casting surprises never found a kindlier mine." Murray's potential Northern Hemisphere readers would benefit greatly from a thin *Selected;* but even his slackest failures may be the sorts of things a poet has to risk to become as original a writer as he has been.

Murray also writes strongly felt verse essays, expository or polemical: their titles can name their genres and topics ("Second Essay on Interest: The Emu"). These poems often rely on special senses of common words, which make up an ideology and an idiolect—call it Murrayese. Its key terms include "sprawl"; "action"; "otherworld" and "dreamworld"; "interest"; "police" (always very bad); and "poem," which denotes an aesthetic construction, realized or unrealized—psychoanalysis is "Freud's poem," modern Turkey presumably Atatürk's. Murrayese generates some of Murray's worst lines, but it also creates some of his most complex effects: here he presents both oil shimmer on water, and the interplay between cognition and imaginative commitment:

> The daylight oil, the heavier grade of Reason,
> reverie's clear water, that of the dreamworld ocean
> agitate us and are shaken, forming the emulsion
> without which we make nothing much . . .

Like half-formed notions, the half rhymes in -*on* pool and dissolve as we read.

Murray also writes allegorical anecdotes. "The New Moreton Bay" celebrates another poet's reception into the Catholic Church:

> A grog-primed overseer, who later died,
> snapped at twenty convicts gasping in a line
> *That pole ain't heavy! Two men stand aside!*
> and then two more, *And, you, pop-eyes! And you!*
> —until the dozen left, with a terrible cry,
> broke and were broken
> beneath the tons of log they had stemmed aloft desperately.
>
> Because there is no peace in this world's peace
> the timber is to carry. Many hands heave customarily,
> some step aside, detained by the Happiness Police
> or despair's boutiques; it is a continual sway—
> but when grace and intent
> recruit a fresh shoulder, then we're in the other testament
> and the innocent wood lifts line-long, with its leaves and libraries.

The first seven lines imagine their scene to perfection; the broad swipe at "Happiness Police" is the sort of thing readers of Murray have to put up with; and the unexpected depths in words like "sway" and "testament" may be more rewards of putting up with it. For Murray this world is a great work gang, its working convicts required to stand together, and anyone who would become a boss is deeply guilty.

Besides verse essays and allegories, he also writes what the eighteenth century would have recognized as (nonlyric) descriptive verse. He is at his best amid working landscapes: he can describe almost anything so as to make it entirely new. Here is Tasmanian mountain runoff, which Murray calls instead "Bent Water":

Flashy wrists out of buttoned grass cuffs, feral whisky
    burning gravels,
jazzy knuckles ajitter on soakages, peaty cupfuls, soft
    pots overflowing,
setting out along the great curve, migrating mouse-quivering
    water,
mountain-driven winter water, in the high tweed, stripping
    off its mountains
to run faster in its skin . . .

Although antimodernist, Murray is no technophobe: the purely enjoyable "Machine Portraits with Pendant Spaceman" applies the same descriptive and mimetic skills to a bulldozer, an electric knife strop, and "the space shuttle's Ground Transporter Vehicle."

Long-standing attention to animals helped Murray virtually invent another genre, that of nonce forms meant to emulate particular animals' modes of perception. Murray wrote such poems off and on beginning in the 1970s, then presented a group of new ones in 1992's *Translations from the Natural World*. "Bats' Ultrasound" gives us the prayers of the bats, whose English includes just one consonant: "A rare ear, our aery Yahweh." "Two Dogs" sounds like this: "Bark! I water for it. Her eyes go binocular, as in pawed / hop frog snack play. Come ploughed, she jumps, ground. Bark tractor, / white bitterhead grub and pull scarecrow. Me! assents his urine." *Translations* can seem like a stunt, but it's more like a few dozen separate stunts: each animal's *Umwelt* requires Murray to select anew from among his aural tools.

Based on a tribal oral form, "The Buladelah-Taree Holiday Song Cycle" (1977) gives Murray perfect venues for his zoological, loco-descriptive, and narrative talents. Its sections concern Australian families' arrivals in holiday country; the automobile traffic that brings them there; the families' ancestors; a barbecue; the holidaymakers' children; mosquitoes; service-industry employees; the ibis; fruit trees; the day-time sky; night and stars. These are the mosquitoes (section 8):

> they find the possum's face, they drift up the ponderous pleats
>   of the fig tree, way up into its rigging,
> the high camp of the fruit bats; they feed on the membranes
>   and ears of bats; tired wings cuff air at them;
> their eggs burning inside them, they alight on the muzzles
>   of cattle,
> the half-wild bush cattle, there at the place of the Sleeper Dump,
>   at the place of the Tallowwoods.

The pace, and the energy, suit the brandished coinages, as if poetry in English has come to Buladelah-Taree for the first time.

The ideal introduction to Murray's corpus is not anything he has written recently, but a sequence of short poems amid his *Collected Poems*: "The Idyll Wheel" (1987) is a contemporary Shepherd's Calendar, recording the life of the Bunyah farm month by month throughout the first year of the Murrays' full-time life there. The sequence includes all of Murray's genuine modes. "December" includes a neat modern nativity scene (in a real manger). "May" yields mimetic description:

> wood coughs at the axe
> and splinters hurt worse,
> barbed wire pulls through
> every post in reverse,
>
> old horses grow shaggy
> and flies hunker down
> on curtains, like sequins
> on a dead girl's ball gown.

"August" provides Australian and local language: "Here, where thin is *poor*, and fat is *condition*, / 'homely' is praise and warmth, spoken gratefully." And "June" hoards compact narratives, like this one:

The garden was all she had: the parrots were at it
and she came out and said to them, quite serious
like as if to reasonable people They are *my* peas.
And do you know? They flew off and never come back.

Fredy Neptune (2000), Murray's second novel in verse, is so compulsively rereadable, and so consistently good, as to make all his previous work—even a standout like "The Idyll Wheel"—seem almost
like mere preparation by comparison. *Fredy Neptune* is a first-person
narrative, in perhaps a thousand eight-line stanzas, about the globe-
spanning misadventures of Freddy Boettcher, a bilingual German
Australian seaman, between the start of the First World War and
the end of the Second. Uneducated, compassionate, and hardworking, Freddy (who spells his own name with two *d*'s) gets drafted into
the German navy aboard a freighter in Turkey, sees Armenian women
burned alive, and contracts, magically, leprosy from the trauma. He
finds, on recovering, that he has lost his senses of touch, pain, and proprioception, and gained superhuman strength: "My body's mad. It's
turned its back on me."

Freddy spends most of the rest of the book as a sort of democratic
superhero, hoping "to find out, without killing, among the killing, /
what my human worth would be." He gets swept into battle outside
Jerusalem; hijacks a British Army plane; falls and stays in love with
Laura, a lively New South Wales war widow; travels to America on
a zeppelin ("Like a windjammer with its sails inside it"); works as a
circus strongman, a steelworker, a log pilot on a Queensland river,
a fisherman, a dredger, and a lion tamer; and finally, in Berlin, encounters Hans, a mentally disabled young man about to be castrated
in accordance with Nazi eugenics laws. Freddy spends the last third
of the book taking care of Hans, first trying to smuggle him back to
Australia, and then trying to protect him there: "the simple ones need
us decent. Some do rise to them."

Fredy incorporates everything Murray's verse does well, and almost
all his obsessions: masculinity, locale, Catholicism, an unsophisticated
persona, Australian identity, "translation," antielitism, and the major
terms of Murrayese—"police," "poem," "presence," "testament." Its
stanzas adapt themselves superbly to action—not just to the ups and

downs of its plot but to pace, physical movement, and the management of attention in a crisis. Here Freddy rides with "a couple of French Greek girls" in a car with a drunk British officer, who

> drove too quick
> on loose corners. The car yawed, climbed a brick-stack
> and turned turtle. Steel bit at me. I flew, swam in gravel
> with Gia, the lively one. Steam and dust were pouring up
> with screaming inside them. I staggered up. I reefed, I
> wrenched the car, up, off them. Held it up,
> walked it to the side. The one boy was busted. Bubbling and dying.
> The wistful girl, Sophie, had a new black knee in her arm.

Murray's filmic quick cuts, long pans, variable pace, and use of stanzas as if they were frames will make some readers think about film. (Freddy does more than think about it: he spends several stanzas in Hollywood, playing Germans in war movies.) Other readers will think (appropriately, too) of moralized adventure novels, like Robert Louis Stevenson's; of comics, with their arrangements of panels and captions; and of photography. Freddy begins the poem by showing us snapshots, tokens of the domestic life he spends most of the poem longing for:

> That was sausage day
> on our farm outside Dungog.
> There's my father Reinhard Boettcher,
> my mother Agnes. There is brother Frank
> who died of the brain-burn, meningitis.
> There I am having my turn
> at the mincer. Cooked meat with parsley and salt
> winding out, smooth as gruel, for the weisswurst.

These photographic ekphrases are the first of *Fredy*'s many inset genres. Murray also incorporates Turkish religious praise poetry; dream visions; Scottish ballads (with fiddle accompaniment); prayers; apothegms; and even a new English version of Rilke's "The Panther," which Marlene Dietrich reads aloud to Freddy on a movie set (though she "really" reads to Freddy in German). Freddy enjoys that first encounter with Rilke, without recognizing the words as Rilke's—he knows almost no high culture, although he is always running across its symbols. Rather than in literary language, Freddy grows proficient in alien dialects, like the nob English of officers "who didn't mean a coward when they said cocktail." (Later Murray has the inspiration to render Swiss German as Scots: *"Yon Hitler's a coof."*)

Despite or because of the crowded plot, Freddy seems deeper and easier to get to know than most characters in poems and novels wholly given to introspection. This scene from Book Two takes place just after World War I; newly returned to Australia, Freddy stands outside his prewar home:

> I started seeing changes around, and untidiness.
> Then out comes a man. Not my Dad, but acting the boss.
> *Good day,* he says, not smiling. *Good day.—What can I do*
>   *for you?—*
> *Well, I live here, or my family do. Where are they?*
> *Gone,* he spits out. *Where all you Hun bastards belong.*
>
> I was clean hopeless.
> King-hit from inside, I stood with my mouth open there.
> His woman came out, and looked frightened in the door.
> *You got it through you head?* he snapped. *You're out.*
> *Get off the place before I sool the dogs on you,*
> and he hitched his trousers up. I remember he hitched his strides.
> The pole barn, the pepper tree,
> the trenched tracks down to the cattle crossing. His belt.

Other characters don't have Freddy's reality, but they're charming enough: Laura, whom we know right away he will marry; dramatically campy, gender-swapping Lula Golightly; the gruff river pilot Matt Garland, who hides a repellent secret; and "Sam Mundine the Jewish Aboriginal / bait-layer from backblocks Queensland." (Murray has less success with characters of higher station, like the aesthete Basil Thoroblood, who keeps a team of strongmen in his private insane asylum.)

Freddy acts out all of Murray's favorite (putatively Australian) virtues: endurance, fellowship, folk democracy, and antipathy to organized violence. (A pair of Australian expats declare forthrightly: *"the Yank story is . . . bringing things to a head / and settling them by killing.—Ours was the opposite, and new; / that violent death's pretentious, that only police natures need it."*) His story also embodies the Australian propensity for round-the-world journeys—it is, among other things, a poem about travel, from Cairo to "Versayles, Kentucky" to Hollywood to Paris to Shanghai. Here is our hero, leprous and begging in Turkey:

> It was chilly at night, about like home
> but there were always trash fires to sleep near. I'd wake up
> and sit around, half there,
> with the carts and dogs and arguments criss-crossing
> as if not around but through me. I was at the bottom
> of wavery air, the birds' sea-floor, my head alight, and notices
> in their running writing saying *jilliby* and *poll-willow*.

"Jilliby" is Freddy's version of Arabic script, one of many ingenious devices by which Murray gets us to see what Freddy sees.

Freddy manages to be in dozens of famous violent scenes, and in the middle of two wars, without losing his mind or his moral compass: this, and not his prowess, is the superstrength Murray wants us to admire. "Never do the impossible near where you like living," Freddy advises: whenever he uses his physical superpower he gets fired or run out of town. Actual comic books have long explored (to the delight of alienated youth) how exceptional abilities stigmatize their bearers; Murray's epic does so, too. In the most striking of Murray's many in jokes, Freddy becomes the real-life model for Superman when he meets the Kryptonian's future creators:

> *Jerry Siegel, sir, and this is Joe, Joe Schuster. [sic]*
> *We heard you lifted a flatcar off of a man?*

> They were nice keen boys in their diamondy sleeveless sweaters
> and their ties, and I'm afraid I had them on a bit:
> Yes, I'd lifted the flatcar. I was from Dungog. Which was a planet.
> We were all strong there. I was under average, if anything.

> We Goggans dressed like so: I showed them a photo from my wallet
> of me from the Golightlys' show, trunks outside my tights.

The next stanza finds Freddy feeling guilty: "I'd brought two boys amusement / and forgot to ask how the man [I saved] fared."

Freddy's strongman act goes over well in Germany in 1932: "the customers were just happy to see heaviness get heaved / up where they might still walk out from under it." Such remark makes the act one of many Big Symbols for the peaceable struggle against fascism. In another, Freddy displays his leprosy to scare off German police: "I opened my clothes and showed my islands and countries, / white, with red crust borders." Risking persecution when Australians take him for German, when Germans consider him a British subject, and whenever anyone finds out his powers, Freddy Boettcher becomes an incarnation (an enflesh-ment, and a reddening) of the bleeding and border-plagued world.

This, of course, also makes him a type of Christ. The book's Christian aspects take over near the end, as Freddy's experience intersects more often with Murray's theology. Christ and the church are for Murray guarantors of human worth and equal dignity. When everyone else considers Freddy either super- or subhuman, only the church will treat him "as just another person, among the Saturday confessors. / It put gravity back under me." (Murray's earlier verse novel, 1980's *The Boys Who Stole the Funeral*, linked its religious ideas to a resentful and slapdash antifeminism: *Fredy* contains no such potential headaches.) The Christianity of *Fredy* arrives through acts of earthly sacrifice and in glimpses of dreamlike other- or afterworlds. Freddy becomes, quietly, an admirable secret savior, with Basil Thoroblood a sort of St. John: one of Basil's strongmen tells Freddy, *"You're the one Thoroblood was waiting for: the body's word."*

Murray's aesthetics are so tightly tied to his polemical stances that it can be trying for someone like me—a non-Australian, secular city lover—to remain of one mind about his whole oeuvre: over and over (it seems to me) the *Collected Poems* places clumsy or merely doctrinaire work right next to some of the best descriptive poetry in the language. I am, however, certain about this verse novel: painful, versatile, eventful, sometimes funny, and finally wise, *Fredy Neptune* is in every sense worth the wait.

Denise Riley
Already Knotted In

Since the late 1970s, Denise Riley has garnered one reputation as a feminist theoretician of history and philosophy, and another, more limited reputation as one of Britain's most admired "experimental" (read: difficult, small-press) poets: her 2000 *Selected Poems* solidified, without expanding, that acclaim. To follow her from her recent prose into her poems is to learn how, and how well, her poems use kinds of argument, versions of political and philosophical abstractions, which many poets still consider hostile territory. Riley's poems are not "theory" by other means. Instead, her theoretical inquiries underpin her poems' verbal and emotional strengths: you do not need to care greatly for "theory" to read her, but her poems may show you how you would feel if you did. Her inquiries often pursue that slippery and much-worried abstraction "the self"; we can begin to see Riley's special merits if we start with "the self," and with one of her poems about it, then move outward to look at the rest of her work.

The *Oxford English Dictionary* defines "self" thirty-seven ways, among them "a permanent subject of successive and varying states of consciousness." Although the *OED* calls that usage "chiefly philosophical," its earliest citation comes from poetry: "A secret self I had enclos'd within" (Thomas Traherne, 1674). More recently Seamus Heaney has called poetry "the revelation of the self to the self." "Theory," of course, tends to call that self into question. Some thinkers deem it a dangerous, bourgeois illusion. Others have done much to place it in history, showing (in the philosopher Charles Taylor's words) that we do not (despite our intuitions) "have selves . . . the way we have heads or arms . . . as a matter of hard, interpretation-free fact." A third group suggests that the self, or a consistent self-identity, is (to quote another philosopher, Derek Parfit) "not what matters" to the way we view our choices and lives.

All these theorists can both produce and describe the sense that one is not, or no longer, oneself: that one's emotions, personality, memories, and beliefs no longer have, or never had, the sort of coherence and agency one took them to have a day or a moment ago. That sense becomes the starting point for Riley's book-length essay *The Words of Selves* (2000). Riley acknowledges the double sense that no self-presentation is me (that I am something else or more than any name for me) and also that I am not under my own control (I'm a product of language, the unconscious, the economy, and time, which may combine to make me somebody else). Riley thus explores a "common compulsion: that once I'm forced to speak about myself at all, I must through my own efforts make it sharply true—yet cannot." She explains that a "self-describing 'I' produces an unease which can't be mollified by any theory of its constructed nature . . . What purports to be 'I' speaks back to me, and I can't quite believe what I hear it say." "The strains of describing the self," she goes on to say, "are also acute within those literary genres reliant on a covert self-presentation: hence it is a liar who writes, and a liar who tries lyric." Riley continues:

> Poetry can be heard to stagger under a weight of self-portrayal, having taken [the self] as its sole and proper object. Today's lyric form, frequently a vehicle for innocuous display and confessionals, is [thus] at odds with its remoter history. What might transpire if this discontinuous legacy in self-telling became the topic of a poem itself?

Even within *The Words of Selves,* this question does not remain hypothetical: Riley includes, amid that book's analytical prose, two fluently post-Ovidian allegorical poems whose characters impersonate the unstable selves she imagines. "The Castalian Spring" turns the poet into a (theoretically sophisticated) frog: "shivery in my cool and newly / Warty skin, I raised this novel voice to honk and boom. . . . Could I try on that song of my sociologised self?" The second poem, "Affections of the Ear," presents "the original Narcissus story" as told by the nymph Echo: "I did things with words until she [Hera] caught me." These long, often very funny poems make a superb introduction to Riley's modes of self-consciousness—though they eschew the technical difficulties that give her shorter poems much of their strength.

Those shorter poems, as gathered in her *Selected*—especially those of *Mop Mop Georgette* (1993)—explore that "discontinuous legacy" at the level of individual words and grammatical turns. One of those poems even bears the title "Lyric":

Stammering it fights to get
held and to never get held
as whatever motors it swells
to hammer itself out on me

then it can call out high
and rounded as a night-
bird's cry falling clean
down out of a black tree.

I take on its rage at the cost
of sleep. If I love it I sink
attracting its hatred. If I
don't love it I steal its music.

Take up a pleat in this awful
process and then fold me flat
inside it so that I don't see
where I'm already knotted in.

It is my burden and subject
to listen for sweetness in hope
to hold it in weeping ears though
each hurt each never so much.

If one has ceased to believe in oneself as an actor, if one has come to regard one's personality as a mere effect of language, one may call that personality a node, a "fold" or a "pleat" in a larger pattern. Taylor and many others argue that such models, while intellectually fascinating and internally consistent, "are not construals you could actually make of your life while living it." Riley's poem appears, at first, to agree: she must, or will, "listen" in future to something called "lyric" in order to find in it "sweetness," "hope," "hurt," and pain. Riley's pronoun "it" refers to "lyric," the poetic genre; to this particular lyric poem; and to the "I" that we expect to govern its lines.

This "it" behaves like an "I," that is, it both seeks and escapes definition; Riley's opening metaphors consider it both as a driven machine (like a motorboat) and as a natural creature who sings like a bird (like Keats's nightingale). And yet not "I" but "my burden" becomes the "subject" of Riley's sentence: "lyric" projects a speaker (or a "subject") able to have (and "hold") experiences without being able to substantiate (or "hold") any firm beliefs about what or who does the experiencing. ("Burden" in sixteenth- and seventeenth-century English can also mean a repeated part, a refrain, in poetry or in song.) Within the poem, grammatical shifts, harsh sounds with their very clear consonant boundaries, and ambiguous pronouns and deictics create for lyric the paradoxical self (the self that flees from self-description, the "I" that cannot find adequate ways to say "I") that Riley describes in her prose.

This kind of dialogue—between "lyric" and "theory," between the dry language of philosophical analyses and the vividly conversational forms of some poems—seems to me Riley's particular contribution to contemporary poetry. It is a contribution that other poets, especially in the United States, have tried to make: few of those poets, though, bring to their own disjunction-filled verse Riley's fruitful experience in discursive, consecutive argument, and the American poets most at home with consecutive philosophical argument—e.g., John Koethe—seem least at home with how Riley sees the world. Riley seems always to have imagined her poems and her prose together, as parallel but distinct vehicles for her investigations of language, identity, and gender. *War in the Nursery* (1982) showed how "working women with children became an invisible category" in 1950s public life. Covering six hundred years of history, and sources from Mary Wollstonecraft to William Empson, *"Am I That Name?"* (1988) showed how the historically variant, semantically slippery category of "'women' is a simultaneous foundation of and an irritant to feminism, and this is constitutionally so." As if to be sure we sought such concerns in her verse, the first poem in Riley's *Selected Poems* is called "A Note on Sex and 'The Reclaiming of Language.'" It thinks about the ways in which ordinary habits of speech cast women as exotic (not ordinary), as nature (not culture), and as icons for men: "The new land is colonised, though its prospects are empty. // The Savage weeps as, landing at the airport / she is asked to buy wood carvings, which represent herself." Riley's handful of exegetes have rightly seized on the poem's illustrations of feminist theory. Yet these sentences—as usual with Riley—do not simply illustrate, but ironize and react. What *should* this Savage do?

> She has ingested her wife
> she has re-inhabited her own wrists
> she is squatting in her own temples, the
> fall of light on hair or any decoration
> is re-possessed. 'She' is I.

"Temples": both the kind that lie next to the forehead, and the kind where idols are set up (or broken), much as the idols of ordinary usage, of inherited, gendered abstract nouns, find themselves broken apart in *"Am I That Name?"*

Such iconoclasm can form a habit; it can also be exhausting for the iconoclast, an exhaustion her poems can describe. "Knowing in the Real World" (a good anthology piece for her; anthologists, take note) makes explicit what emerged, by the 1990s, as her best subject: the unease of continual, and politically alert, self-analysis. "In my room / I hear cars and the snow flying around the street. // I'm not outside anything: I'm not inside it either." The poem then asks (without a question mark), "Where do I put myself, if public life's destroyed." With the crack of a spondee, Riley then returns to vivid minutiae, which she now makes into symbols (perhaps) of "public life":

Sliced into the shine of now, a hand on a blade.
A wound, taproot in its day, its red blossom in light.

The wind sheets slap the sea to ruffled wheatfields.
Angel, fish, paradise, rain of cherries.

Riley tries to describe the attractions, and the disabilities, of her particular abstracting, inquisitive temperament, her particular, self-scrutinizing sort of "self": "What does the hard look do to what it sees? / Pull beauty out of it, or stare it in?" She also warns herself against that temperament's intellectualizing excesses: "Don't make / yourself into such a fine instrument of knowledge," she cautions, "that you slice uselessly back into your own hand."

Beside most other poets she seems difficult, demanding, harsh; beside the American poets who share her interests in avant-garde styles, in false consciousness, poststructuralism, demystification, Riley sounds notably careful, uncertain, even diffident, willing to look again at all the evidence and at the rules for what constitutes "evidence" in a given situation, a given speech act. Despite their long itineraries, her trains of thought can be jumpy, with hairpin turns and rickety brakes. "Dark Looks" begins with forbidding seriousness but soon enough becomes dizzyingly, almost flirtatiously, evasive:

Who anyone is or I am is nothing to the work. The writer
properly should be the last person that the reader or the listener
    need think about
yet the poet with her signature stands up trembling, grateful,
    mortally embarrassed
and especially embarrassing to herself, patting her hair and
    twittering If, if only
I need not have a physical appearance! To be sheer air, and
    mousseline!

These lines, again, hunt the paradoxes of "the self," banished as soon as invoked, and greeted with relief upon its rapid return.

Because Riley's interests, and her effects, so often seek to upset common assumptions, because she affects the mien of a scientist, busily testing alien hypotheses, an uncareful reader might find her poetry sterile, verveless, subject to what Riley herself calls (in her poem "Wherever You Are, Be Somewhere Else") "a modern, what, a flatness." "Speaking apart, I hear my voice run on," a short work from the 1980s opened: another ("The ambition to not be particular speaks") began "'I cannot tell what gives each voice its tune.'" Riley's resistances to ordinary speech, to ordinary kinds of decoding, seem integral to a poet so interested (as anyone drawn to "theory" must be interested) in what insights our ordinary habits of conversation and "voice" might prevent. Yet Riley does not (as so many of her peers do) ask us to accept nonsense as "resistance," toneless chaos as "subversive": her forms of self-consciousness instead create strange and dissonant ways to say and mean.

These forms maximize the poems' intellectual sophistication while minimizing any air of authority: the poems strive to sound hurried, diffident, unsure. And if Riley writes an intellective poetry, one discontented with feelings unanalyzed, she also writes a poetry of exasperation, harried frustration, social awkwardness, and other everyday concerns: "Well all right, things happened it would // be pleasanter not to recall, as a deeply embarrassed dog / looks studiedly at a sofa for just anything to do instead." Skeptical readers may find themselves won over by that quiet humor, or by Riley's moments of explicit invitation: "Draw the night right up over my eyes so that I / don't see and then I'm gone." And even the most skeptical of readers might enjoy the compression of a poem like "Not What You Think," here in full:

wonderful light
viridian summers
deft boys
no thanks

A witty snapshot, or a serious blow against compulsory heterosexuality? An attractive teenage memory, or a grown-up painter's holiday? A riposte to the boys, or a riposte to misreaders who believe Riley cares only for abstractions, and not for impressions and scenes? A rebuke to the thought that all poems portray "the self"? Or a lesson in the careful skepticism that Riley herself pursues?

John Tranter

Write Another Party

John Tranter is one of those poets with one reputation in the United States and quite another in the country where he lives. Here, he's known largely as the founding editor of the Internet journal *Jacket*, probably the best—and surely the largest, both in total word count and in page views—of the Web-only journals that cover poetry now. In Australia, though, he remains well known—he was well known when the Internet was just a Darpanet—as a leading light of "experimental" or difficult verse, writing (and helping to publish) it since the late 1960s. Americans used to reading John Ashbery will recognize some of Tranter's verbal devices; he is to Australia nearly what Ashbery is to the United States. Yet to look back over Tranter's poetry is to see why Americans (and Britons and Canadians and Singaporeans and so on) might read him—what he has done with words that Ashbery has not. The language of the self, of the inner life, which we expect to find in a (lyric) poem comes from the talk of our friends, the conversation of strangers, the books and even the newspapers we read: many poets draw on that range of sources, but few make the heterogeneity of those sources one of their subjects. That is what Tranter does. He takes from Frank O'Hara his sense of the poem as itself a social occasion, and from Ashbery his skill in grafting heterogeneous phrases. Yet in Tranter, more than in his North American sources (and more than in his Australian peers), the poems give us a sense that they include not just free-floating words (or "discourse") but the words someone else has said, or might say.

If poetry always exists between speech and music, Tranter's poems have always hewed closer to speech, and they have always imagined fractured, indistinct, or multiple speakers. The somewhat labored early *ars poetica* "Conversations" offers "'Give up life, my boy, there's nothing in it!'" (Tranter adapting Pound adapting Arnold Bennett) but also more ordinary talk: "'More news from the front,' whispered a friend"; "'Drink. / The drinks are free.'" One later poem explores "Men's Talk," keeping the poet "one step ahead of the plausible talkers" whose "fragments make up the town's speech." Another late poem pivots repeatedly on the poet's ear for other people's words: "I keep hearing the word 'workaholic.'" "I think he said 'phenomenology.'" "I keep hearing the word 'histrionic.' . . . I keep hearing polysyllables, / then jackhammers."

The preceding unambiguous "quotations," marked by indicators such as "he said" or "I keep hearing," make unusually explicit samples of Tranter's approach to poetic language in general. Tranter reminds John Kinsella in an interview that "a poem only has meaning because of the history of the language it's written or spoken in." His poems flaunt their reliance on that history. The poems sound like something somebody has just said, except that nobody would ever say just that: they are speech deformed, or bits, stuck together, of normally incompatible speech:

God, here I am, hungover inside
the little café near the markets, jittery,
scribbling a babble of sentimental language
in my purple notebook emotion container—

Tranter's later poems can even become, briefly, indistinguishable from dialogue in a novel:

"We went and looked at a place," he said,
"a place to get away to."
"It's no holiday, we both grew up here," his wife put in.
. . . .
Her dry and colorless speech upset her guy,
reinventing the old times when art was a big deal.

Except in his (disappointing) long narrative poems (collected in *The Floor of Heaven*), Tranter rarely produces, for the length of a whole poem, coherent naturalistic speakers who are not the poet. Instead, he flirts with their presence and torques their terms: "Hey, you there with the scented lipstick, / take me to the bosses and their club, if / they exist." A stanza from the important late poem "Dark Harvest" modulates between attributed speech and a lyricism that tempts us to attribute it to the poet himself:

> Listen to those guys
>
> rattle and blather, he said, and you didn't remember
> that melancholy, the twilight autumn air, then
> the rumpled nameless force pushing us out
>   towards the horizon?

Tranter's poems do not only complicate our ideas about who has said what; they blur distinctions between the poet's own utterances and those of others. His 1968 mimeograph project, *Free Grass*, presented Tranter's own work under a variety of pseudonyms; the recent chapbook *Borrowed Voices* adapted poems from European predecessors into Tranter's contemporary Australian diction. For Tranter, not only our speech but our inner lives may be a collection of quoted or acquired experiences—we are not organic growths, or sensitive plants, but "notebook emotion containers." And yet someone, somewhere, seems to have had those experiences, to be speaking those words.

The sonnet sequence *Crying in Early Infancy* (1974–77) is perhaps too capacious, and too various, to reward analysis as a unit. (Tranter told Kate Lilley that he composed them over several years, that some of the poems were not first intended as sonnets, and that the editor and critic, Martin Duwell, determined their order.) Yet its first few poems, taken together, look like keys to his methods. The first sonnet likens Tranter's "book" (of poetry) to a party on a beach (with war noises nearby):

> Now the party is over the beach dissolves
> in a morbid and equivocal Brazilian atmosphere
> I have especially constructed in the hope
> that the book will write itself, but Bill screams
> at my efforts. Write another party, he flashes . . .

Tranter's poems may appear automatic, or effortless, but are in fact "constructed"; their causes include occasions on which people talk to one another, angrily or festively (or both), so that Tranter's writing itself resembles a social event, full of overlapping and conflicting strands. The poem goes on to suggest, and reject, punning metaphors for its own effects: "Once I loaded the magazine, I ran out of paper"; "Once I was happy, at the middle of the party." Neither instrument (the gun never fires) nor social occasion (the party is over), a Tranter poem (like an Ashbery poem) wriggles out of the speech genres and occasions that have produced it.

In this aspect a Tranter poem resembles a picture without fixed-point perspective, a picture or object with "Non-Euclidean Geometry," the title of the sequence's second sonnet. As that poem opens, a horizon's "strange / colour . . . belongs to you, even though / it will always be too far away / to be of any use." If the poem resembles an object glimpsed from afar (an object more like an impression than like an instrument), and a party (but a party that has ended or gone sour), it also implies a speaker who is and is not the poet himself—who is, perhaps, "Your Lucky Double," the title of sonnet 3. That double is not he or she, but "it":

> It is heavy with the breath of bad images
> it is more than you deserve it is easy
> like a news lesson in Portuguese it has
> a taste for racing alcohol and other

delicacies how lucky you are how lucky
or maybe it reads how disreputable and diseased
it is easy to read like a polka dot it is
madly in love like a silly kid good night

it cries and wastes away utterly . . .

Tranter's attraction to Rimbauldian drunkenness (and to other drugs)
would recede as he grew older, along with the rest of his urban bohemian
props. His interest in how "a silly kid" might talk, in kinds of speech
that seem excessive, improper, or inappropriate, would prove fundamental to his "non-Euclidean," post-Ashberyan sense of line and poem.

In *Crying in Early Infancy*, implicit quotation, *déjà pensée*, the
sense that our words and thoughts already belong to somebody else,
became at once Tranter's subject and his source of stylistic invention.
Take the middle lines from the sonnet "The Hollywood Version":

We all saw *The Invasion of the Body Snatchers*
and quickly went out for a drink. Why,
we've been snatching at bodies ever since,

haven't we? We saw the Indians
dying like flies, but things have changed.

Tranter's choice of movie proves uniquely appropriate, since the very
phrases "we" use seem "snatched" from previous speech: "went out
for a drink," "dying like flies," "things have changed." Yet these lines,
assembled from clichés, do not sound clichéd overall: they sound disturbing, because they do not belong together. "Things have changed"
is, after all, a shockingly understated way to say that movies no longer
celebrate genocide, or that white Americans (and Australians) no longer practice it openly.

Such teasingly or shockingly juxtaposed clichés (like quotations
from disparate speakers), and the tonal dissonance they generate,
recur throughout Tranter's verse. "Intonation that isolates others'
speech (in written speech, designated by quotation marks) is a special
phenomenon," wrote the literary theorist Mikhail Bakhtin: "it is as

though the *change of speech subjects* [in conversation] has been inter-
nalized." Tranter's poetry offers such intonations constantly (and only
sometimes flags them with quotation marks). My next few quotations
italicize the clichés or apparent quotations within Tranter's verse:
"A vicious man jumping off a building— / *you could make something of that*"; "*It's goodbye to* the glue // that used to *hold everything together / it's goodbye to* the trembling Rotarians." The same
features occur in Ashbery's verse, especially in his late poems, but far
less insistently; what for the introverted American is an important ornament becomes for the more extroverted Australian a basic unit of
construction.

Tranter perhaps discovered the aesthetic potential of tonal dissonance, its ability to call new attention to (and cast new doubt on) any
language in its neighborhood, while writing poems against the war in
Vietnam: "*it's time for / Christmas bombing, / could you do that?*"
Tranter reminds one interviewer (Ted Slade in 1998) that American
"language writing" "started . . . partly as a reaction against the
ghastly debasement of language by the Nixon administration during
the Vietnam War." Yet as early as *Crying*, Tranter extended his tonal
dissonance into poems with no clear political force: "The Chicago
Manual of Style is *really neat*." Later poems extend these effects further, encompassing tones from outrage to bemusement to saddened
puzzlement at the disorganization of everyday life:

> You know it's *dumb hippie magic,* but you try
> the Zen Bingo *Method of Prediction*
> developed by a gambling vet for the *Women's Weekly.*
> Your girl-friend goes catatonic
> and *leaves home,* so you *burst into tears*
> like a *pop star. "You will grow old, then die."*
> *So what?*

Tranter titled that poem "Telephone," invoking both the household device and the party game (which, by its alternate title "Chinese
Whispers," later gave its name to John Ashbery's book). A more frequent Tranterian figure for the social transmission, and transformation,
that all language undergoes is radio. (Tranter worked in Australian

radio for many years, starting in 1973.) In his best book, *Under Berlin* (1988), radio can stand for everything about contemporary talk and culture that connects us as citizens, readers, or listeners. The apologetic lover in "Crocodile Rag" moves from rejection ("you blew it. Sorry") to a renewed plea for tenderness after "hearing your voice last night / on the radio, hoarse with sorrow." And in "South Coast After Rain, 1960," not the necking teenagers in a parked car, but rather their "radio / fills the car with emotion." Poems from the 1970s with the collective title "Radio Traffic" liken Tranter's style to a radio spun among stations. These poems rely on words or phrases (I put them in bold) at which the poem switches from one "program" to another:

> Over Lisbon the Aussie navigator bought it but
> the tail gunner's a good kid & finds **the way**
> stockings ladder among a flurry of limbs in
> the back seat of an Austin **Seven's** a sign
> of the times, & he's not often wrong.

> A eucalyptus tree has branches & **gum leaves**
> a sticky mark on the footpath, & these are paradigms
> for how a tired but happy athlete enters & **leaves**
> follow on a gust of wind: "Double Exposures" is
> a clue but doesn't tell us what he's thinking of.

The transitions in such lines (Tranter suggests) differ from ordinary conversation and thought only in degree. Such transitions reappear in later work: "Absolute type of a gentleman. Wouldn't / hurt **you with** a barge pole"—a "Double Exposure" compounded of "wouldn't hurt a fly" and "wouldn't touch him with a barge pole." Such "double exposures" impress on us the arbitrariness, and the preexistence, the pre-owned nature, of language as Tranter encounters it.

Tranter's dependence on speech as against music, his sense of the poem as a place where discourses and attitudes clash, reinforce (and perhaps once grew from) his hostility toward the "well-made poem," the poem whose every enigma implies a solution, which models a balanced or self-contained world. For Tranter, such poems seem not only false to experience (in which, as Henry James put it, "really, universally, relations stop nowhere") but ethically suspect. Tranter's hostility to so-called academic writing drives another sonnet from *Crying,* "The Student Prince"; it ends:

> I went to college like a privilege
> and learnt to wield a metaphor in each hand
> and got a kiss on the arse for being good.
> Who made a million? The Student Prince?
> Who made a profit from a lasting work of art?
> Who was improved by the perfect landscape?

Tranter's aggression extends from the "droll town" with its lack of culture to the hollow "privilege" college promised to the "perfect" art it seemed to demand. As with other educated poets who have wanted to reject everything "academic," Tranter discovers (as if in the course of writing) that he cannot block off what he knows; he can, however, embrace a model of writing that says that all poems ought to reveal their dependence on other sorts of language, that no piece of writing (and no writer) is "perfect," that no work of art should pretend to stand alone.

This attitude (whether or not it is fair to the university) has obviously contributed to the rough edges in Tranter's own best work. Tranter and Les Murray are, within Australia, famously hostile opposites—oil and water, thesis and antithesis, raw and cooked. Yet much of the anger in "The Student Prince" is Murray's property, too. (Tranter told Kinsella, describing the poets' rural upbringings, "Les and I are more alike than different.") The greatest difference between them has to with their attitudes toward language: Murray and his imitators seem to believe that they can wield—against the untrustworthy, metropolitan center—an uncorrupted or an honest language as if they were its first speakers. Tranter insists by contrast that every part of speech is already quotation; his poems show how familiar (or overfamiliar) phrases can be redeployed. His poem "The Un-American Women" begins:

> One, they're spooking, two, they're opening letters,
> three, there's a body at the bottom of the pool

labeled "Comrade X," and you've been asked to
speak up truthfully or not at all.

The poem speeds up, as if almost overexcited, from an end-stopped
first line up to the extreme enjambment of "to / speak." Tranter's most
original poetry sees no bright line between "speaking truthfully" for
and about oneself (on the one hand) and (on the other) putting words
in somebody else's mouth. "The Un-American Women" begins and
ends by worrying at just such distinctions:

> You make a movie,
> I'll write the dialogue: One, we're laughing,
> two, we're breaking rules—I'm finished, you're
> dead, and as the cipher smoulders on the lawn
> a cold glow rises from the bottom of the tank:
> our Leader starts to speak, and so will you.

What here sounds almost paranoid, implying that a "Leader" con-
trols "your" speech (the movie could be *The Manchurian Candidate*),
would later seem to Tranter simply a condition of social life: I speak,
but what I speak responds to, and may incorporate, words of yours.

When Tranter imagines official or ordinary language as a target, he
invokes an audience of allies: "You're not alone," he tells them; "you
have / the rhetoric of fiction for your adversary." As with much of the
so-called avant-garde (in America, in Australia, on the moon), Tranter's
poems can invite too-easy assent to a project that seems merely destructive: once the ordinary ways of thinking and talking have been
disassembled, what will the poet put in their place? Can we find satisfaction in poems composed, as Tranter's works of the 1970s were,
wholly of middles, or of disassembled parts? "Can this kid resist //
the Demolition Derby where the Poem breaks down?" The structural
problem that Tranter then faced—a search for a positive principle by
which to put together (to give beginnings and endings to) poems organized as reactions *against* other texts—came with tonal problems, too:
Tranter could not remain *only* a satirist, only an attacker, without laps-
ing into sub-Swiftian nihilism or theory-driven aridity.

The Tranter of *Under Berlin* and afterward solved this problem in two ways. One (discussed later here) involves poetic genres. The other involves the difference between official or institutional language, and the wider field of preexisting usage; if Tranter's response to the first required a sometimes sarcastic hostility, he could also stitch poems together—using the same slippery, "non-Euclidean" methods—out of the second, without discrediting it. Tranter's acceptance of artifice as second nature, of constructed feelings as genuine, of characters as comprising multiple voices they did not create, accompanies the acceptance of family life, middle age, suburbia, on which his poems of the 1980s and '90s can turn. "Having Completed My Fortieth Year" discusses the life of the poet, his disillusion and his subsequent goals, in surprisingly unadorned (for Tranter) terms; he compares his own work to the "naive" (in Schiller's sense) work, his own life to the lives, of

<blockquote>

                                writers

    who live on another planet,

    their droppings bronzed like babies' booties
    and we're glad to see things so transmogrified
    though we suspect that life's not always rhymed
            quite as neatly as that . . .

</blockquote>

Despite the tonal dissonances ("babies' booties"), one might consider un-Tranterian this poem of unified reflection in propria persona, of an unaffectedly personal voice. On the other hand, the poem, Tranter says, "is a stanza-by-stanza reply" to Peter Porter's poem of the same title, a poem itself derived from Byron's "Having Completed My Thirty-Fifth Year." Even the most personal utterance, for Tranter, grows from previous language, previous texts, in ways that his poems (seams and stitches still showing) point out.

Tranter's strongest later poems ("Fortieth Year" among them) often adapt his as-if-quoted, faux-collage style to what looks like an unsuitably earnest kind of poem: the Romantic ode. "If the eighteenth-century poet proved himself to be a poet by writing an ode," the critic Paul Fry explains, "the Romantic poet proved himself *still* to be a poet by writing an ode, but no longer a poet gifted with unmediated vision," nor with "the natural holiness of youth." Worried "about growing old or growing up," "in place of ecstasy" the poet of the Romantic ode (such as Wordsworth's "Intimations" or Coleridge's "Dejection") instead "gains knowledge, a new awareness of the role played by determinacy in consciousness" and a new set of expectations about his future creations, or failures.

Such losses and gains recur throughout Tranter's poems of the 1980s and 1990s, where they are often tied to the Sydney suburbs. Take "Country Veranda":

> Behind that ridge of mist and blowing eucalypt tops
> > the world waited once:
> > exotic, inexhaustible.]
>
> You've been there now, and found that it's not much fun.
> > On the veranda, silence
> > fills the long afternoon.

Tranter's crisis odes pursue the vocational doubt of middle age, with the destructive verve of the earlier poetry now behind him: instead, he offers his agile diction and his awareness of the disappointment that has come to him, and may come to us soon. "The Other Side of the Bay" attributes that disappointment not only to "I" ("am I / imagining this") but also to "we" and to "she," a professor who

> > > leaves the centre
> > for the ventures on the edge, accepting a job
> > in a provincial college and a gift pen
> > carved out of turquoise, representing
> > the imagined and the real, displaced
> > through the grammar of the "hidden future" . . .

Such long sentences' deferred endings, as each phrase leaves the grammatical subject farther away, track her (or "our") continually fading expectations, and the growing disappointment they produce. Tranter makes that disappointment, partly hers, partly ours, and partly the property of an Ashberyan "you," with whose dissatisfied longing the poem concludes:

> To the border,
> who cares if it's far away, the other side
> of the bay, across the black water, that's
>
> where you wished to travel,
> that's where you wanted to go, and vanish.

Fry observes that the Romantic ode takes place at evening, in whose "decline" it "accepts a diminished calling." Tranter here absents himself (his first-person pronouns) from the scene in order to let his "lucky double," his reader, share his evening, his acceptance, his sense of loss.

Language preexists any one language user, even if it exists only as it is used; Tranter's poems recognize that double-headed truth in prominent ways. One of those ways involves the everyday conversation and nonpoetic language that surrounds us all. Another way—one just as productive for Tranter's late work—involves the conventions and precedents specific to poetry: in other words, genres and subgenres, and precursor poems. Many of Tranter's poems adhere self-consciously to particular genres—not only Romantic crisis odes, but nostalgic love poems, epigrams in the style of Martial (and of the Australian poet Laurie Duggan), and funeral elegies. The poem of suburban disillusion appears in Tranter's oeuvre over and over (often coupled to the Romantic ode); so do the poem-written-in-an-airplane, and the parody or answer poem. Tranter also uses external forms strongly associated with particular subgenres, or particular poets: Sapphics, the Burns stanza, sestina, pantoun, haibun, the thirty-line "trenter." He even takes up the form of the faux-fragmentary Greek text, dependent on the effects of omitted words and derived from modern misreadings of Sappho:

> I am restless for your
> . . . skin burning . . .
> touch!" A grass fire
> and . . . fever . . .

The scholar Alastair Fowler describes a line of poems about paintings "primarily developed from a single influential poem," W. H. Auden's "Musée des Beaux Arts," which begins "About suffering they were never wrong, / The Old Masters." Tranter's contribution to this subgenre affirms that artworks are put together from preexisting parts: "a work of art," Tranter's "Old Masters" agree,

> collectively
> lies in a kind of mud:
>
> gossip, bad faith, someone else's
> wife, phone bills, a little happiness. And so we
> go on, they said, doing what we can . . .

Strangest, and most representative, among the kinds of poems Tranter invents is the "terminal," a poem that appropriates all the end words, in the same order, from a previous poem. Among Tranter's "terminals," the pair derived from "Dover Beach" deserve special attention. "Dover Beach" is itself a Romantic crisis ode, a poem about Matthew Arnold's loss of all sorts of faith (in a Christian God, in romantic love, in his own powers): "Ah, love, let us be true / To one another!" Arnold declares in his ending, which a century's worth of readers have memorized:

> for the world, which seems
> To lie before us like a land of dreams,
> So various, so beautiful, so new,
> Hath really neither joy, nor love, nor light,
> Nor certitude, nor peace, nor help for pain;
> And we are here as on a darkling plain
> Swept with confused alarms of struggle and flight,
> Where ignorant armies clash by night.

Early on, in the 1970s, Tranter rewrote the ending of "Dover Beach" to describe his own (and his generation's) unease: "So we slog on / to navigate the fading resonance of our capacities / and find the luminescent map of armies / burning on the plain." Other poets have also used "Dover Beach" to reconsider the Romantic heritage: consider Auden's

"Dover," Anthony Hecht's "The Dover Bitch," or Mark Levine's "About Face (A Poem Called 'Dover Beach')." Tranter likes to remind us not only that poems are made of words but that poems are made of words we have heard before, words other people have used. Funnier and more ambitious than his previous rewritings of "Dover Beach," Tranter's pair of Arnoldian "terminals" flaunt that reminder. "Grover Leach" takes Arnoldian nostalgia to a provincial American setting, making it comic without (quite) inviting us to reject it:

> And so the farm sleeps, waiting for a new
> owner, and Rover waits too in that yellow light
> that seems to paint the wet sand with pain
> so it resembles a watery plain
> where screaming seabirds dash their reflected flight
> over the glitter of the State Fair, Saturday night.

In "See Rover Reach"

>   we thought
> Jim was loyal to Jenny—instead he was all at sea
> with a dozen different women, and no faith
> in any of them. Listen, are you sure
> you want another highball?

These lines answer not just the Arnoldian lines with corresponding end words ("The Sea of Faith / Was once, too, at the full, and round earth's shore . . .") but Arnold's later plea for fidelity. With these sarcastic musings (these half-quoted speakers) out of the way, the poem responds to Arnold's vista of disillusion by lauding, only half-ironically, its built-up suburban landscape:

> Only a parson, you said, would find it drear,
> the vista from our back porch, the whole world
> stoned on diesel fumes from the expressway. It's true!
> Ugly? No, I'm glad we bought here—it only seems
> ugly in the daylight.

Again, the constructed, even the tawdrily constructed, becomes a back-drop for the genuine; again, Tranter shifts from sarcasm to tacit accep-tance. And, again, a poem about inherited language with multiple voices becomes a poem about middle-aged settling down, as Tranter's "own" poetic voice comes about by imitating multiple speakers' speech.

Australians connect Tranter, for good enough reasons, to all sorts of fashionable postmodern thinkers, some of whom (Michel Foucault, for example) Tranter even names in his poems. Yet if you are look-ing for a thinker whose ideas will help you see what Tranter does, you may not do better than Erving Goffman's *The Presentation of Self in Everyday Life* (1959), the one academic work Tranter, in that long interview with Kinsella, unambiguously recommends. Goffman's volume examines social interactions as theatrical performances, in which people collaborate in order to save face, keep up fronts, or af-firm certain roles and allegiances: "the expressive component of so-cial life" is for Goffman "a source of impressions given to or taken by others." From this point of view, "this self . . . does not derive from its possessor, but from the whole scene of his action, being generated by that attribute of local events which renders them interpretable by wit-nesses." And yet, Goffman adds, this sense of the self as performed does not deny the reality of the perfomer, nor the good faith of the per-formance. "Attributes of the individual *qua* performer" (such as "fan-tasies and dreams," "gregarious desire," or "deeply felt shame") "are not merely a depicted effect"—our emotions are not like our clothes; we cannot take them off and remain recognizably ourselves. And yet even the most intimate emotions "seem to arise out of intimate inter-action with the contingencies of staging performances": for Tranter, as for Goffman, we make, from the prop closet and the wardrobe of language and habit, ourselves, whether or not we know that is what we are doing.

It is not a knowledge, or even a hypothesis, that we find easy to ac-cept. People in Tranter's poetry are disappointed to find their lives less original, less romantic, and less certain, more prefab, more slapped together, much more like conscious performances, than they have thought—and then, often, the people get over it. The elegiac tones in the later Tranter work in tandem with his dissonances, "in a kind of memory theatre," so that the people or characters he imagines can attend to their senses of artifice and move beyond them:

> looking back, the old people weren't real—
> that's what they felt; since the kids left home
> they'd mutated into an ideal. Then at least
> we'll have been made up, they say, a tale
> telling us about our sad and radiant feelings,
> so we can own them again.

Thom Gunn

Kinesthetic Aesthetics ⁻

Thom Gunn declared in 1978: "My life insists on continuities—
between America and England, between free verse and metre, between vision and everyday consciousness." By the time he died in
2004, his intercontinental style had given us a brace of odd Gunns to
enjoy. Gunn was born in 1929 in England and attended Cambridge;
his first book, *Fighting Terms* (1954), landed him almost accidentally
in the Movement, the set of unmodernist, plainspoken British poets
that included Philip Larkin and the young Donald Davie. Following his
American life partner, Mike Kitay, Gunn moved to California in 1954,
where he studied with Yvor Winters at Stanford. In 1960 Gunn and
Kitay settled in San Francisco, whose evolving street life—motorcyclists
(already present in his fifties poems), then LSD, bars, street fairs, hippies, bathhouses, and proudly gay neighborhoods—furnished frequent
subjects for Gunn's poems.

Some readers have regarded Gunn as a racy verse chronicler of
"Romantics in leather bars" and "badboy uniforms." Others admire
him as a strict craftsman, for his quatrains and sonnets and heroic couplets, indebted to Ben Jonson (whom he edited) and to Thomas Hardy.
A few younger poets (notably August Kleinzahler) seemed to model their

own work on Gunn's tough free verse (Gunn insisted that Kleinzahler in-fluenced him instead). Some reviewers found in everything Gunn does a Brit reacting to America. And since *The Man with Night Sweats* (1992), with its poems about friends who died of AIDS, many readers consid-ered Gunn first as a dignified gay elegist: that view remained in place after his final book, *Boss Cupid* (2000), and after his death. When I read Gunn I hope first of all for none of these; instead, I thrill at his senses of touch and kinesthesia, of skin and limbs and muscles, poised or excited, at rest or "on the move" (as one early title puts it). Any poet can talk about his or her body; Gunn gets his into his verse.

"Rhythmic form and subject-matter are locked in a permanent embrace," Gunn has written. He imagines the elements of verse as human bodies: his most characteristic rhythmic effects reflect or copy or respond to physical actions people take. Gunn likes the purpose-built stanzaic forms of the seventeenth century, partly because their lengths and breaks can replicate walking or reaching or jumping and falling—as they do in "Three," a charming, serious poem about nud-ists at a California beach. Their three-year-old son

> Swims as dogs swim.
> Rushes his father, wriggles from his hold.
> His body which is him,
> Sturdy and volatile, runs off the cold.
>
> Runs up to me:
> Hi there hi there, he shrills, yet will not stop,
> For though continually
> Accepting everything his play turns up
>
> He still leaves it
> And comes back to that pebble-warmed recess
> In which the parents sit,
> At watch, who had to learn their nakedness.

The verbs race and pause along with their characters: Gunn knows the flex and pull of his line lengths and consonants, and puts them all to work to show the child at play.

Gunn rarely shows us a scene without people. At a construction site, he tracks the workers' supple, near-jerky but confident motion in one-syllable rhymes:

Downtown, an office tower is going up.
And from the mesa of unfinished top
Big cranes jut, spectral points of stiffened net:
Angled top-heavy artifacts, and yet
Diagrams from the sky, as if its air
Could drop lines, snip them off, and leave them there.

On girders round them, Indians pad like cats,
With wrenches in their pockets and hard hats.

The self-sufficient, balanced workers earn their own grammatically self-sufficient couplet. "From the Wave" begins with the "concave wall" of a wave front approaching the beach, and ends in the smooths between the swells:

Clear, the sheathed bodies slick as seals
    Loosen and tingle;
And by the board the bare foot feels
    The suck of shingle.

They paddle in the shallows still;
    Two splash each other;
Then all swim out to wait until
    The right waves gather.

Wave and beach, spray, crash and tide (along with Gunn's army of re-treating *l*'s) frame the happy surfers as they enjoy not only the breakers but one another.

Gunn makes his energy tangible by giving it forms and limits—his free verse seems as tight and worked out as his meter and rhyme. And Gunn's unmetered verse loves to hold action: racing, crawling, shoving, swimming, ambling, flying a plane, having sex, having an argument, or hewing a new path across a wet lawn:

The snail pushes through a green
night, for the grass is heavy
with water and meets over
the bright path he makes, where rain
has darkened the earth's dark. He
moves in a wood of desire,

pale antlers barely stirring
as he hunts.

Enjambments shove these syllabics slowly along beside their snail, leaving a brief crawl space between sentences. Gunn also takes on inertia, momentum, acceleration, and deceleration: the poet and his brother on their bicycles, in "Hampstead: The Horse Chestnut Trees,"

rode between them and
down the hill and the impetus
took us on without pedalling
to be finally braked by
a bit of sullen marsh
(no longer there) where the mud
was coloured by the red-brown
oozings of iron. It
was autumn
        or was it?

Gunn zooms his readers downhill with him. And brakes. Only after the bikes stop can he remember, or try to remember, the season.

In John Varley's short story "The Persistence of Vision," deaf-and-blind people establish a commune, with its own customs and tactile language. If Varley's communards composed poems in their "bodytalk," Gunn would be the candidate to translate them. Although (of course) Gunn's poems describe what he sees, he tries hard to do as little as possible with the purely or merely visual, to rely on other, neglected senses. Sometimes he delves into scent, as in "Fennel":

I stand here as if lost,
As if invisible on this broken cliff,
Invisible sky above.
And for a second I float free
Of personality, and die
Into my senses, into the unglossed
Unglossable
Sweet and transporting yet attaching smell
—The very agent that releases me
Holding me here as well.

But usually (as book titles like *Touch* and *The Sense of Movement* announce) touch and kinesthesia take control. And they do so through sounds, as much as through direct description: they have to, since English has fewer words for tactile and kinesthetic feeling than for sight. (Look up the meaning of "comfortable" in *Roget's,* then look up "blue" or "red," and you'll discover what kind of handicap Gunn gives his language when he eschews the seen.) In "The Hug," the lines interlock and rely on each other as Gunn and his lover do:

It was not sex, but I could feel
The whole strength of your body set,
        Or braced, to mine,
     And locking me to you
As if we were still twenty-two
When our grand passion had not yet
        Become familial.

The near-total lack of visual detail makes the vowels and consonants, the elements of aural mimesis, do much of the descriptive work; the poem strives to present the weight and the tactile qualities of the hug it describes— what he would feel even if he had closed his eyes. The divide between "distant" and "close-up," or "impersonal" and "personal," senses—sight and hearing as against touch, smell, taste—is hardly Gunn's discovery: what he has discovered are ways to use that divide in poems.

Downplaying sight, exalting touch, motion, or smell, Gunn invokes the convention that regards the bodily, "lower," earthier senses as less deceptive, closer to the unconscious or to the soul. Machiavelli wrote that "men in general judge more by the sense of sight than by the sense of touch, because everyone can see but only a few can test by feeling" (*The Prince*, trans. Robert M. Adams). Kenneth Burke, more than four hundred years later, wrote (in *Attitudes Toward History*): "The eyes are the 'remotest' of the senses. They lack the immediacy that goes with experiences of taste or contact. . . . Vision, compared with touch, has a quality of 'alienation.'" Why does vision seem, to these writers as to Gunn, less trustworthy than touch? Sight works from far off and treats people just as it treats things; it also sets up an asymmetry between looker and looked at. (You cannot see yourself as others see you, unless you arrange to look in the same mirror.) Touch, however, distinguishes people from things—a Duane Hanson sculpture looks like a human being, but won't ever feel like a person. And touch is uniquely recip-rocal: I can spy on or overhear you, but if you touch me, I'm touching you, and in all likelihood we both know it. We use our sense of sight on strangers, and watching strangers can make Gunn nervous about their privacy: "What am I doing to this man in the yellow jacket?" he asks himself, "Reading him, pretending he is legible, / thinking I can master what is self-contained," though in fact "I know only his outer demeanor, his clothing and his skin": unknowable through sight alone, self-contained, "this man" stands apart from the poet, "a shimmering planet sheathed in its [i.e., his] own air."

Sight, for Gunn, often alienates; touch unites. We rarely pay much attention to how we touch strangers, or spend a long time touching them; the habits of ordinary life make us associate our own tactile sense with friends and lovers—the people whom we touch, the people we want to touch us. Gunn uses this property of touch to present, and to analyze, friendship, erotic love, and the finally unerasable boundar-ies between even the closest selves: in "Jack Straw's Castle," Gunn and his lover

> lie sheetless—bare and close,
> Facing apart, but leaning ass to ass.

And that mere contact is sufficient touch,
A hinge, it separates but not too much.
An air moves over us, as calm and cool
As the green water of a swimming pool.

"Mere contact" cools Gunn down, secures him. Gunn can pack linguistic power, physical strength, kinesis, friendship, and the (male) sex drive so tightly together that they behave like synonyms. "A trucker" fits into his rig as if it were one "enormous throbbing body." In "Saturnalia," "the whole body pulses / like an erection, blood / in the head and furious / with tenderness." Even Gunn's vegetables can grow muscular: the eponymous naturalist in "Thomas Bewick" strikes through woods with his walking stick to find "Gnarled branches reaching down / their green gifts; weed reaching up / milky flower and damp leaf." The fascinated Bewick

> loses himself
in detail,
>   he reverts
to an earlier self, not yet
separate from what it sees

Bewick's communion with the vegetation copies Gunn's communion with flesh. It is a communion savagely parodied in the poems from *Boss Cupid* that attracted the most attention (though they were not its best poems): the stanzaic lyrics spoken by the gay cannibal-murderer Jeffrey Dahmer, who wanted to take into himself the flesh of his victims, and who could not understand (let alone respect) the boundary separating his flesh from theirs.

When Gunn speaks in his own person, he makes clear both his avidity for touch, for fleshly pleasure, and his respect for the boundaries between persons, for what in each self another self cannot know. Gunn likes to imagine, and praise, the preconscious, "not-yet-separate" collectivity he sometimes sees in animals, in nonhuman nature (with Bewick), or in happy crowds. But Gunn rarely lets his own voice blur or fade. He prefers moments when people barely touch, or almost merge.

And he loves to demonstrate ecstasies, appetites, mergings, in other people, or even in animals. When Gunn admires the pig in "Meat" he knows he sounds funny, but we know he means it:

> My brother saw a pig root in a field,
> And saw too its whole lovely body yield
> To this desire which deepened out of need
> So that in wriggling through the mud and weed
> To eat and dig were one athletic joy.

The pig may be ugly if we merely look; consider its motile pleasures, and it turns beautiful. But the human being nearest to that kind of bliss is "the sand man," a brain-damaged beachfront derelict:

> He rocks, a blur on ridges, pleased to be.
> > Dispersing with the sands
> He feels a dry cool multiplicity
> > Gilding his body, feet and hands.

The golden sand's feel on the skin makes it, for the sand man, more precious than gold. His "mere innocence / Many have tried to repossess" amounts to, equals, the pleasure he takes in his senses. No one would want to become the sand man, or a pig (though Gunn's poem "Moly" explores just that change). The aggressive biker boys and street kids who populate all his books run closer to Gunn's ideals: those strong, hot-blooded heroes—skateboarders, club kids, often so naive they make him self-conscious—inspire Gunn as few subjects can.

Gunn was not always so confident, or so comfortable, as I have thus far made him sound. In his first books—up through *My Sad Captains* (1961)—control became a grim end in itself: allegories of exiles and prisoners, in stiff, boxy stanzas with end words like pistons, spelled out Gunn's early dogmas:

> Much that is natural, to the will must yield.
> Men manufacture both machine and soul,

And use what they imperfectly control
To dare a future from the taken routes.

These books get called "heroic" and "martial," but they are also desperate: as Gunn has acknowledged, some of his best early poems look
now like plaints from the closet. Before 1965 Gunn's characters are
mostly enduring loners, suffering, tortured, or "numb past pain": a
teen werewolf; a trucker and his truck; bikers; Nazi foot soldiers; polar
explorers; centurions; "Tamer and Hawk"; and St. Martin (who hu-
manly and justly keeps half his cloak for himself so he won't freeze).
In 1965 Gunn finished the sequence "Misanthropos," whose protagonist thinks himself the last man alive on earth, and learns otherwise
in the final lines. Soon after, Gunn began to choose happier alter
egos—flowers; a satyr; the centaur of "Tom-Dobbin"; fiercely playful "Apartment Cats"; an inquisitive dog; nudists en famille; surfers;
a newborn; an American pioneer couple; transient hippies "discovering" the Pacific; a small plane banking and rising in the wind; the sun;
and a seed.

What happened? The sixties? Gay liberation? Certainly both: several
poems in *Moly* (1971) bear the subtitle "LSD." But what those times
and movements did for Gunn, they could do for no other poet. Because
Gunn started with such an understanding of his own body, of how to
get its rigors into verse, the countercultures of the 1960s—which elevated community, unself-consciousness, pleasure—showed Gunn how
to use his proprioception, and his sense of his skin, to welcome other
people into his poems. Asked to pick a single swivel point in Gunn's career, I'd nominate "Back to Life," from *Touch* (1967)—a book broken
up, in his 1994 *Collected Poems*, into the sequence "Misanthropos"
plus a handful of "Poems from the 1960s." In "Back to Life," Gunn
walks in a "little park" in San Francisco, smells limes, watches branches
and streetlights, and traces their three-dimensional solidities:

Touching the lighted glass,
Their leaves are soft green on the night,
The closest losing even their mass,
Edged but transparent as if they too gave light.

Next Gunn notices the other walkers, "boys and girls . . . jostling as they grow, / Cocky with surplus strength." Gunn's earlier rebels and heroes could be themselves only alone. But these kids' energy, their adolescent unease, help them create a social life. Kids hold hands, limes brush streetlights, and Gunn feels, briefly, in touch with them all:

> I walk between the kerb and bench
> Conscious at length
> Of sharing through each sense,
> As if the light revealed us all
> Sustained in delicated difference
> Yet firmly growing from a single branch.

The oscillating meters expand and contract as if to let in other minds. Later "Back to Life" remembers that all of us fall from the branch, "sooner or later separate"; nonetheless, from here on Gunn will seem far more at home with us, far friendlier, more confident, more inviting.

The later, better Gunn thus uses his muscles and bones and finger-tips to make himself a social poet. Gunn loves the gay street fair in "At the Barriers" because there "we stretch our sympathies, this is a day of feeling with"—the line makes explicit the serious pun Gunn often asks his readers to make, between "feeling" other people's emotions, and "feeling" the limits and shapes of their skins. Gunn's conversational tones can sound forced: "Time to go home babe, though now you feel most tense." But the same poem ("Fever") that throws up that clunker boasts one of Gunn's best bits of venom:

> Your mother thought you beautiful, I suppose,
>   She dandled you all day and watched your sleep.
> Perhaps that's half the trouble. And it grows:
>   An unattended conqueror now, you keep
> Getting less beautiful toward the evening's end.

Barely hinted at before 1970, Gunn's talent as a psychological observer informs excruciatingly true poems like "Dolly," about (I think) a heroin addict who is "out to end his choices / for good and doesn't realize it." He does not understand his own deep motives, nor does the more attractive man whom Gunn examines in the second half of the poem:

> I know someone who
> was never let play with dolls
> when he was little, so now
> (he thinks to spite his father)
> collects them.
> But it's the crippled ones
> he cherishes most, particularly
> the quadriplegics: they loll
> blank stomachs depending from blank heads
> with no freedom
> >   ever, ever
>
> and in need.

The longest line lobs out the only real image, "blank stomachs depending from blank heads." (What horrifies Gunn first? Their posture.) Four elegant sentences set up all the characters—"you," "I," the addict, the sad "someone" of the second half, the father, the healthy dolls, and the sick dolls, who reveal the half-hidden motives of the rest.

All of Gunn's descriptions include justifications: he says nothing he can't understand and makes no verbal move he can't explain. His habit of judgment gives him the depressing habit of tacking moral tags onto poems that hardly need them: "we savour the approaching delight / of things we know yet are fresh always"; "I tingled with knowledge. / The swiftly changing / played upon the slowly changing." But I trust Gunn as I trust few poets of his generation. If his commitment to knowing what he is doing—and his skittishness about seeing—debars him from the visionary, fantastic power of, say, Hart Crane, Gunn offers instead the modest virtues of clarity and reliability, and the ability to bring into language the senses that most language, most poets, ignore.

Gunn's motto might be "no trust without risk; no risk without trust": each depends on the other to make it worthwhile. "Trust" and "risk" during the 1990s became his favorite words: Gunn's

HIV-positive "man with night sweats," looking back over his sexual rovings, recalls:

> I grew as I explored
> The body I could trust
> Even while I adored
> The risk that made robust,
>
> A world of wonders in
> Each challenge to the skin.

Trust and risk, for the man who speaks the poem, have come in and through flesh, though others (see "His Rooms in College") might find those virtues in literature.

Gunn insists on the likenesses between poems and persons, minds and bodies, and (even in his LSD-prompted poems) on the material, physical grounds of even the most outré event. He defines "miracle" (in "The Miracle") first as a partner so sexy and "so slim / That I could grip my wrist in back of him," and then as a cum trail that stays for months:

> "Then suddenly he dropped down on one knee
> Right by the urinal in his only suit
>
> And let it fly, saying Keep it there for me,
> And smiling up. I can still see him shoot.
> Look at that snail-track on the toe of my boot."
>
> —"Snail-track?"—"Yes, there."—"That was six months ago.
> How can it still be there?"—"My friend, at night
> I make it shine again, I love him so,
> Like they renew a saint's blood out of sight.
> But we're not Catholic, see, so it's all right."

A sacrament? A guy with a hard-on? Love? All three: their conjunction-disjunctive ties the poem to Donne's "The Relic," the blasphemous, worshipful, erotic, anti-Catholic precedent Gunn has in mind. (Donne's poem ends: "All measure, and all language, I should pass, / Should I tell what a miracle she was.")

Gunn enjoys the Metaphysicals far more than he does metaphysics. "I'm not very spiritual!" Gunn exclaimed in an interview. His thorniest abstractions grow from his forays into psychology, when his fierce, lovely, loving struggles among erotic partners probe the bounds of the ego. Gunn reminisces, in "The Differences," "So when you gnawed my armpits, I gnawed yours / And learned to associate you with that smell / As if your exuberance sprang from your pores." He enjoys shocking us—how many lovers gnaw armpits?—but he's also mulling what the psychoanalytic thinker Jessica Benjamin calls "the problem of domination": how can I love somebody without wanting to control, or to be controlled? Most of his best love poems take up the same question: most of them answer with tableaux of adjacent, barely touching bodies, either excited or sated. "The Differences" gets wacky in the middle, declaring, "love is formed by a dark ray's invasion / From Mars," which turns out to be translated Cavalcanti. But Gunn's ending grows quietly serious: the skin, the flesh's surface, stands for the borders of respect between lovers, which we can learn to accept and appreciate:

> We lay at ease, an arm loose round a waist,
> Or side by side and touching at the hips,
> As if we were two trees, bough grazing bough,
> The twigs being the toes or fingertips.

It's like Gunn to clarify where all the limbs ended up, and (as in "Jack Straw's Castle") just how toe touched toe.

Because he knows so thoroughly what male bodies can enjoy when they stay healthy, his verse can show how they fail when they turn ill. His poems about people with HIV and AIDS make not death but illness weirdly vivid. And because his poems of the seventies and eighties so often found forms for gay friendships, parties, and neighborhoods, Gunn can depict how HIV and AIDS menace not just individuals but a milieu. The man in "Still Life" becomes a heraldic symbol of all dying men, a crest (like a lion couchant) on a "field," as his exertions strain Gunn's phrases:

He still found breath, and yet
It was an obscure knack.
I shall not soon forget
The angle of his head,
Arrested and reared back
On the crisp field of bed,

Back from what he could neither
Accept, as one opposed,
Nor, as a life-long breather,
Consentingly let go,
The tube his mouth enclosed
In an astonished O.

Disyllabic rhymes (neither, breather) shrink to one-syllable rhymes inside two-syllable words (opposed, enclosed), and then to the desperate gasps of go and O.

Gunn's exertions in *The Man with Night Sweats* strive against the deaths he describes: the Man of the title poem pulls himself back to the flesh that threatens (like an unreliable lover) to leave him:

I have to change the bed,
But catch myself instead

Stopped upright where I am
Hugging my body to me
As if to shield it from
The pains that will go through me,

As if hands were enough
To hold an avalanche off.

We barely see the Man, but we hear what he feels: "to," "as," "if," "from," all carry scary, unaccustomed weight, making for linefuls of spondees, and sentences as effortfully tough as wrestlers' holds. "The Missing" remembers the happy crowd from "At the Barriers," in the same half-numb, determined tones:

Contact of friend led to another friend,
Supple entwinement through the living mass
Which for all that I knew might have no end,
Image of an unlimited embrace.

To be alive means, here, to be "entwined." The scariest people in *The Man with Night Sweats* are not the AIDS patients in the elegies, but the nameless dead in "Death's Door," who belong in death, to death, because they no longer care about bodies, nor care for their friends. In their purgatorial TV room,

The habit of companionship
Lapses—they break themselves of touch:
Edging apart at arm and hip,
Till separated on the couch,

They woo amnesia, look away
As if they were not yet elsewhere,
And when snow blurs the picture they,
Turned, give it a belonging stare.

Even at his most harrowed, Gunn remembers other poetry, in this case Larkin's "The Winter Palace," which ends, "Soon there will be nothing I know. / My mind will fade into itself like fields, like snow." Against Larkin's forgetful mind of winter, against the dead in their indifferent armchairs, Gunn uses his poems to show his strength, his friendships, and his turnings "Back to Life." Where the childless Larkin of "Dockery and Son" wanted no son, no social bonds, one of Gunn's ex-lovers chose to adopt one. When Gunn sees the son, in the last poem in *The Man with Night Sweats*, he makes the adoptive father into another alter ego:

What I admired about his self-permission
Was that he turned from nothing he had done,
Or was, or had been, even while he transposed
The expectations he took out at dark

—Of Eros playing, features undisclosed—
Into another pitch, where he might work
With the same melody, and opted so
To educate, permit, guide, feed, keep warm,
And love a child to be adopted, though
The child was still a blank then on a form.

The blank was flesh now, running on its nerve,
This fair-topped organism dense with charm,
Its braided muscle grabbing what would serve,
His countering pull, his own devoted arm.

That handclasp, with its measured "countering pull," declares that parents and children—like friends, like readers, like lovers, like generations of writers—can care for others while respecting their independence. It is the unerotic, chastened version of the "ass-to-ass" contact that guaranteed love and trust twenty years earlier in "Jack Straw's Castle."

Gunn ends his saddest book—and the one that seems, now, to remain the basis of his U.S. reputation, the book through which the future will encounter the rest of Gunn—with a man who looks forward, who holds on to somebody else and repudiates none of himself. In the same way, Gunn did not repudiate, did not have to choose between, American life and English tradition, Nor did he choose between meter and free verse, tradition and counterculture, old and new, consciousness and instinct, the pull of feeling and the rule of thought. His tactile talents let him get all these supposed opposites into the bodies his poems imagine, the people they create. And Gunn grabs and holds even those abstract virtues in terms of physical sensations—muscles; strength; warmth; a tug on somebody's willing, living hand.

Paul Muldoon, Early

If—as Randall Jarrell put it—poets are in the beginning hypotheses, in midcareer facts, and in the end values, Paul Muldoon is at least a fact: those of us who are convinced he's important no longer need to get everyone to read him. But we, or he, may still have to defend his work against the charge that he's frivolous or overwitty, or to show that he does have a soul. If the celebrated, and surprisingly direct—in places almost Whitmanesque—elegy "Incantata" (from *The Annals of Chile* [1994]) was one sort of demonstration, his 1996 *New Selected Poems* is another. Poets selecting from their own work are inevitably advising readers: *don't read X without reading Y,* or, sometimes, *don't bother with X.* Thus Elizabeth Bishop, refusing anthologists permission for "The Fish" unless they took other poems along with it; thus Muldoon, leaving out all but one page of "Madoc," and including, whole, both earlier detective-story sonnet sequences, "Immram" and "The More a Man Has the More a Man Wants." Muldoon's second *Selected* is a chance to look again at the shape of Muldoon's career, a new perspective on the earliest poems, and an oblique, memorable account of the growth of a poet's soul.

Growth implies a starting point: how did Muldoon begin? The earliest poems suggest Frost and Heaney, but with a mysteriousness not present in either; if Frost, with his ironic rural mythographies, served the young Muldoon as a suitably distant model, the only-slightly-older Heaney seems now to have been both model and rival. The first half of "Hedgehog" seems to compare the two poets, with Muldoon in the title role and Heaney as snail:

> The snail moves like a
> Hovercraft, held up by a
> Rubber cushion of itself,
> Sharing its secret
>
> With the hedgehog. The hedgehog
> Shares its secret with no one.
> We say, Hedgehog, come out
> Of yourself and we will love you.
>
> We mean no harm. We want
> Only to listen to what
> You have to say. We want
> Your answers to our questions.

For all the echoes and debts, rereading early Muldoon now reminds me less often of *North,* or of *North of Boston,* than of what Muldoon became. The fear in "Good Friday. Driving Westward 1971" is Frostian: did Muldoon, driving across the border, hit and kill a pedestrian, or was his hitchhiker seeing things? But the abrupt confrontation with uncertainty, the self-interruption, could only be Muldoon's:

> I glanced back once
> And there was nothing but a heap of stones.
> We had just dropped in from nowhere for lunch
>
> In Gaoth Dobhair, I happy and she convinced
> Of the death of more than lamb or herring.
> She stood up there and then, face full of drink,
> And announced that she and I were to blame
> For something killed along the way we came.
> Children were warned that it was rude to stare,
> Left with their parents for a breath of air.

Muldoon's later habits start here: his slippery metrics and half-rhyme (*once / stones*), allowing full rhyme to signal climaxes or special effects; his almost compulsive allusiveness (Donne's "Good Friday," like Muldoon's, explaining why the poet did not want to look behind him). Paths of development run straight on from the insistent hitchhiker to the accusatory companions or ex-wives in "Sushi" and "Capercallies," and from the "iffing and butting herd / Of sheep" in "Good Friday" to the self-begetting "metaphysicattle of Japan" in "Cows." Here, too, is his willingness to give his accusers the last word.

Muldoon's early work forecasts his late achievements quite as much in themes as it does in tones and verbal props: the early poems include (oddly Gaelic) American Indians; the poet and his surrogates on the lam or in hiding; doubled or hybrid identities; and the insistence (more familiar from novels and plays than from poems) that the same events can tell, for different eyes, many contradictory stories. From *Mules* (1977) on, Muldoon represents himself as a fusion of opposites, a half-man, a double, or two people at once, each discovering his doppelgänger or counterpart. Everything from a bisexual ménage to a provincial circus becomes an emblem of division, and the middle poems are a forest of single lines describing self-contradictory states: "A dwarf on stilts" and "what was neither one thing nor the other." In "Merman," Muldoon is "sowing winter wheat" when he meets a merman "ploughing his single furrow": the poem's "I" asks the merman (citing, I think, Tolstoy), "Had he no wish to own such land / as he might plough round in a day? / What of friendship, love? Such qualities?" The merman's nonanswer is that—having lived, in the past, on land—he "remembered these same fields of corn or hay / When swathes ran high along the ground, / Hearing the cries of one in difficulties." Muldoon is the practical, earthy, domestic-minded half of himself; the merman is the other half, the abstract aspirant transfigured by ambition. Uncertainty, "wonder," or even evasive shuttling proves more attractive, and more poetically interesting, than any stance on either side: the poet's quarrel with himself ends, provisionally, with the supposition that it should not really end, should not produce a moral, only sharpened terms in which to state a dilemma.

Although Muldoon has stated that the families in his poems are often whole-cloth fictions, "The Mixed Marriage" will comfort the sorts of readers who want to trace a poet's personae to his upbringing, since its speaker's lineage suggests Muldoon's own teacher mother and practical-minded farmer father. ("She" and "he" are the parents in the poem; farcy is a cattle disease.)

> She had read one volume of Proust,
> He knew the cure for farcy.
> I flitted between a hole in the hedge
> And a room in the Latin Quarter.

The "hole in the hedge" is rural play, as distant from books as possible, but it is also the Irish-language hedge schools of eighteenth-century Irish Catholics; the geographically impossible commute Muldoon describes is another paradox of division, the young poet really thinking himself—as he put it later in a sonnet—"two places at once, or was it one place twice?" Muldoon is, famously, "the man who can rhyme knife with fork," an appellation he mocks in another sonnet: "Not for nothing would I . . . rhyme (*pace* Longley) 'cat' / with 'dog' . . ."; even his famously casual, Byronic virtuosity with rhyme words might be seen as standing for divided selves, a flaunted *discordia* that's never quite *concors*. Heaney's own poem about a boundary, "Terminus," sounds now like a belated assent to Muldoon's definition of a poet's mind—or of an Irish, or Ulster, poet's mind?—as one beset by contraries: "Is it any wonder when I thought / I would have second thoughts?"

From *Mules* on, Muldoon has been a master of proper nouns. Earlier these were seeming inventions: the comically resolute, would-be hardman boy Will Hunter, the Eliotically displaced "Mrs de Groot from the bridge set," and Joseph Mary Plunkett Ward—young, self-appointed, impossibly apt heir of the Easter martyr Joseph Mary Plunkett. But increasingly names have denoted real places and identifiable, or even famous, people. Louis MacNeice, Christo, President Kennedy, the Royal Victoria Hospital, Knut Hamsun, the oyster bar in Grand Central Station, and the rest not only resonate in the poems they serve but also connect the poems to a larger universe of "real" fact and incident. The weirder Muldoon's poems became, the more they included names you'd recognize, or want to look up: the poems, for all their evasions and involutions, have wished to be part of the world of all of us, and do not even try for—do not claim to want—the self-sufficient clarity and wholeness we expect from the mature products of Heaney, or even of William Carlos Williams.

But the increasing allusiveness and fragmentary quality of the poems from *Why Brownlee Left* (1980) on, had another not cause, but precondition: if it can be good practice for inexperienced writers to start with "easier" poems, it is also a discipline imposed on all but the most self-involved young poets by the restricted or local audience with which most young writers begin. The increasing (or increasingly obvious) difficulty, and the undeniably increasing allusiveness, of Muldoon's poetics from *New Weather* to *The Annals of Chile* now sound less like consequences of changing ambitions than like consequences of the *permission* that already-existing, at least notionally appreciative readers give. "Mink," for example ("A mink escaped from a mink-farm / in South Armagh / is led to the grave of Robert Nairac / by the fur-lined hood of his anorak"), presupposes readers who will have learned from more conventional, earlier epigrams—say, "Blemish"—to appreciate this one.

A writer who already has readers can also start to allude to his previous work, to bind his poems together into an oeuvre. (Eliot's quirky criterion for "major" writers, that any bit of their work help us with the rest, fits Muldoon better than it fits anyone else alive.) By the mid-1980s Muldoon had a whole landscape of self-quotations: "It seemed that I would be forever driving west" ("Immram") points backward twelve years to "Good Friday"; "The Right Arm" shakes hands with the "one good arm" in an earlier poem about linguistic isolation, "The Narrow Road to the Deep North"; and the fiction of Muldoon's father's flight to Brazil or points south spawned a whole colony of interrelated poems, from "Immramma" to "Immram" to "Yarrow." The narrative poems become the world's most literate, violent pulp serial, featuring the ill-starred mercenary Gallogly, aka Golightly, Gallowglass, English (see, again, "The Right Arm"). And the poems grow thick with in jokes, only some of which I get: in the aside from "Immram," about an Irish American cop,

His laugh was a slight hiccup.
I guessed that Lieutenant Brendan O'Leary's
Grandmother's pee was green,
And that was why she had to leave old Skibbereen.

Discolored urine can indicate venereal disease, but the real secret is that Muldoon's narrator is playing a (drinking) game called "Skibbereen," which consists in thinking up outrageous first lines (e.g., "They took away our good Pope John and they gave us Fulton Sheen") to rhyme with the phrase "And that's another reason why I left old Skibbereen."

Even during the 1970s, readers met a brace of Muldoons before the hard, long poems begin: the fabulist, the literary critic ("Standish O'Grady? Very old fashioned"), the bohemian adventurer, the shy boy (see "Profumo"), and the crime reporter; they also met a social satirist and a dirty joker, the poet for whom "Once he got stuck into her he got stuck / Full stop" provides a suitable occasion. (It provides, too, yet another metaphor for Northern Ireland: the medically unfortunate tryst takes place in the Belfast Botanical Gardens, and the couple are "manhandled onto a stretcher / Like the last of an endangered species.") We have, too, met the signature grammatical moves—the Muldonian "or," which establishes deep uncertainty about what is being described, rather than (like the Elizabeth Bishop "or") increasingly accurate perception over time. There is also the Muldonian optative—the wary "I would have" or "it might as well"—and the tantalizingly overspecific apposition "not an A, but a B," "not by A, but by B," one of whose effects is to set a reader immediately to imagine whatever the clause excludes: "We *might* have been thinking of the fire-bomb . . . We *might* have wept with Elizabeth McCrum. / We *were* thinking only of psilocybin" (italics mine). And we may sigh, or delight, at Muldoon the lexicographer, who sends readers to the *Oxford English Dictionary* for *thrapple, sheugh, gowk, borage, kedlock* (meaning, in order, throttle or strangle; furrow, trench, or ditch; cuckoo or fool, but also a variant for "gawk"; a wildflower; field mustard). All these Muldoons have stayed with us, writing the beautiful-by-anybody's-standards short work, anthology pieces in the best sense—say, "Cuba," "Meeting the British," "Holy Thursday," "Milkweed and Monarch." But the mature Muldoon felt able to make another, and a larger, kind of poem: the dense, sprawling, frustrating modernist narrative that sends its readers not only to the OED but to encyclopedias before (if not instead of) sending them to copy it out.

If the "I" and the eye of the lyrics from the 1970s located themselves definitively in Ulster, the "I" of the early 1980s lays an equal claim to

New York and California, and to an America derived as much from film noir, detective fiction, and eccentric biographies as from anything you could actually see in the United States. When the Muldoon of *Quoof* thinks about Dublin, he writes a poem ("The Frog") about moral dilemmas and political cruelty, one so serious you can see the brows knit; when he thinks about New York ("The Unicorn Defends Himself"), he thinks about art museums and anal sex, and the poem sounds, well, *naughty*. "Immram" is full of American properties, in the Hollywood and the prop closet sense of "properties"; its style comes from the impatient, waggish prose of Flann O'Brien, who shared Muldoon's interests in recursion, self-reference, hallucinations, and taking the piss out of the Celtic Revival. As in O'Brien, the pulp and the science fiction aspects of "Immram" and "The More a Man Has" and "Madoc" permit disjunction, hallucination, sensational antiheroes, and a litter of puns: it must have been a fun style to write in, maybe even more fun to write than to read. But the America of "Immram" and of *Quoof* is the America of Raymond Chandler and of Quentin Tarantino: anyone who lived in it and thought about it only in that way would probably not be choosing to write *poems*.

And when Muldoon came to live in America, he started finding other ways to write about it. We get in the *New Selected Poems* nothing either of "Madoc" or of "*7, Middagh Street,*" two long poems about Irish and British writers self-exiled in the United States, both obsessed with exile, nationality, and political responsibility, and both hard for new readers to swallow. Instead, Muldoon's mellower, lived-in America consists in single scenes from Toronto ("Ontario") or Manhattan ("The Briefcase") or New Jersey—seven pages from *The Prince of the Quotidian,* the 1994 assemblage of chatty one-a-day sonnets largely about the poet's domestic and academic life in Princeton. The sonnets *do* read like a journal, but a witty, fun-to-read journal, expert, self-confident, and invitingly informal sketches of a poet surprised by his own satisfaction:

After two days grading papers from the seminar I taught
on Swift, Yeats, Sterne,
Joyce, and Beckett,
I break my sword across my iron knee:

in the long sonata of *The Dead*
ceremony's a name for the rich horn—
those images fresh images beget—
and custom for the hardy laurel tree . . .

I wouldn't trade "Meeting the British" for these lightweight jokes against Yeats's "A Prayer for my Daughter," but I would not willingly part with the jokes. And even the least satisfying sonnets—like the least of late Lowell—show us the creative process of fermentation. Reading these stacks of jotted-down proper nouns is like seeing the flattened ferns in ancient forests halfway to being coal—you know they'll contain more energy later, but right now you can appreciate the outlines of the leaves.

New Selected ends by reprinting most of *The Annals of Chile,* bar the hardest and longest poem ("Yarrow"). "Incantata" is surely Muldoon's least guarded and most sincere big work, and probably the decade's best elegy in English. (Or mostly in English: readers without suitably bilingual acquaintances might want to look up the 1994 *Times Literary Supplement* whose footnotes translate Muldoon's Irish.) With the giant narratives left out of *New Selected,* Muldoon stakes, and wins, his recent claims on his lyric. The omissions also make the work of the 1990s seem more like his earlier poems: his career, circa 1996, looks tough in the middle, and tender at each end. I was surprised to see (tender) bits of Muldoon's libretto *The Shining Brow,* especially since the verse play *Six Honest Serving Men* gets no space at all: but the opera belongs here because it is Muldoon's most sustained self-critique, his attack on the Modernist Genius in him. The author of *Madoc* is the opera's Great Man Frank Lloyd Wright, obsessed with his ambitious making and willfully ignorant of its potential human uses. The best of the three excerpts in this book is the ten-line, Audenesque "Workmen's Chorus":

Hand me up my spirit-level, my plumb-line and my plumb.
Hand me up my spirit-level, or I'll lose my equilibrium.

When the whistle blew at lunch time, I opened my lunch-pail.
It was completely empty. That's why my mouth is full of nails.

The workmen in the Workmen's Chorus are saying—in the flattened, accessible way appropriate to lyrics for music—something like Sidney's "But oh, Desire still cries, give me some food," and even more like St. Paul's "Though I speak with the tongues of men and of angels, if I speak without love, I am nought but a gong." This is the worst thing we could say about the Muldoon who wrote "The More a Man Has the More a Man Wants," and it is to his entire credit that he has, by now, said it himself.

What will surprise old fans and new readers even more than the relevance of the opera are three poems newly rescued from the 1984 pamphlet *The Wishbone*. "The Bear" is mostly in-jokes, "The Main-Mast" is OK, and "The Ox" is far better than OK:

> They had driven for three hours non-stop
> that April afternoon
> to see the Burren's orchids
> in bloom.
>
> Milltown Malbay. They parked
> in front of a butcher shop.
> "A month too early. I might have known."
> "Let's find a room."
>
> They reversed away from the window.
> To the right hung
> one ox-tail,
>
> to the left one ox-tongue.
> "What's the matter? What's got into you?"
> "Absolutely nothing at all."

The pamphlets have deliberate sequences, even more than the full books do, and this one would probably benefit from its context, which also makes clear that the questioner is a woman, the questioned speaker the real-life "Muldoon"—though the poem gives them equal time. Again Muldoon is two people at once, divided over whether to turn tail, or to come out with whatever he has against himself. A better question to ask the reticent partner might be, "What have you gotten yourself into?" or "Do you see any way out?" or even "Let's split up: what are we waiting for?" One can split up with oneself, though, only in poems: poems like Muldoon's self-divided best, of which there are now more in bookshops than there were before. This is a fair, accessible, up-to-date sampler for one of the best poets alive, and while there are poems I wish he had put in ("Elizabeth," the useful "Identities," "Gone"), the only omission I really regret is the entire absence of explanatory endnotes, a coy move common to all his books, and one that has hurt his American reception: surely his power to exceed interpretation would not be very much damaged if he told readers who wrote "Pythagoras in America" or "The Alchemist and Barrister," or who Bernardo O'Higgins (or is it Kevin O'Higgins?) was, or how to play a game of skibbereen.

Paul Muldoon, Late

Coming to Paul Muldoon for the first time must feel like tuning in to an especially complicated, well-regarded television series midway through its seventh season. While devotees praise or deprecate each new twist, newcomers need help figuring out who is who, which parts even fans find baffling, and which—to the well informed—make immediate sense. It seems only fair, then, to start a consideration of Muldoon's *The End of the Poem* (2007) and *Horse Latitudes* (2007) with a sketch of his prior career. Raised in County Armagh, Northern Ireland, Muldoon attended Queen's University in the early 1970s and lived mostly in Belfast until 1986; he then moved to the United States, settling at Princeton University. The move divides the uneasy, often cryptic or terse, sometimes violent, verse that set him among the most admired (and most emulated) poets of Britain and Ireland from the no less cagey, more obviously virtuosic verse he wrote in the United States. The first phase—*New Weather* (1973) through *Meeting the British* (1987)—included unhappy love affairs, rural settings, precarious and unsettled youthful protagonists, shaggy-dog stories in verse, other sorts of self-canceling, incomplete narratives, and much-remarked half- and off-rhyme. The second phase, obvious since *The Annals of Chile* (1994), maintained the odd rhymes and half-finished adventure stories, but added difficult forms with repeated end words (especially the sestina); flotillas of proper nouns, seemingly designed to send readers to encyclopedias; and celebratory occasional verse.

Where the earlier poems could sound curtly querulous, the later have been teasingly loquacious; where earlier poems portrayed disgruntled lovers, the later depicted Muldoon's happier adult life as a husband, teacher, and father. At one end of his life—as it appeared in the poems—lay Armagh, the strivings of adolescence, and the poet's admirable but close-mouthed farmer father; at the other, transatlantic success, most recently reflected in his position (from 1999 to 2004) as Oxford University Professor of Poetry. The distance itself gave Muldoon plenty to consider: whether the parts of his life may be seen as connected, whether he can understand how he got from one end to the other, has become one of the problems his poems explore.

Elected by Oxford graduates, the Professor of Poetry must give three public lectures per year for five years: *The End of the Poem* collected Muldoon's fifteen. Each save the last considers, at length, one poem, among them W. B. Yeats's "All Souls' Night," Elizabeth Bishop's "Twelve O'Clock News," Eugenio Montale's "The Eel" (in several translations), Arnold's "Dover Beach." (The last takes up three poems, all by prior Professors: Robert Graves, C. Day-Lewis, and Seamus Heaney.) *The End of the Poem*, as a title, signifies the imputed, disputed purpose of poetry; the condition of closure or termination for a poem; the way interpretation can go on forever; and the boundaries (if there are any) between poem and poet, poetry and biography, information relevant to a poem and information of no pertinence. Always inventive, Muldoon is best not when examining individual poems but when speculating about how poems in general get made. He nevertheless proposes memorable, plausible arguments about, for example, Emily Dickinson and circumpolar exploration; about Matthew Arnold, Thomas Arnold, and Thucydides; about Heaney and Robert Lowell.

Other arguments sound absurd. As in Muldoon's only prior book of criticism, *To Ireland, I* (2000), no association can be ruled out; any likeness of sound or contiguity of experience in Muldoon's mind can become as relevant to someone else's writings as it would be to his own. Thus "lees" (of wine) in "All Souls' Night" suggest Georgie Hyde-Lees (Yeats's wife); "there's a connection in Yeats's mind" among "the 'poetic line' and the 'line of descent,'" linen (for shrouds), and (by way of Keats) the linnet, which eats the seeds of flax, the plant from which linen can be made. The date appended to "All Souls' Night," "Oxford. Autumn 1920," is for Muldoon "an astonishingly direct reference to [Keats's] 'To Autumn'" (published in 1820, though written earlier), which makes the lees in Yeats a version of the "last oozings" from Keats's cider press. In the second lecture, Ted Hughes's failure to use the word "loom" in a catty poem about Marianne Moore supposedly shows that Hughes has been thinking about Harold Bloom, whose theories of literary influence supposedly tie Moore to Hughes's earlier book *Moortown*. The "fern" in Moore's own "Spenser's Ireland" sounds like the "fen" in a poem she published in college, "fen" being a synonym of "marsh" or "moor," which makes the fern "a subliminal version" of the poet, whose "own name, with its m, r and double o, is a near version of that 'mirror' held up to nature."

And so on. Muldoon's filters and search engines remain alert not for what Yeats would find relevant to a poem by Yeats but for what Muldoon would find relevant to a poem by Muldoon—coincidences, puns, hidden barbs, and jokes, what Auden called "the luck of verbal playing." (Muldoon has read widely but not always deeply in the relevant scholarship: hearing, at the beginning of Lowell's "Quaker Graveyard," echoes of Gerard Manley Hopkins, he overlooks Lowell's documented source in Thoreau.) The lectures come off best if we see them as Muldoon's effort to show us how we should read him, and in turn to show us how he sees the world: a dense constellation of words, delightfully rich if we take it for what it is, and frighteningly unstable, disorienting even, if we expect, from its multifarious patterns, clues that tell us how to live.

Even the lectures' exhilarated—and therefore unreliable—self-confidence of tone is part of that point: we do not know how seriously to take the points he makes, because he does not quite know what he ought to take seriously himself, which verbal overlaps and mental links are evidence of anything outside his head. Such uncertainty may be unusual for critics, but it is almost ordinary for poets, who can rely on nothing outside themselves as they decide what to make of their unfinished poems: connecting the word "expiation" to the word "expedition" in Dickinson, Muldoon does what many writers do when they misread their own handwriting, then accept on purpose what they have created by accident.

So evasive himself, Muldoon does well with the chameleonic Portuguese modernist Fernando Pessoa, unearthing Pessoa's bizarre but apparently productive dealings with Aleister Crowley, the English Satanist, self-promoter, minor poet, and enemy of Yeats. Pessoa's self-reinventions suggest, and Muldoon's slippery lines perhaps confirm, "that each and every poem invents both its writer and its reader, and that both writer and reader are engaged in an endless round of negotiations from which no true peace may ever result." The best poems, in other words, pose questions without answers; they draw us to problems that always remain to be solved.

An ally of questions, Muldoon is no friend to answers, and his enmity bears ethical and political points. Writing on Marina Tsvetaeva's "Poem of the End," Muldoon advances what has been a theme in his own verse for decades: the ineradicable opposition between any language we might call poetry, and any attempt, as of a political, religious, or philosophical faction, to pin that language down. The end of the poem (in the sense of its extinction) is "the beginning of propaganda," such as the Bolshevik ideology "with which . . . Tsvetaeva was forced to contend." Later Muldoon quotes Graves: "membership of any political party or religious sect or literary school deforms the poetic sense." Muldoon's earliest poems said, again and again, *non serviam* ("We answer to no grey South // Nor blue North"), and his heroes are still saying it: celebrating "Bob Dylan at Princeton, November 2000" in a new poem, Muldoon awards him not an honorary but "an ornery degree," praising "his absolute refusal to bend the knee."

Muldoon's talk on "Dover Beach" deserves special note. Arnold's own first lecture as Professor of Poetry invoked, in phrases Muldoon quotes, "that impatient irritation of mind which we feel in presence of an immense, moving, confused spectacle which, while it perpetually excites our curiosity, perpetually baffles our comprehension." Arnold thought that he had described one station on the way to understanding great art; for Muldoon, that station is the end of the line. Muldoon also quotes Jean Baudrillard: "'Might we not transpose language games on to social and historical phenomena: anagrams, acrostics, spoonerisms, rhyme, strophe and catastrophe?'" In such games, "meaning is dismembered and scattered to the winds": to represent history and experience by transparently arbitrary verbal play is to imply, as Muldoon all too plausibly implies, that the sufferings historians seek to explain are themselves arbitrary, their patterns without use and without end.

The whimsical quality in such transpositions dominates Muldoon's new prose; their frightening, sometimes fatal arbitrariness animates his new poems. Plenty of features in *Horse Latitudes* look familiar: the sonnet sequence ("Horse Latitudes") and long stanzaic poem ("Sillyhow Stride"), which flip and swivel from context to context, in which distractable wit plays off against anguish; the handful of lucid, winning domestic lyrics; words that barely made the *OED* ("mummichog and menhaden," which are Atlantic food fish; "sillyhow," which means a caul); glamorous, doomed, drug-addicted friends or ex-girlfriends; half-hidden sex jokes ("As I was bringing up her rear"); echoes of Irish history in the Americas; bravura rhyme schemes (each sonnet in the titular sequence rhymes *abcd dcb eeff abc*); a brisk, lengthy set of haiku ("90 Instant Messages to Tom Moore").

Horse Latitudes also offers much that is new, or else unseen since *Quoof* (1983): compared to the rest of Muldoon's American oeuvre, it is harsh, slightly morbid, and shockingly topical. The opening sequence takes its matter from the bouts with cancer of a friend or ex-girlfriend named Carlotta, its digressions from the life of her emigrant grandfather, and the titles for sonnets from battles beginning with B: Bannockburn, Bunker Hill, Basra. "Carlotta would . . . set a spill / to a Gauloise as one might set / a spill to the fuse of a falconet . . . The French, meanwhile, were still struggling to prime / their weapons of mass destruction." A lesser but revealing sonnet sequence, "The Old Country," seems to have fallen together from the grating clichés that many of us store involuntarily in memory:

> Every wishy-washy water diviner
> had stood like a bulwark
>
> against something worth standing against.
> The smell of incense left us incensed
> at the firing of the fort.

Every heron was a presager
of some disaster after which, we'd wager,
every resort was a last resort.

"Wishy-washy," "stood like a bulwark," "last resort": these are the preassembled ideas to which George Orwell's "Politics and the English Language" objected, and Muldoon's point is Orwell's: glibness kills. (George W. Bush, March 2003: "As a last resort, we must be willing to use military force.")

Muldoon's eighth book (by my count) to reflect his life in America, *Horse Latitudes* is also the first in which he seems not to admire his adopted home: much of it reflects the United States of 2003–5, determined to fight terrorists, or specters of terrorists, here, there, and everywhere, and to reelect the architects of such designs. *Horse Latitudes* also reflects the illness and death, from cancer, not of any one friend or former lover (as in his earlier masterpiece "Incantata"), but of several: Muldoon has reached the age when friends' illnesses come not as single spies but in battalions, and his new, sadder tenor reflects that change.

All of Muldoon's collections reveal motifs, words, and images that turn up, over and over, in apparently unrelated poems. Here he offers a stable's worth of horses: various stallions; the titular latitudes ("regions of calm" where ships get stuck, where sailors kill horses for food); stallions; heroin ("horse"); "chevaux-de-frise" (medieval fortifications meant to disable cavalry); a "wooden horse head fitted with some kind of spike"; the morin khur (a Mongolian stringed instrument made from a horse's skull); Glaucus, the mythical king who fed his horses "human flesh / to give them a taste for battle," and who wound up "eaten by his own mares." The horses in *To Ireland, I*— that is, in Muldoon's overview of Irish literature—seem always either bound for, or returning from, the land of the dead; the equine element in Muldoon's own new verse may point us there as well.

These horses join other gloomy leitmotifs: paired stones, often gravestones, to mark the book's repeated mournings ("I fell between two stones / that raised me as their own"); turtles and tortoises (who may live longer than we do, and who remember what we forget); buzzards. The one-sentence, four-page poem called "Turkey Buzzards" sees "the theologian's and the thug's / twin triumphings // in a buzzard's shaved head and snood." The volume-closing elegy, "Sillyhow Stride," concludes with those North American birds' scientific name, *Cathartes aura*: the macaronic pun suggests both that the arts have lost their aura, their magical meliorating power, and that the truest elegy offers neither apotheosis nor catharsis, only scavengers above a corpse.

As sad as it gets, *Horse Latitudes* also gets angry. Theologians are thugs; a sheep is "the avatar / of no god we know of, always the best kind." The morin khur's traditional musical "call . . . may no more be gainsaid / than that of blood kin to kin / through a body-strewn central square": the music that binds us to whatever old country may also lead us to kill in its name. Nor does Irish heritage escape: "Hedge School" links the often-valorized secret schools for eighteenth-century Catholics to "those rainy mornings when my daughter and the rest // of her all-American Latin class may yet be forced to conjugate / *Guantánamo, amas, amat.*" To say the Pledge of Allegiance, in those years, was to say that you loved a torture camp. Nor are all the angers here political: when a coyote mauls the family dog, his bloody eye reminds the poet of a marital quarrel, of the figurative "ring where you and I knuckle down."

The sexual and political frustration that suffuses *Horse Latitudes* also marked *Quoof*; readers who thought (unfairly) that Muldoon had gone soft should think this book his best since that one. A feeling that we have learned nothing from prior conflicts such as the Troubles in Northern Ireland, that we learn nothing no matter what, animates perhaps the best short poem here, "Turtles." In it, a "cubit-wide turtle acting the bin lid" reminds Muldoon first of the "lid-banging" used as an informal local alarm in Belfast, and then of carnage elsewhere:

> Nor am I certain, given their ability to smell the rot
> once the rot sets in,
> that turtles have not been enlisted by some police forces
> to help them recover corpses.

Muldoon finds sigils of strife even in Bermuda: "The black W / on the cicada's wings? War. / Hence the ballyhoo." "90 Instant Messages to

Tom Moore," like Muldoon's prior excursions into miniature forms, suggests that the illusion of order can come, if at all, only in very small units: on any larger scale, all is "Flux, Tom. Constant flux." ("Tom Moore" names both the author of *Irish Melodies* and a tortoise.)

"Sillyhow Stride," on which the volume ends, mourns both Muldoon's sister Maureen and the rock songwriter Warren Zevon (1947–2003), with whom Muldoon collaborated. Zevon's songs—and his rock-and-roll, addiction-and-recovery life—give Muldoon a prototype for all art, which either makes otherwise aimless life worthwhile, or simply distracts us from grisly death: "two true, plain hearts like yourself and Maureen . . . struggled to fend off the great crash that has us end // where we began, all strung out on heroin." Stride, a style of jazz piano, requires the player's left hand to alternate chords with octaves or tenths in the bass; Muldoon's terza rima "stride" alternates reactions to Zevon's and to Maureen's dying with quotations from John Donne, one in almost every stanza. Muldoon wants to liken the witty songwriter to the dean of metaphysical wit, but the device makes Muldoon seem more like Donne instead: riddling, wildly variable, wildly learned, passionate, unpredictable, and frustrated by the violence that he observed close at hand and early in life.

The literary ghost that haunts the volume, though, is not Donne, much less any Moore, but the Yeats of "Nineteen Hundred and Nineteen," who found that he could believe in his own art, but not in much else, as he watched his country at war. "The Old Country" even attributes Yeats's lines to the Christian Savior: "Christ was somewhat impolitic / in branding as 'weasels fighting in a hole,' forsooth, / the petrol smugglers back on the old sod." Those smugglers may include Muldoon's ancestors, but they are also the people who disrupt pipelines in the modern Middle East, and perhaps the all-too-legal oil company veterans who helped plan the invasion of Iraq. (Yeats: "We planned to bring the world under a rule / Who are but weasels fighting in a hole.")

For all the death and foreboding in this new book, Muldoon's shorter poems still do well in depicting the comfort—always mingled with anxiety, faint hope, and absurd regret—in which New Jersey's affluent towns (Princeton, for example) specialize, and in depicting the sexual comedy and anxiety of middle age. Alarmingly, the poems of love and sex here, like those from *Quoof,* chronicle spats and extra-marital affairs ("As Your Husband Looks Up to Our Window"): one does not want to know which are drawn from life. In another new, domestic poem, a toy for Muldoon's son, newly assembled, becomes an "imperspicuous game / that seems to be missing one piece, if not more." This forever-unsolvable problem suggests both the unsolved mysteries left to us by deceased parents, and the enduring riddles in all good poems: "The game. The plaything spread on the rug. / The fifty years I've spent trying to put it together." It would be puerile to argue that Muldoon's puzzling art represents confusion by confusion, incomprehension by bafflement: rather, Muldoon pursues—as Robert Frost pursued—both curiosity and bafflement, both the ways in which the world's games, problems, and riddles draw us in, and the ways in which they will not let us out alive.

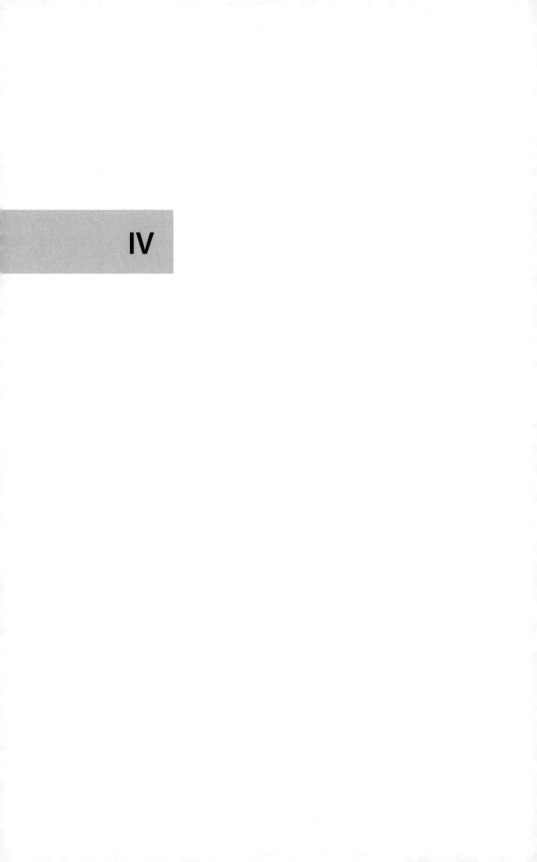

IV

John Ashbery

Everything Must Go

The great inventor of a style fluid enough to reflect our uncertain times, a helpless symbol of those times, an incomprehensible hoax, a clear-as-glass poet of loneliness and dejection, the greatest living surrealist, the last Romantic, a frequent influence on poets much younger than he (he was born in 1927): since 1975, when his *Self-Portrait in a Convex Mirror* won almost all the awards a book of American poems could win, readers and reviewers have bestowed on John Ashbery all these labels. Meanwhile Ashbery has gone on writing his poems, and writing them faster than most of us can read them. *A Worldly Country* (2007) is his eleventh book of new verse in twenty years; *Notes from the Air* selects from the previous ten, from *April Galleons* (1987) to *Where Shall I Wander* (2005), beginning where his last *Selected Poems* stopped. Together, the new books portray a sad decline—but not, by any means, a decline in Ashbery's imaginative powers. Rather, their wealth of poems portrays the decline to which all of us are subject, the fact, realized over and over in any life, that we will lose all the people and things we love, that they must, as we must, grow old and die.

The verbal bounty in Ashbery's recent work reflects the treasure of memory and the bodily impoverishments of late life. Ashbery's may be the best poems of old age since Wallace Stevens's, and if they do not even seek the kinds of formal completion we find in Stevens, they make up for it in their range of tones—befuddled, affectionate, bubbly, chastened, somber, alarmed, and then befuddled again. In one fifteen-line poem from *A Worldly Country,* Ashbery imagines himself dying, and then dead, enclosed in a coffin from which his spirit has departed:

> oh quiet noumenon
> of my soul, this is it, right?
> You lost the key and the answer is inside
> somewhere, and where are you going to breathe?
> The box is shut that knew you
> and all your friends,
> voices that could have spoken in your behalf . . .
>
> Why, what did you want me to do with them?

Another new poem, "The Gallant Needful," instructs the next writer who hopes to devise a late style: do not try to remain in fashion ("the clothes gave out. No one / wanted to wear them any more"), think of yourself as a patchwork, a palimpsest ("Mended with gay stuffs, they'll serve"); don't worry if your drafts make sense only to you ("as soup is to stew, / so the sea to bubbling chasms that prop up the 'meaning'"); finally, "don't expect thanks." The last poem in *A Worldly Country* even concludes, in an unmistakably posthumous mode, by telling us that whatever Ashbery has not done, another poet may yet do: "Those places left unplanted will be cultivated / by another, by others. Looking back it / will seem good."

The longest poem in *A Worldly Country,* "The Handshake, the Cough, the Kiss," joins earlier poems beloved of Ashbery's critics in describing the arc of a poet's career. Here is the brilliant schoolboy, attracting local notice with his apprentice work:

> They all knew him in that ancient, wondrous and miserable town
> as the local amateur historian and vendor
> of a kind of chili only the houris knew about.

Then, turning his face away, he'd try
to guess the answers to their riddles. If correct,
a kiss would reward him. If not, a retreat
to a sheet of paper or promise to better himself
in huge academic halls some kilometers away, but they
didn't tell him this.

"The Handshake" later turns away from one poet's career to address poetry in general, which cares nothing for cliques and claques (for "muddy groups" and their rivalries) and which will outlast even its hardiest practitioner, as rivers (which share a Latin root with "rival") outlast dwellers on their banks:

O songbird! You asked us to believe
in you but the way was short. Our quondam companions persist,
a small, muddy group, adhere to the rival shore, ravenous,
and expire.

Believe it, they feel the air.

The note of self-satire, so frequent in Ashbery, fades before such figures' serious force.

To look back on a life spent making art is to think again on the shapes of artistic careers, but also to think about what remains of a personal past. Even the least consequential recollections seem precious, decades afterward: "We loved that too, / as we were a part of all that happened there, the evil and the good / and all the shades in between, happy to pipe up at roll call / or compete in the spelling bees." (Spelling bees!) Well-treated, bright children, Ashbery implies in "The Ice Storm" (one of his best prose poems), see life as a series of tests, with competent examiners and set texts: "I tell myself it all seems like fun and will work out in the end. I expect I will be asked a question I can answer and then be handed a big prize. They're working on it." Yet really the judges are no smarter than we are, and the only prize at the end is oblivion: "I am going, and they are going with us, with us as we go."

So insistent on late style and old age, *A Worldly Country* demonstrates, like a crystal dropped in supersaturated solution, how much those topics suffused his works of the 1980s and '90s. Half the poems in *Notes from the Air* could be called (as one really is called) "Avant de Quitter Ces Lieux," or subtitled with the Wordsworthian phrase that *A Worldly Country* quotes three times: "Was it for this?" The title *Notes from the Air* suggests overheard music, or outlines (notes) for a treatise unwritten. The poem of the same name emphasizes (with a nod to Shakespeare's Ulysses) the ephemerality of everything: "Look, it says, // it has to be this way and no other. Time that one seizes / and takes along with one is running through the holes / like sand from a bag."

The same poem begins with nonsense, as a mock lecture: "A yak is a prehistoric cabbage: of that, at least, we may be sure." Ashbery often begins absurd and ends sad: even the silliest turn of phrase, pursued long enough, leads him back to isolation, yearning, or mortality. The involutions, changes of topic, and failures of pronoun reference—what is "it"?—by which we recognize his style point to the failures and disorientations that characterize a distracted, dispirited mind, one that cannot accommodate (as who can?) the knowledge that everything we cherish must someday go. Even the greatest friendships or works of art are in the long run the fleeting thoughts of a cloud: "This cloud imagines us and all that our story / Was ever going to be, and we catch up / To ourselves, but they are the selves of others"—so says a poem called, appropriately, "Riddle Me."

Against a confessional model, in which we feel closer to a poet the more he reveals of his biography, Ashbery suggests that we see further into his soul the less we know about the person outside the poems: lyric poetry, of the kind that he writes, works not by telling us all about poets' documentable, material lives but by revealing only the inner man. "Now I have neither back nor front," he writes, "I am the way certain persons are / who never tell you how they are / yet you know they are like you and they are."

Some readers must see such writing as gay code. Much gets made now of Ashbery's homosexuality—fair enough, given the camp effects, the pre-Stonewall traditions of covert signals and open secrets, and the semisecret assignations intimated so often in the parks, parties,

beaches, and bathrooms ("In the bathroom there was considerable em-
barrassment") of Ashbery's late verse. But his poems are (compared to,
say, Frank O'Hara's) rarely sexual. They evoke, instead, more diffuse
affections, remembered, offered, or bestowed, and they evoke them
with an intensity proportional to their lack of explanation: "We never
knew what prompted us to smile / or to embrace." Amidst all the gener-
ality and all the symbols, all the jokes and all the evasions, it is a shock
to discover "The History of My Life," a bleak outline of Ashbery's real
biography (he did indeed lose a brother in childhood):

> Once upon a time there were two brothers.
> Then there was only one: myself.
>
> I grew up fast, before learning to drive,
> even. There was I: a stinking adult.
>
> I thought of developing interests
> someone might take an interest in. No soap.

Ashbery's flirtatious nonsense and rococo cartoonishness are, these lines
suggest, defenses against the deep-freeze isolation that the poet might
otherwise feel.

Yet poems like that one are exceptions. Usually Ashbery's late work
looks back—digressively, distractedly, confusingly, or confusedly—on
a life that could be (they imply) anyone's, gay or heterosexual, male or
female, yours (as in his book title *Your Name Here*) or Ovid's. The author of *Ars Amatoria* turns up by name in *A Worldly Country* as the
star of "an infomercial" in which he recalls his life in the second person: "You were careful about choosing your companions, did what /
was expected of you, rose early to greet the punching ball" (i.e., the
sun), and yet he, too, must die: "the good stuff was poised to return,
but the screen crashed, / and there is no help in us, over and under the
now receding water."

The poems return constantly to the largest possible subjects—loss,
love, helplessness, and death—but they can scrutinize smaller ones,
too. "Redeemed Area" concerns the ways in which the old check one
another, and themselves, for signs of dementia: "Do you know where

you live? Probably. / Abner is getting too old to drive but won't admit it." "Objection Sustained" reflects fears about global warming: "The can of ice slipped and cracked. / All my worldly belongings weren't / so worldly anymore." Ashbery elsewhere represents the approaching end of a life with self-conscious vagueness, with images of contraction and departure, and by portraying hypnopompic states, as in "The Business of Falling Asleep": "Yes, but a weird creepy feeling came over me that you might know about all this, not [have] wanted to tell me but just know. It's amazing how the past shrinks to the size of your palm, forced to hold all that now."

For each poem that sticks to one clear topic, though, there are three that, on first reading, have none: some include language that sounds computer generated ("Avuncular and teeming, the kind luggage / hosed down the original site"), though few remain in that frustrating mode for long. Ashbery's non sequiturs throw us back on the reasons we have tried to follow them, on why we take, or try to take, an interest in any topic at all—on our desire for conversation, for companionship, for evidence that we are not entirely alone. He seeks such evidence in our artistic inheritance, and in the flimsiest components of daily speech, stitching into his shimmery fabric a host of phrases we might, without him, think incompatible with serious verse:

> Surely, passing through the town,
> we contributed a little to the regional economy,
> received credit for showing our faces.
> So what if the only theater in town
> had been turned into a funeral parlor?
> There are few things more theatrical than death,
> one supposes, though one doesn't know.

No modern poetry half so original incorporates half so many clichés. I count at least five in those seven lines, each a reminder that our language—ugly or beautiful—is never ours alone. Rather, a language, a sociolect, a culture, is something that we inherit, something we then (after "passing through" and dying) bequeath.

Ashbery seems more contemporary, more topical, now than when he started writing, though the culture has changed around him more than he has changed: he has become the poet of our multitasking, interruption-filled, and entertainment-seeking days. "I wish I could help but I've a million things to do," Ashbery explains, "and restoring your peace of mind isn't one of them. There goes my phone . . ." (In such effects of overlap and overhearing—more important now than they were in Ashbery's verse before 1990—he has, in a sense, caught up with the discoveries of John Tranter, the Australian poet who had in the 1970s learned so much from him.)

If you see Ashbery as a recorder not of his life but of his times, you will see both how he appropriates modern catchphrases (another poem says it will "take a commercial break") and how fast those catchphrases collide. A poem called "Mottled Tuesday" announces, "I'll add one more scoop / to the pile of retail," then addresses someone (a beloved? a reader? a child?) as "my sinking laundry boat, point of departure, / my white pomegranate, my swizzle stick." "Racked by jetsam, we cry out for flotsam," he protests elsewhere, "anything to stanch the hole in the big ad." Critics make heavy weather of the flow of information through Ashbery's poems—almost any piece of news or slang, as well as any shard of old high culture, may turn up, as if brought in by those tides. But Ashbery's sustained interest lies more with the tides than with anything they bring in. You can find Emerson and Jacques de Vaucanson, Sibelius and Shakespeare, John Dewey and Admiral Dewey (see the very funny "Memories of Imperialism"), and much else in his lines if you want them:

> Once, on Mannahatta's bleak shore,
> I trolled for spunkfish, but caught naught, nothing save
> a rubber plunger or two. It was awful,
> at that time. Now everything is cheerful.
> I wonder, does it make a difference?

Here Ashbery evokes Walt Whitman and T. S. Eliot and Elizabeth Bishop and Hart Crane (and the waterfronts where Crane looked for rough sex) all at once. Yet to chase allusions, or to seek a continuous tradition, is to miss the point. Where other poets ask us to look everything up, or berate us for not being as learned as they, Ashbery implies that life is too short for him to expect us to learn what he knows:

"Where do the scraps / Of meaning come from? . . . It was all going / To be scattered anyway."

The same anything-goes, anything-could-come-next qualities that make his verse so hard to memorize give the same verse its peculiar mimetic virtues. Our thought includes both remembering and forgetting, both concentration and distraction, and Ashbery's poems get closer to the moment-by-moment way that our minds work (at least to the way that we now believe they work) than earlier poets have ever come. If we find ourselves holding a firm belief, Ashbery says, it's not because we have found solid proof: rather, a belief, like a memory, "gets worn into the mind like a crease in a road map that has been folded up the wrong way too many times." If his poems work as our minds do, can we understand them any better than we understand ourselves? "I don't understand myself," Ashbery writes, "only segments / of myself that misunderstand each other." His readers may feel the same way, even though (perhaps because) his poems tell us over and over how much he wants to reach us: "I need your disapproval, / can't live without your churlish ways."

Ashbery would be the most whimsical poet now writing were he not also the loneliest: he needs us, and tells us he needs us, as few poets do. Most of his recent books end with romantic gestures addressed to a "you" who may only be any reader, and whose companionship he yearns to retain: "That's all any of us gets, / why I am happy with you, alone, just us." Or, in a more extravagant (sillier) mode that sounds like wishful thinking: "You wore your cummerbund with the stars and stripes. I, kilted in lime, held a stethoscope to the head of the parting guest. Together, we were a couple forever." The poet's urgent solicitations and his ruminations on mortality are of a piece, since poems survive—and traces of their otherwise vanished authors survive within them—only if they portray (whatever else they do), for later readers, some elements we recognize in ourselves: that "is why I am you, why we two / never quite seem to escape each other's shadow." If you do not feel that the poems address you, such claims are hubris. If you do, then those lines describe what happens when you read a poem, and so do these: "We are the people we came to see / or might as well be, bringing cabbages as gifts, / talking nonstop, barbed wire stringing the trees."

As unthinkable as Ashbery's creations would be without modernism, his late poems just as often set him beside Edward Lear. Ashbery quotes Lear repeatedly and titles a cento—a poem made of lines from other poets—"The Dong with the Luminous Nose" (a double entendre for Ashbery, though not for Lear). As in Lear, without the absurdities we could not face the profundities, and it may be from trivial or bizarre chances and hobbies that most of the joys that make our lives worthwhile come. Like Lear, late Ashbery tries to make his most formally intricate poems feel like games, or like jokes: a pantoum called "Phantoum" (it ends "you had to be a ghost to appreciate it"), a poem written to be inscribed on a Minneapolis bridge (see Eric Lorberer, "The Ashbery Bridge," *jubilat* 13, 2007), a poem in two-part lines (imitated from the Finnish *Kalevala,* and reminiscent of biblical Hebrew) in which the second half always restates the first: "The one who runs little, he who barely trips along / Knows how short the day is, how few the hours of light." Here the redundancy (what medieval writers called *copia*) feels like a way to keep going; here, as often in Ashbery's later poetry, the onward procession of hard-to-process sentences renders pathetic, even tragic, the command familiar to radio announcers: keep talking, no matter what—as if the plug would be pulled, the channel changed, the life ended, at the first sign of dead air.

The last figure whom half the English-language poets alive thought a great model, and the other half thought incomprehensible, was probably T. S. Eliot. But Eliot, by the time he became famous, came with instruction manuals, moral directives, claims about good and bad taste and about right and wrong. Ashbery comes instead with an early, self-satirical poem titled "The Instruction Manual," and with a career-long sense that there are no wrong answers, only more or less interesting possibilities. He is the ideal poet to preside over our antihierarchical age, a wistful, affectionate democrat with our entire word hoard at his command, so contemporary that we may overlook his frequent (and Eliotic) returns to famous bits of the past—for example, his rewrite, in *A Worldly Country,* of "Where are the songs of spring?":

Spring is the most important of the seasons.
It's here even when it's not here.
All the other seasons are an excuse for it.
Spring, idle spring,
you poor excuse for summer—

Did they tell you where they mislaid you,
on which arterial road piercing the city,
fast and faster like breath?

Here, where the rush of images that characterizes so much of his work
drops out, we may hear other kinds of variation in which John Ashbery
specializes: each line has a different pace, and a different tone. Which
one fits the absence of spring, the advent of adulthood, the long-ago
disappearance of our own youth? None, singly: all, together, might do.

Because he invented a style that can incorporate almost anything, because he so often returns—whatever his modulations—to the same tonic
and dominant of loneliness and nostalgia, and because that style rarely
demands (it more often precludes) the kinds of closure that make poems
by other good poets seem like one-of-a-kind creations, Ashbery's short
poems can seem like excerpts from his long ones (such as the book-
length *Flow Chart*), or like bolts of arbitrary size cut from one decades-
long tapestry, its pronouns and moods repeating like patterns in fabric.
The poems are indeed too much like one another—one sacrifices, especially in his last few books, variety among the poems, but gets instead
variety within them. Wildean remarks and Sophoclean pronouncements,
amusement park gimmicks and desperate homages, collide or interlace
all on one page, and almost always the poet reminds us that he, like his
page, must come to an end. "You will leave empty-handed, / others will
know more than you," a poem called "Cliffhanger" warns, and then
concludes: "Now even the farthest windows have gone dark. And the
dark / wants us, needs us. Thank you for calling."

When you interpret Ashbery at all, you risk having skeptics tell you
that you made it all up: that the poems demonstrate ingenuity not from the
poet but from his interpreters, who find music in static, meaning in randomness, synthetic silk in a succession of sow's ears. The same objections
used to be (and occasionally still are) leveled at people who spent time rereading Eliot, or rereading Gertrude Stein (whom Ashbery admires). No
one can prove that Ashbery's poems mean anything. But no one can prove
that your life means anything, either: on a good day, you feel able to keep
on living it, as John Ashbery has kept on writing, following a plan where
a plan seems to fit, but otherwise making it up as you go.

Richard Wilbur

Not Unlike You

Besides the Richard Wilbur that all serious American, and many British, readers know, there are at least five others no one talks about. The familiar Wilbur presents a technically flawless paradigm of dignified, mostly stanzaic, mostly rhyming verse, much of it devoted to beautiful forests, statuary, easel paintings, married love, and parenthood, a paradigm to which young poets disenchanted with recent styles resort. This Wilbur detects "a poignancy in all things clear," likens poets to architects and jugglers, and advises that "a heaven is easier made of nothing at all / Than the earth regained." This Wilbur is real, valuable, and at least as talented as his acolytes suggest. But there are others, all valuable in themselves. His 2004 *Collected Poems* (his third overall, and the first to include his verse for children) offers the juggler-architect along with five more: a shocked (even shell-shocked) American soldier; a fiercely partisan political liberal; a deft wit; a versatile translator; and a thoughtful, almost Hardyesque singer of subdued grief.

Take the beautiful craftsman first. This is the once-influential, easily caricatured Wilbur who dominates *Ceremony* (1950) and *Things of This World* (1956); when Randall Jarrell wrote that too many 1950s poets "came out of Richard Wilbur's overcoat," or distinguished him from imitators by writing that Wilbur himself "obsessively sees, and shows, the bright underside of every dark thing," it's this Wilbur whom Jarrell had in mind. Rarely have vowels and consonants seemed so purely melodic, or so expertly managed, as in "A Storm in April," perhaps the best of Wilbur's many seasonal set pieces:

> This storm, if I am right,
> Will not be wholly over
> Till green fields, here and there,
> Turn white with clover,
>
> And through chill air the puffs of milkweed hover.

If he would avoid monotony (and Wilbur would), a poet devoted to perfection of form must also devote himself to variety, and so Wilbur's collections double as sparkling cyclopedias of forms—not just sonnets and villanelles but taut quatrains, couplets of all sorts, Provençal ballades, flawless terza rima, comically polysyllabic exact rhyme, lyric dialogue (think Blake's "The Clod and the Pebble"), Anglo-Saxon accentual meters ("Lilacs," "Junk"). His pastoral love poems even boast actual pastures:

> You, in a green dress, calling, and with brown hair,
> Who come by the field-path now, whose name I say
> Softly, forgive me love if also I call you
> Wind's word, apple-heart, haven of grasses.

For all his appreciation of conventionally admirable things ("A Baroque Wall-Fountain in the Villa Sciarra," various temperate climate trees, his wife) some of his triumphs in the genres of praise concern things and events few others would notice:

> when somebody spoke and asked the question
> Comment s'appelle cet arbre-là?
> A girl had gold on her tongue, and gave this answer:
>   Ça, c'est l'acacia.

Wilbur's introduction to Europe came at a less golden moment: he served with the U.S. Army in the Second World War and drew fire near Monte Cassino, "living in a hole on a hillside subject to harassing artillery fire," as he recalled in 1995. Like other cold war poets (but slightly earlier, and to better effect), Wilbur saw the beauties of postwar France and Italy—from the cedilla to the Villa Sciarra—through a wartime lens. No one should read Wilbur's first book, *The Beautiful Changes* (1947), without seeing how often it evokes 1943 and '44. In "Mined Country," "boys come swinging slow over the grass," gracefully manipulating not baseball or cricket bats but metal detectors. The "night guard" in "First Snow in Alsace" loves how the new flakes muffle the recent deaths:

Absolute snow lies rumpled on
What shellbursts scattered and deranged,
Entangled railings, crevassed lawn.

As if it did not know they'd changed,
Snow smoothly clasps the roofs of homes
Fear-gutted, trustless and estranged.

Wilbur's war service informs his sense (which Jarrell scanted) that we need all the effort of intellect, aesthetic detachment, and studied technique to stem the panic in our wounded hearts. "Man Running" imagines the day when protopeople first "descended from the trees / Into the shadow of our enemies, / Not lords of nature yet, but naked prey." "A Barred Owl" depicts a negative apotheosis of supposed innocence, "A small child . . . dreaming of some small thing in a claw / Borne up to some dark branch and eaten raw."

Wilbur lauds self-restraint, sociability, charity, and views with suspicion all violence, all aggression, and all crowds (his "nature" is almost the inverse of D. H. Lawrence's); Western civilization seems to Wilbur an impressive, though bloody and clearly imperfect, inheritance. In other words, he's a stalwart American liberal, concerned about the tyranny of the majority, protective of civil liberties, and generally opposed to invading small countries, Vietnam very much included. As James

Longenbach has, almost alone, pointed out, Wilbur's poems repeatedly defend the theory and practice of American liberalism, from the anti–Red Scare "Speech for the Repeal of the McCarran Act" to the anti–missile defense poem "A Fable" (supposedly the only poem Wilbur wrote in his year under Reagan as U.S. poet laureate). The best of these poems on practical politics remains "For the Student Strikers" (1970), written in response to campus unrest at Wesleyan University in Connecticut, and published in the students' "alternative" newspaper there; the stanzas are worthy, and durable, advice. "Go talk with those who are rumored to be unlike you," Wilbur advises his pupils:

> Doors will be shut in your faces, I do not doubt.
> Yet here or there, it may be, there will start,
> Much as the lights blink on in a block at evening,
> Changes of heart.
>
> They are your houses; the people are not unlike you;
> Talk with them, then, and let it be done
> Even for the grey wife of your nightmare sheriff
> And the guardsman's son.

The poems take not just topical positions, but deeper ethical ones to match. Over and over they remind us that nobody has all the answers, that people will hate and kill unless they agree to disagree: "The Undead" even portrays "extremists" as vampires, "Preferring their dreams . . . To the world with all its breakable toys," and "fearing contagion of the mortal." Like other liberal thinkers from John Stuart Mill on, Wilbur reminds us that the world is far more various, and far less organized, than any one representation, any single idea of the good life, or any one work of art can represent. "The use of strict poetic forms," he wrote in 1950, can "serve to limit the work of art, and to declare its artificiality; they say, 'This is not the world, but a pattern imposed upon the world or found in it; this is a partial and provisional attempt.'" Wilbur's careful stanzas, "blessed by doubt," therefore delight in checks and balances. Sometimes they declare that they have nothing to declare, and always they present their care as a rebuke to confident fanatics, in poetry, governance, cuisine, or anything else. Such rebukes even prompt parables. In "A Wood," dominant oaks discover dogwoods and witch hazels, learning that they themselves are not the only beauties under the sun:

> Given a source of light so far away
> That nothing, short or tall, comes very near it,
> Would it not take a proper fool to say
> That any tree has not the proper spirit?
> Air, water, earth and fire are to be blended,
> But no one style, I think, is recommended.

Note that "I think," delighting in doubt within doubt; note the hint of pleasure in its tone.

Three Wilburs so far. The fourth is, simply, a wit. "I am for wit and wakefulness," Wilbur rightly says: you can find his humor, his sense of how light verse works or should work, uncut in his translations of Latin riddles, or in the very enjoyable children's verse of *Opposites* and *More Opposites:* "The opposite of *post,* were you / On horseback, would be *black and blue;* // Another answer is *to fail / To put your letters in the mail."* ("The opposite of *opposite?* / That's much too difficult. I quit.") You can also take the wit mixed with grim social criticism, historical sense, and taut stanzaic closure, as in "Matthew VIII, 28ff." a sixteen-line epistle to Jesus from the Gadarenes:

> It is true that we go insane;
> That for no good reason we are possessed by devils;
> That we suffer, despite the amenities which obtain
> At all but the lowest levels.
>
> We shall not, however, resign
> Our trust in the high-heaped table and the full trough.
> If you cannot cure us without destroying our swine,
> We had rather you shoved off.

Wilbur can apparently wield all (and only) the rhymed or metered forms the language offers; it would be a shame if he could use them only for subjects of his own devising. Fortunately almost all his books include translations—from Spanish, Russian, French, Italian, Bulgarian; almost all the translations show the polish and thoughtfulness of his original work. (Renaissance poets, of course, often blurred distinctions between translations and originals; it makes sense to call these poems "original," too.) Wilbur's Brodsky-in-English sounds better than Brodsky's Brodsky-in-English (admittedly some people think that's not so hard). Familiar French poems sound fine, if still familiar (Baudelaire, Villon). The real gems are poets of whom you've probably never heard, whose works let Wilbur try out attitudes he might not otherwise attempt: Valeri Petrov's nearly flippant complaint about his advancing age, for example, and Vinicius de Moraes's scary cradle song. The latter sets the poet's real infant daughter against her fictive counterpart:

> The firstborn child within me,
> That cold, petrific, dry
> Daughter whom death once gave,
> Whose life is a long cry
> For milk she may not have.

The last Wilbur—not the most complex, but the most moving—informs certain translations (like the Moraes), certain public poems (say, "Advice to a Prophet"), and many pastoral lyrics, then comes into his own in the most recent work. This Wilbur writes quiet poems of memory, elegy, human diminishment, and the passing of time. At his best he reminds me of Larkin and of Hardy (and of the perpetually underrated Englishman Peter Scupham, the other poet active now whom Wilbur most resembles). It takes awhile to find this sad, personal Wilbur amid the greenery and burnish of his earlier work, and most readers seem not to have found him yet. But follow the recollections of childhood, or the accumulation of poems about branches losing their foliage, and there he is—in "Alatus," say, when, "Their supply-lines cut, / The trees go down to defeat." Here he is in animatedly mimetic blank verse from *Mayflies* (2001), recalling a night drive with his mother and father:

Wild, lashing snow which thumps against the windshield
Like earth tossed down upon a coffin-lid,
Half clogs the wipers, and our Buick yaws
On the black roads of 1928.

And here he is in "Crow's Nests" (also from *Mayflies*), with an extended metaphor, and a pun (on ships' lookouts and carrion crows), that ought to outlive him, and you, and me:

That lofty stand of trees beyond the field,
Which in the storms of summer stood revealed

As a great fleet of galleons bound our way
Across a moiled expanse of tossing hay,

Full-rigged and swift, and to the topmost sail
Taking their fill and pleasure of the gale,

Now, in this leafless time, are ships no more,
Though it would not be hard to take them for

A roadstead full of naked mast and spar
In which we see now where the crow's nests are.

Robert Creeley

Counting the Days

For a spell during the 1960s, Robert Creeley's "I Know a Man" may have been the most often quoted, even the most widely known, short poem by a living American. Here is the poem:

As I sd to my
friend, because I am
always talking,—John, I

sd, which was not his
name, the darkness sur-
rounds us, what

can we do against
it, or else, shall we &
why not, buy a goddamn big car,

drive, he sd, for
christ's sake, look
out where yr going.

Written around 1954, the poem got wide notice after *For Love* (1962), Creeley's first trade collection, and it is not hard to see why. Sad and funny at once, with a trick ending, it undercuts the pretensions of high culture: what earlier poet would admit "I am / always talking," or suggest that his own verse exemplified mere "talk"? Better yet, "I Know a Man" undercuts hip counterculture, too: old and new art, Romantic despair and groovy enthusiasm, seem comically and equally irrelevant to the hurried American who just wants to get safely down the road.

Robert Hass, later the U.S. poet laureate, called "I Know a Man" "the poem of the decade" (he meant the 1950s). "Drive, He Said" became the title for a 1964 novel by Jeremy Larner, which in 1971 became a Jack Nicholson film; the same title later served an anthology of poems about cars, an episode of at least one television show, and at least a dozen magazine columns, including a May 2007 *New Yorker* piece about congestion pricing ("Don't Drive, He Said"). "I Know a Man" is a poem about poetry's impotence, and about artistic obsolescence, and a warning against pretension, addressed in particular to would-be Beatniks who wanted to talk the way it sounds. It is also the poem of a man with a very good ear, averse to big words, alert to colloquial speech, and uneasy, if not ashamed, of his art.

"I Know a Man" seems like a good introduction to the vast opus Creeley, who died in 2005, left behind: thousands of poems, dozens of essays and interviews, a bitter novel, a book of short stories, and hundreds of pages of hard-to-classify prose. Yet "I Know a Man" also leaves out much of what made Creeley notable in each of the three phases of his career: his early focus on lust and shame, the diary-like verse-and-prose books of the 1970s, and the quiet achievements in his late poems of retrospect and solitude. We recognize Creeley's poems first by what they omit: he uses few long or rare words, no regular meters, and almost no metaphors. The young Creeley aspired to write in Basic English: "he very nearly does," his friend Cid Corman wrote, except for the slang. Creeley kept for five decades a way of writing whose markers include parsimonious diction, strong enjambment, two- to four-line stanzas, and occasional rhyme. What changed over his career was not his language but the use he made of it, the attitudes and goals around which the small, clear crystals of his verse might form.

Robert Creeley was born in 1926 and grew up in "a small sort of farm town about 25 miles from Boston" with his mother and sisters (his father died in 1930). "With five women in the house," he recalled, "I didn't have a clue as to what men did." At the age of four, he lost an eye to infection: he wore an eyepatch, like a pirate, as a young man. Although he loathed Robert Frost—he liked to say so in interviews—the parallels between them are remarkable: Both came from rural New England, whose "apparently laconic way of saying things" (as Creeley put it) marked both men's poems. Both attended Harvard, from which neither received a degree. Both liked to talk about American speech, and to say (correctly) that their poems captured that speech more than their peers' poems could. Both achieved popularity despite the grim attitude in their best poems, and both discovered too late that their biographers despised them. (In Creeley's case, the culprit was Ekbert Faas, whose unwieldy tome stops halfway through the life of a poet he paints as a hostile philanderer.)

At a Harvard College full of incipient talent—his classmates included Frank O'Hara, Kenneth Koch, John Ashbery, and Donald Hall—Creeley felt discouraged and alone. "My eager thirst for knowledge, almost Jude-the-Obscurian in its innocence, was all but shut down by the sardonic stance of my elders," he recalled. He left college in 1944 for noncombatant service, driving ambulances in India and Southeast Asia, then returned to Harvard but dropped out. "From 1946 to 1950," he remembered later, "I was frankly doing almost nothing else but sitting around listening to records." Creeley was also "smoking pot pretty continuously" and drinking a lot; he got in fights, too, including one abortive dustup with Jackson Pollock. Partly to escape urban temptation, Creeley, his wife, Ann, and their two young sons relocated in 1948 to a farm in New Hampshire, where he bred pigeons and poultry and tried to write. "I learned more about poetry as an actual activity from raising chickens," he said, "than I did from any professor."

The Creeley of those years modeled his verse on William Carlos Williams's, his sensibility on recent jazz (he listened to Charlie Parker while composing), and his fiction on that of D. H. Lawrence, "my own mentor, finally the only one I can have." Creeley later claimed that he picked up his sense of line from the mistaken assumption that

Williams, when reading his own poems aloud, paused at every line end. But imitating Williams was not enough: like most young poets, Creeley needed an attentive, sympathetic reader with just a bit more experience than his own.

He found one. "It is really Charles Olson I must thank for whatever freedom I have as a poet," Creeley said, "and I would value him equally with Pound and Williams." Olson and Creeley began corresponding in 1950—Williams seems to have put them in touch. Olson was then a former federal official, the author of a vivid book about Melville, not yet the theorist, impresario, and cult figure of *The Maximus Poems*. The Olson–Creeley letters now comprise ten published volumes; Olson's most famous slogan, "Form is never more than an extension of content," originated in a letter from that first year, when Olson had published one book of verse, Creeley none.

In 1951 the Creeleys decamped to rural France, where Robert and Ann could live cheaply, and then to Mallorca, where Creeley became tutor to Robert Graves's children. While abroad, he cofounded small presses and little magazines—Divers Press (with Ann), *Origin* (with Corman), and then (with Olson) *Black Mountain Review,* named for Black Mountain College in North Carolina, where Olson became rector and in 1954 brought Creeley to teach. Creeley, Olson, and Corman would soon see themselves, with some justice, as part of a rising tide, an antiacademic neomodernism in American letters, led in part by the journals they had helped found. In 1955 Robert and Ann split up; in 1956 he left Black Mountain for New Mexico, where he taught in a boys' school, married his second wife, Bobbie, and established a steady flow of poems and prose that continued for fifty years. For most of those years he made his home in Buffalo and taught at the state university, whose reputation as a haven for avant-garde writers he helped create; he also undertook frequent, sometimes yearlong trips to Europe, Australasia, and the American West Coast.

Among all the poets of the American 1950s who wanted to learn from Williams, only Creeley had anything like Williams's ear. He learned early (compare Williams's "To a Poor Old Woman") how to repeat and how to vary the simplest of phrases within a stanza: "Time we all went back home, / or back, / to where it all was, / where it all was." Creeley often seems to have thought not in lines or sentences so much as in quatrains, which he called "both a semantic measure and a rhythmic measure," and to which he gave remarkable aural finish: "Sun on the edges of leaves, / patterns of absent pleasure, / all that it meant / now gathered together."

Despite his acoustic gifts, Creeley in his twenties "thought that my work as a writer would be primarily in prose." His stories pursue a stuttering interest in the repetitive monologues that take place deep inside his baffled protagonists' heads: "I love you, he said, and echoed it in invariable silences saying, each time, I love you, but never feeling very much . . . He would have spoken, but couldn't, and looking to his wife, wanted to push, then at her, to explain, but did not know what he wished explained." His 1963 novel, *The Island,* set on Mallorca, presents a marriage grinding its way to collapse. Both the author and his apparent stand-in, John, subscribe to a Lawrentian sense that men and women live in different worlds; John displays, too, the paralyzing self-consciousness that in Lawrence and elsewhere afflicts men who cannot be masculine. Fighting insomnia, John contemplates "some necessity he never got the hang of, or the feel of, the place of. One wants to ask a simple question, do I do it right, is it enough."

The young Creeley called his poems "signs of inadequate love"; their topics were the topics of his fiction. Those early poems portray quarrelsome lovers, stranded travelers, impoverished New Englanders ("we are practical / —but winter is long & . . . there is never enough"), a failed violinist, and a whole cast of grim characters who cannot find their instincts in the authentic Lawrentian way. Creeley could be frank, like Lawrence, not only about sex and bodies but about our shame and confusion concerning them. Probably no other serious English-language poet wrote multiple poems about urination. Nor had any other male poet before him written well about sanitary pads: "What should the young / man say, because he is buying / Modess?"

Creeley was not always ashamed: the perfect casualness of sexual joy has rarely been as ably captured as in "A Wicker Basket," in which sudden rhyme and hip lingo show a fleeting ease:

Out the door, the street like a night,
any night, and no one in sight,
but then, well, there she is,
old friend Liz—

And she opens the door of her cadillac,
I step in back,
and we're gone.
She turns me on—

To mock such words, such attitudes, Creeley suggests ("certainly / they are laughing at me" while "I make it") is to miss all the world's fun.

But "A Wicker Basket" is an exception. Usually the early Creeley's pace is slower, his tone less confident, his women hard to please, and his men baffled. He wrote a "Ballad of the Despairing Husband," a "song of the sleeping wife," "who wouldn't even hear you if you asked her," and a horrifying poem that opens: "Let me say (in anger) that since the day we were married / we have never had a towel / where anyone could find it." His men are not just *post coitum triste* but sad or anomic before sex, too: "It / hurts / to live / like this, / meat / sliced / walking."

If you want to know whether you will like Creeley's early poetry, a better test than "I Know a Man" lies in the closing stanzas of "The Rain":

Love, if you love me,
lie next to me.
Be for me, like rain,
the getting out

of the tiredness, the fatuousness, the semi-
lust of intentional indifference.
Be wet
with a decent happiness.

The passage gathers almost all the qualities that typify Creeley up through the late 1960s, and by which he sometimes excels: irregular line lengths, regular stanzas, restricted diction, intermittent medievaliz-ing (note the echo of "Western wind"), only the simplest sensory detail, and a genuine attempt at tenderness, with resentment underneath.

With *For Love* and *Words* (1967)—his ninth and eleventh books of poetry but his first and second from a trade press—Creeley deserved, and received, attention as a maker of spare free verse and as a poet of modern sexual love. Yet by the time he got that attention he was already abandoning those goals. "Tonight let me go / at last out of whatever / mind I thought to have," he prayed in *Words,* "and all the habits of it." It is a very 1960s prayer. "Sometime in the mid-1960s," Creeley recalled, "I grew inexorably bored with the tidy containment of clusters of words on single pieces of paper called 'poems.'"

What else was a poet to write? Not more narrative fiction: perhaps a series of unfinished texts, "pieces" if you will, whose vagueness testified to the inadequacy of all representation. "Composed in a journal as daily writing," the still controversial *Pieces* (1968) reflects its times as much as it reflects its author. It reflects, too, a kind of fatigue common to the period: "I was so damned tired of trusting my own opinion as to whether or not this was a good piece of poetry or a bad piece of poetry," Creeley remembered. For years he all but gave up on writing distinct and individual poems: instead he wrote stanzas, sentences, phrases, and then pages, series, books. Often those pages explore not what we mean and how we feel but what it is to expel sound from the larynx, to have a body, to stand in a room: "What a day / it is—what // one of many days"; "Where it is / was and / will be never / only here."

Creeley collaborated, then and later, with many prominent visual artists, most of them quasi pop or figurative: Robert Indiana, Jim Dine, R. B. Kitaj, Marisol. Yet his middle-period writings, with their stark and almost featureless units, now seem to place him closer to minimalism—to Donald Judd, for example, with his sets of identical boxes. A few Creeley poems might almost be reviews of Judd's sculptures: "Singular, / singular, / one / by one"; "This / and that, that / one, this / and that." The Creeley of these years declared war on "the damn function of simile, always a displacement of what is happening," adding, "I hate the metaphors." As paint for some painters must be always and only paint, metal stand for nothing except metal, Creeley's words had to be always and only themselves.

Pieces and its sequelae also recall the drug culture, more important to the arts in those years than to poetry in English before or since. In the right chemically enhanced frame of mind, even such banal couplets as "Walking / and talking. // Thinking / and drinking," such openings as "There is love only / as love is" can seem to disgorge infinite wisdom. If the poems of the 1950s show the theorizing, technique-oriented influence of Olson, those of the 1970s reflect frequent parties with famous hosts and guests, none more so than Allen Ginsberg, repeatedly named. It's no surprise to discover, in *A Day Book* (1970–72), a poem titled "On Acid," nor to discover within it a mantra: "End, end, end, end, end, end." Creeley called one of his first minimal poems, "A Piece," "central to all possibilities of statement"; that poem read: "One and / one, two, / three." If you like that, you'll love, well, almost anything.

Yet the man who wrote "A Piece" wrote, in the same years, genuine, memorable, almost equally minimal poems. One is "The Farm": "Tips of celery / clouds of // grass—one / day I'll go away." Another is "Xmas Poem: Bolinas," set in the California town where Creeley and other countercultural writers (Tom Clark, Aram Saroyan, Ted Berrigan) then lived:

All around
the snow
don't fall.

Come Christmas
we'll get high
and go find it.

It's misleading to call Creeley "experimental," as if other poets served as his control group; it's useful, though, to see his career as an experiment in how little a poet can say outright, how few techniques and how few words a poet can use and still end up with durable poems. His middle period, with its tiny nonpoems ("Wigmore / dry gin / kid"), is in this view a useful negative result: it showed what happens if you give up too much, and it enabled him to learn, in *Later* (1978) and after, what was just enough.

Creeley's work after 1978 reflects his intercontinental travels, his consciousness of his own advancing age, and his more settled life with his New Zealand–born third wife, Penelope (Pen). (Creeley's style also helped shape such New Zealand poets as Ian Wedde, Bill Manhire, and Andrew Johnston.) The later poems are more traditional than their predecessors in their sounds and in their goals. They rhyme more often. They have recognizable closure. Few are so short as to pose conceptual puzzles about what a poem is. When they are bad they are prosy or repetitive, not insubstantial or nonsensical. They never sound like Olson (much less like Ginsberg), and at their best they recall Thomas Hardy: they are, in the end, mostly poems of old age.

Devoted to stripped-down, quiet effects so early, Creeley seems to have prepared for most of his youth to write about feeling old. At just sixty, he published a poem called "Lost": the "here and now of all," he mused, gave him the choice "to look back to see the long distance / or to go forward, having only lost." Old age is, for Creeley, solitary, melancholy, and surprisingly reminiscent of childhood: it is, he wrote in 2003,

> Like sitting in back seat,
> can't see what street
> we're on or what the
> one driving sees
>
> or where we're going.
> Waiting for what's to happen
> can't quite hear the conversation,
> the big people, sitting up front.

Creeley's last essay considers Whitman's late, short poems of ebb tides and declines: "Daily, it would seem, the persons one has lived with go, leaving an inexorable emptiness." His own late poems make peace with their purported inconsequence, their unshowy, unhurried manner revealing a late style that knows all too well how late it is: "Amazing what mind makes / out of its little pictures," one page concludes, "the squiggles and dots, / not to mention the words."

The early Creeley rarely depicted landscapes; the late Creeley often does, but with odd simplifications. Almost all his sites—Helsinki,

Berlin, Auckland, Massachusetts—look alike, and all their colors are muted or sad: a "grey / iced sidewalk"; "yellow / light with low sun . . . against far-up pale sky"; "sheen of water at evening"; "snow, day old, like thin curdled milk." Even in tropical East Asia, the poems find the same "faint dusky light / at sunset," the same matte off-whites and grays. The colors Creeley saw everywhere in the world brought, in their subtle variations, a visual correlative for the subtle effects in his palette of small words.

So averse early to any English tradition, the late Creeley names or quotes Chaucer, Wyatt, and Wordsworth, and even writes his own "Versions" of Hardy's "The Voice": "Why would she come to him, / come to him, / in such disguise." Such a poem means not to outdo its model but to transcribe Hardy's melancholy into Creeley's new American metric, almost as a musician might transcribe a piano score for woodwind or strings. Creeley's late simplicities, like Hardy's, revoke old hopes and offer few replacements:

> Were you counting the days
> from now till then
>
> to what end,
> what to discover,
>
> which wasn't known
> over and over?

The stoic warning completes itself with "known," but the poem does not end till the half-rhyme "discover" and "over," as if Creeley were only restating, once more, what life says to us in its last half, again and again.

It is a consolation to see, amid all the late gray poems of advancing years, flashes of comedy about straight male desire, that subject in which the earlier, more self-serious Creeley specialized: the boy called "Bozo," for example, grew up to "see . . . all / he'd wanted to, aged four, // looking up under skirts, / wearing ochre-trim western shirts." But mostly the poems are sad. The 1950s Creeley seems to have been hard to handle: often drunk or stoned, a skirt chaser (in the language of the time), with frequent, extreme ups and downs. Such reports sit oddly with the many prose tributes—and the spate of elegies—that honor the older Creeley not just as a poet but as a colleague and friend: the change in his poetic aims perhaps reflected a changed personality, too.

Creeley's quiet poems demand that we read them slowly, even when they appear brief and simple. Taken too fast, or too many at a time, his poems (and there are a lot of them—almost fourteen hundred pages in the two-volume *Collected Poems*) can sound cramped, monotonous, and repetitive. Read at leisure, the best poems are subtle, musically gifted, memorably terse. Such an oeuvre places unusual pressure on the editor of a posthumous selection: Ben Friedlander has done it right. The 2008 *Selected Poems* represents all of Creeley's periods and everything Creeley did well: *For Love* rightly dominates the early going, and every late volume gets at least some space, while the prose-and-verse journals and collaborations (such as *A Day Book*) are mined for what gems they hold. Friedlander's introduction emphasizes the continuity of Creeley's efforts, making a case on behalf of the work as a whole. Only the table of contents indicates which poems came from what volume; the poems themselves appear as a continuous stream, which rightly draws the focus away from books and phases and toward individual poems—I had never noticed how good "People" was, for example, until Friedlander reframed it here.

Creeley said that he and Olson were trying "not only to realize themselves" in their poems "but to realize the potentiality and extension of words as a physical event in the world." He and his allies believed for a while that modern poems could express without representing, that figurative language only got in the way. This belief led at its worst to a literature as limited and unwieldy as the language of objects in Swift's Laputa, where only a kettle itself can signify "kettle." Yet this unsustainable (if not anti-intellectual) attitude let Creeley focus as few modern poets have on sound, which is to say on the sound of speech: on the ways intonation and rhythm carry attitude and emotion, and on how to put those ways down on the page.

To say this is to make Creeley sound much like Frost, who said he could hear "the sound of sense" in "voices behind a door that cuts off the words." And to listen to Creeley at his best is to listen, often uncomfortably, to men and women speaking behind closed doors, to hear what they say to themselves and to each other when they do not know what else to do. Creeley arrived—he wanted to arrive—as part of an anti-Frostian, antitraditional wing of American verse: Olson, and Black Mountain, and postwar jazz helped him develop his sense of line, his sparse, even teasing placement of words on a page. And yet Creeley now seems to belong to a much older and nearly continuous enterprise. He dedicated *Collected Poems 1975–2005* "with love, for Herrick and Zukofsky": affiliation with late-modern innovators, such as Louis Zukofsky and Olson, first got Creeley noticed, but his likeness to earlier makers of lyric poems—to Herrick, Housman, Hardy, Gurney, Frost—will help his verse endure. Few poets have had their receptions more affected by the wind of the times, which at one point seemed to blow right in Creeley's direction. Yet we read not a zeitgeist but a book of poems, and behind the poems, a man: shy at the core, aggressive in the beginning, melancholy at the end. Few writers have done more with fewer words.

James Merrill

Becoming Literature

James Merrill died in 1995, aged sixty-nine, just before his last book of new poems, *A Scattering of Salts,* appeared. Since the 1970s he had been one of America's best-known serious poets: the formal agility of his shorter poems inspired legions of imitators, and his book-length poem *The Changing Light at Sandover* acquired a flock of interpreters. Even as Merrill's admirers (me, for example) treasured that last book, new questions arose: When would there be a book of all the poems? Were there post-*Salts* poems, and would we see them? What would his work look like as a whole? Would important facts about the man emerge? Merrill's monumental *Collected Poems* answers the first three questions, while Alison Lurie's brief, frustrating memoir, *Familiar Spirits,* tries to answer the last. Both books remind us how, and how often, the poems depict, and reflect on, Merrill's life.

It was a life marked by advantages. James Merrill's stockbroker father, Charles, became the Merrill in Merrill, Lynch; Charles left his second wife, James's mother, when the future poet was twelve. (Merrill remembered the wealth, and the breakup, in "Economic Man": "Forty floors down is Wall Street; forty years / Ago, the merger of Heart & Hurt / That made me.") James was educated, and partly raised, by a

European governess, then at a New England prep school, and then at Amherst College, where he was already writing the poems of his first books. Soon afterward, in 1950, began the influential months of European travel—and of thinking about his homosexuality—that Merrill recalled in his memoir, *A Different Person* (1993).

By the mid-1950s Merrill had met David Jackson, who became his lifelong partner; the two settled first in Amherst, then on Water Street, in Stonington, Connecticut, where they would make their home for more than three decades. Merrill also spent many winters in Greece, where the friends, lovers, and virtual family he gathered would enter many of his poems. By 1972 he had published two novels, two plays, and six full books of verse. He had also begun book one of *Sandover,* whose three sections chronicled Merrill and Jackson's joint communications, via Ouija board, with spiritual and extraterrestrial beings. After completing the long poem in 1982, Merrill and Jackson moved to Key West, which joined Greece, Stonington, and Manhattan as frequent settings for Merrill's poems. We see in them, and in the whole *Collected,* not simply Merrill's life, with its privileges and its sadnesses, but the virtuosic and inviting works he made from it.

They did not start out inviting. Up through *The Country of a Thousand Years of Peace* (1959), Merrill's verse can seem positively hermetic, devoted to form—to its own forms—above all else. The eponymous bird in "The Black Swan" "outlaws all possible questioning: / A thing in itself, like love"; the swan is a poem, the kind of poem the young Richard Wilbur (another Amherst man) made popular—a stanzaic thing of self-referential beauty. For all their "splendid curvings of glass artifice," though, the works of art in early Merrill yearn to make contact with some outside world. A statue feels "a zest for life / Peculiar to those not quite alive"; a mirror says to a parlor window:

> *you* provide examples,
> Wide open, sunny, of everything I am
> Not. You embrace a whole world without once caring
> To set it in order. That takes thought.

One of Merrill's many early masks, "Mirror" combines in its reflective protagonist a playful artifice, a tacit sadness, and a desire to be more outgoing and less artful. Another 1950s poem remarks of some sculptures, "for a long time now / I have wanted to be more natural / Than they."

The young Merrill worried so much about what counted as "natural" partly because he was, and would remain, a childless gay man. "The Broken Home" (from *Nights and Days* [1966]) opens when Merrill sees parents and their child entering his apartment building. Soon he addresses, indoors, a single lit candle: "Tell me, tongue of fire, / That you and I are as real / At least as the people upstairs." Later on Merrill grew comfortable, even confident, in calling his own reflective, gay experience as real as anyone else's. He did so best in longish poems that juxtaposed several scenes, or several stories. "Chimes for Yahya" (from *Divine Comedies* [1977]) weaves together five or six tales about disguises and gifts: one involves the elaborate prank Merrill's Arab friends play on an earnest graduate student named Gloria, "doing fieldwork in the tribe." Hussein and his compatriots stage an "authentic" childbirth, with a midwife (in drag) and "Maternal invocations and convulsions." Finally Gloria is permitted to hold the infant:

> Into her credulous
> Outstretched arms laid—*not* a wriggling white
> Puppy! Horrors twinkled through the brain.
> Then the proud mother bared her face: Hussein.

The joke is on Gloria, whose research methods suppose clear divisions between the real and the constructed, as between play and productive, or reproductive, adult life.

Merrill found his metier by rejecting that division. He remained devoted to form, or to forms; but his mature aestheticism, if that is the right name for it, is resolutely sociable, closer to Wilde than to Stevens. The later poems thus define art as costume, or as necessary ornament— poems and persons are represented by robes, kimonos, outerwear, even (comically) a roving armoire. "Dreams about Clothes" supplied the title for *Braving the Elements* (1972). The poem addresses a dry cleaner named Arturo, in an eloquent stanza whose every term is a pun:

> Tell me something, Art.
> You know what it's like

Awake in your dry hell
Of volatile synthetic solvents.
Won't you help us brave the elements
Once more, of terror, anger, love?

"Brave," Merrill would have known, meant flaunt before it meant dare; Merrill's best poems dare to flaunt their artifice—they are, so to speak, avant-gaud. For him, poetry goes furthest in acknowledging how we feign; our costumes and conscious performances are not barriers to our truer selves but instead the conditions for the creation of those selves. "Seldom do we the living . . . feel more 'ourselves,'" Merrill wrote in "Prose of Departure," "than when spoken through, or motivated, by 'invisible forces.'" "The School Play" recalls the similar discoveries a younger Merrill made by means of *Richard II*:

I was the First Herald, "a small part"
—I was small too—"but an important one."
What was not important to the self
At nine or ten? Already I had crushes
On Mowbray, Bushy, and the Duke of York. . . .
Later, in adolescence, it was thought
Clever to speak of having found oneself,
With a smile and rueful headshake for those who hadn't.
People still do. Only the other day
A woman my age told us that her son
"Hadn't found himself"—at thirty-one!

Mother and son (like Gloria) commit the fallacy of authenticity, the error Merrill's style refutes: he who would find himself must lose himself first in other performances, amid the flexible rules of social life, or the rules of art. Another poem of the 1980s compares its author to a "Hindu Illumination," whose

artist made his elephant
Entirely of interlocking
Animal and human avatars:

Antelope, archer, lion, duck, each then
Reborn as portion of the whole
Proverbial creature—wisdom, memory—
Shown dancing on a crimson field.

We are made up of others, and of roles, as elephant is made up of archer and duck. To love, or to understand, us is to master those avatars: Merrill's companion thus appears, in the poem's last line, as the elephant's mahout.

If Merrill saw people as compositions of other people, of social experience, he saw them, too, sometimes, as compositions of language, through which that experience is imagined, reinterpreted, conveyed. Stevens explained that a poet must love words with all his power to love anything at all. Merrill fit the prescription perfectly: his mature poems love human beings and words. They love, moreover, the slippery fit between one and the other, which Merrill tried to represent with puns. No poet since Shakespeare has loved puns so much, or put his readers through so many. In "McKane's Falls," a river, once panned in a gold rush, now flows into a dam with electrical turbines; Merrill makes the river water ask:

Where's my old sparkle? Of late
I've felt so rushed, so cold.

Am I riding for another fall?
Will I end up at the power station
On charges, a degenerate?
Have my spirit broken in a cell?

Must I grow broad- and dirty-minded
Serving a community, a nation
By now past anybody's power to shock?

Almost as dear as puns to Merrill's technique are macaronics, comic or pathetic effects achieved by colliding languages and bad translations: "'Eh, Jimmy, qui sont ces deux strange men?'" To understand somebody else is to translate from her language into yours. To understand one's younger self, moreover, is to translate his terms into yours—as Merrill's "Lost in Translation" understood. The poem begins with Merrill as a boy, spending a summer with a governess:

> A card table in the library stands ready
> To receive the puzzle which keeps never coming.
> Daylight shines in or lamplight down
> Upon the tense oasis of green felt.
> Full of unfulfillment, life goes on,
> Mirage arisen from time's trickling sands
> Or fallen piecemeal into place:
> German lesson, picnic, see-saw, walk
> With the collie who "did everything but talk"—
> Sour windfalls of the orchard back of us.
> A summer without parents is the puzzle,
> Or should be. But the boy, day after day,
> Writes in his Line-a-Day *No puzzle.*

As he remembers the boy he was, the grown-up Merrill worries at a new puzzle: he has been trying to translate Paul Valéry's "Palme"— did Rilke translate it into German? Can Merrill find Rilke's version before he leaves Greece? The jigsaw puzzle, when it arrives, turns out to be a Near Eastern scene with animals and "a hundred blue / Fragments" of sky. Boy and governess assemble it ("Quite a task, / Putting together Heaven"), then take it apart to exchange it for another. Yet,

> Before the puzzle was boxed and readdressed
> To the puzzle shop in the mid-Sixties
> Something tells me that one piece contrived
> To stay in the boy's pocket. How do I know?
> I know because so many later puzzles
> Had missing pieces—Maggie Teyte's high notes
> Gone at the war's end, end of the vogue for collies,
> A house torn down; and hadn't Mademoiselle
> Kept back her pitiful bit of truth as well?

The governess speaks French, but is secretly German, "a widow since Verdun," of English descent. (When the puzzle arrives, "Mademoiselle does borders.") Is the lost piece of the puzzle like her lost past, like the lost milieus of prewar Europe? Are all three like the "warm Romance" of Valéry's French, abandoned when Rilke rendered "Palme" in German?

> But nothing's lost. Or else: all is translation
> And every bit of us is lost in it . . .
> And in that loss a self-effacing tree,
> Color of context, imperceptibly
> Rustling with its angel, turns the waste
> To shade and fiber, milk and memory.

Memory, autobiography, time lost or past: these are Merrill's themes as they were Marcel Proust's. Like Proust, Merrill could see the self both as something to be recaptured, retrieved, and as something to be continually reworked in social life, even remade. Merrill wrote his Amherst thesis on Proust: the novelist would emerge, alongside W. H. Auden, as Merrill's chief influence. (Others have noted debts, too, to C. P. Cavafy, whose poems of gay love and lust lay behind Merrill's "Days" titles—"Days of 1935," "Days of 1971," etc.) "For Proust" sets the French writer's life into quatrains Merrill invented: the first and fourth lines rhyme, but the second and third end on the same word. Late in the poem Merrill watches Marcel "make"

> for one dim room without contour
> And station yourself there, beyond the pale
> Of cough or of gardenia, erect, pale.
> What happened is becoming literature.

Events from Proust's life repeat themselves—but altered, made into "literature"—in his book; in the same way, Merrill's end words return, transformed.

Merrill found many other ways to incorporate into lyric Proustian time schemes and Proustian themes. One way was sheer grammatical elaborateness: Merrill's cascading dependent clauses, odd verb tenses and verb moods, and multiple appositions show how everything in the poet's memory informs, stands for, or stands in for something else. (Readers who think Merrill's self-remakings and his interest in recollection stand at odds rather than work together might think about how they edit their own retold memories—or look up what Proust had to say on the subject.) Other poems find visual symbols for retrospect. In "Lorelei," the passage of a life resembles a series of rocks laid over a stream: "The stones of kin and friend / Stretch off into a trembling, sweatlike haze." A longer poem enunciates "Proust's Law":

(a) What least thing our self-love longs for most
Others instinctively withhold;

(b) Only when time has slain desire
Is his wish granted to a smiling ghost
Neither harmed nor warmed, now, by the fire.

As in Proust, in Merrill we become who we are not through single, exceptional moments, but in a back-and-forth play of experience and understanding, without which our present-day social enjoyments, our comic remakings and new loves, might merely seem hollow.

The same poems can ask whether Merrill's dependence on memory, understanding, and anticipation—his devotion to *temps perdu*— might be a human universal, or whether it is instead peculiar to him. "Chimes for Yahya" remembers how young James once learned, before Christmas, what his Christmas gifts would be: come December 25,

I mimed astonishment, and who was fooled?
The treasure lay outspread beneath the tree.
Pitiful, its delusive novelty:
A present far behind me, in a sense.
And this has been a problem ever since.

Merrill is both comic and Proustian in his insistent returns from present to past—to previous lovers, friends, or poems, and even to previous parts of the same poem. ("Mirror" thus generates, thirty years later, a response poem called "Big Mirror Outdoors.") "Strato in Plaster" re-visits a Greek ex-lover:

> Out of the blue, in plaster from wrist to bicep
> Somebody opens a beer, pretending to be
> My friend Strato. Years or minutes—which?—
> Have passed since we last looked upon each other.
> He's in town for his sister's wedding
> To this elderly thin-lipped sonofabitch
> Who gets the house for dowry—enough to make
> A brother break with the entire family.
> Considering it, his eyes fairly cross
> With self-importance. That, I recognize.
>
> Here at hand is a postcard Chester sent
> Of the Apollo at Olympia,
> Its message *Strato as he used to be. . . .*

When the pair finally converse, Merrill asks:

> Was the break caused by too much malakía?
> Strato's answer is a final burst
> Of laughter: "No such luck!
> One day like this the scaffold gave beneath me.
> I felt no pain at first."

Merrill's view of his once-ideal companion, we see, has suffered a similar fall. The break, and the breakup, were sudden, then painful, now funny: comedy, Merrill (inverting the usual formula) suggests, may be what happens to tragedy, given time.

Perhaps uniquely among modern poets in English, Merrill thus became at once a poet of social comedy and a major poet of autobiography. As with other poetic autobiographers, from Wordsworth to Adrienne Rich, the more we know about Merrill's life, the more we can see in the poems. As with Wordsworth or Rich, Merrill's poems provide much, though not all, of the data we want. Lurie's prickly memoir offers some more. Her first chapters describe Merrill and Jackson in the 1950s, when Lurie and her then-husband were neighbors of Merrill and Jackson's at Amherst. Lurie recalls the couple as shy, then friendly, and as much more fun than Amherst's straight men. Without children or financial worries, Merrill and Jackson's became "the happiest marriage I knew": their amusements, in Amherst and then in Stonington, ranged from psychedelic mushrooms (disappointing) to amateur theatricals (delightful) to the Ouija sessions from which *Sandover* would grow.

As Merrill's reputation rose in the 1960s, Jackson kept writing novels, which never saw print. His frustrated novelistic energies, Lurie argues, created the spirit disclosures from which Merrill built his poem: the Ouija board work was, Lurie writes, Merrill's "last-ditch effort . . . to save their marriage." Suggesting that Jackson "was in an essential sense the co-author of *Sandover*," and that the long poem excluded their friends, Lurie says with asperity just what Merrill says in "Clearing the Title," a 1982 poem that celebrates the "co-authors'" move to Key West. The epic becomes "Our poem now. It's signed JM, but grew / From life together, grain by coral grain. / Building on it, we let the life cloud over."

Lurie knows something about Ouija boards, having researched séances and mediums for her 1967 novel *Imaginary Friends*. The best part of her book, and the least personal, shows how *Sandover*'s otherworldly messages—and thus its elaborate cosmology—follow patterns common to spiritualist practice. At first, dead friends and obscure historical figures appear with reassuring news. As participants devote more time, belief, and energy to the séances, more celebrities turn up; "the spirit tutors become more . . . grand and authoritative." The magico-religious system that the spirits unfold absolves the human participants of doubts about the conduct of their lives: those participants learn they are better than everyone else, with extraordinary hidden talents and a special, secret mission. Fans of *Sandover* are hereby challenged to show how parts two and three do not fit these depressing patterns. Part one, "The Book of Ephraim," seems to me (as it has to other readers) a fine, complete poem on its own.

Readers of Lurie who haven't read Merrill might expect his early poems to be merry, while his late work grew turbulent or grave. In

fact, the reverse is more nearly the case. As he got older, Merrill—
or Merrill's poems—seemed to have more fun: more fun with verse
forms, and more fun with the groups of friends the poems depict. "A
Tenancy" (1962), set in a new apartment, ends: "If I am host at last /
It is of little more than my own past. / May others be at home in it."

A good Merrill poem often tries hard to be a good host, to invite
us into, and help us appreciate, the stories and terms that it comprises.
Merrill the comic autobiographer thus relies on Merrill the maker of
forms, who translates the life we don't see into words we do. Auden
suggested that comic rhymes seem to put words in charge of events,
while serious poems do the reverse; Merrill shows how hard, even impossible, it can be to divide artificial from natural, comic from serious,
verbal play from the real thing, not just in literature but in life. The
mature Merrill can even entertain the perspective (advanced in Wilde's
"The Decay of Lying") from which art trumps life, and a sunset looks
like a bad Turner: "To the Reader," for example, presents "Each day"
as if it were a new book, "hot off the press from Moon & Son":

If certain scenes and situations ("work,"
As the jacket has it, "of a blazingly
Original voice") make you look up from your page
—*But this is life, is truth, is me!*—too many
Smack of self-plagiarism. . . .
And what about *those* characters? No true
Creator would just let them fade from view
Or be snuffed out, like people.

That is (put less comically and less elaborately): all of us die for no reason; there is no God. But of course the comedy is the point. Merrill
sought (he wrote in one late poem) "Uprightness, lightness, poise"; the
poems hope to make life, thought, feeling, at their worst seem lighter
and more bearable by placing technique, form, jokes (in jokes, even) on
the other end of the scales.

Part of Merrill's comedy is his irreverence, and part of that irreverence is the way he upends clichés, not just of language but of emotion:
"The day I went up to the Parthenon / Its humane splendor made me

think / So what?" Other irreverent jokes involve literary history: one of the characters in "Nine Lives" declares, parodying *The Waste Land,* "No, no, I am Greek, / My husband was a Hamburger. He spoke / The Ursprache." The comic temper also governs Merrill's substantial poems on sexual love, and on public affairs. "I rarely buy a newspaper, or vote," Merrill admitted in "The Broken Home." Yet he later became an accomplished poet of citizenship, investigating the private emotions created by political events. One poem from the Reagan era asks,

> Is my dread of the electorate
> Justified or fatally naive?
> What relation has the mother cat
> To (a) her litter, (b) the barrio
> Women who corner her, and (c)
> The TV coverage of their meal?

Almost all the gravest topics our era has produced can be found in Merrill—nuclear apocalypse; terrorism; Third World development and underdevelopment; the gradual forgetting of the past; existential meaninglessness; solipsism; aging and death. He challenged himself to show not how dreadful or scary these prospects can be but instead how we do, in fact, live with them all. At its best the involuted cosmology of *Sandover* (involving radioactive isotopes, reincarnation, prehistory, and demonic superbats) furnished a way of living with, and thinking about, the nuclear threat. "Santorini" (another poem of the 1980s) wishes instead and touchingly for a "companion who might / Act on a hushed injunction, less to ignore / The worst than stroll through it by evening light."

That "worst," by Merrill's last decade, meant three things. The first was global ecocatastrophe—coral reef bleaching, extinctions, the greenhouse effect—to which his time in Florida made him alert. The second was AIDS, whose growing casualty list animates *The Inner Room* (1988) and especially its sequence "Prose of Departure," a combined travelogue and elegy cast in the Japanese sequential form haibun. The third was Merrill's own mortality. All three topics merged in *A Scattering of Salts,* his last book and his best. Its introductory poem sees the earth as a bath (with bath salts) on which humankind accidentally pulls the plug; its valedictory lyric presents a posthumous speaker rising above his home, his life, and his loves: "O heart green acre sown with salt / by the departing occupier"—a figure as sad, and compact, as Merrill could be. In between came, among others, the sparkling narrative of "Nine Lives"; one of the best of Merrill's poems about opera, and two of his best poems about New York; excellent, lightish verse about cats and dogs; the brilliantly intricate sentences of "Pearl"; and a perfectly realized ten-line lyric connecting the word "body" in turn to cosmetics, theater, astronomy, birth, adulthood, religion, and death.

The huge *Collected Poems* holds about 675 pages, including all the books of short or midlength poems Merrill published. Excluded, the editors tell us, are "many occasional poems and . . . minor verse." Also excluded is *Sandover,* still in print separately and enormous on its own. Included, on the other hand, are a double-handful of verse translations—from Montale, from Cavafy, from the Dutch poet Hans Lodeizen, a friend of Merrill's who died young. Here, too, lives all the never-reprinted work from *The Black Swan* (1946) and *The Yellow Pages* (1974), a limited-edition volume of leftover poems from as far back as 1947. Among these stand a letter-perfect imitation of George Herbert; some earliest attempts at political verse; a villanelle about telephone phobias; a sestina whose six repeating end words are "one," "two," "three," "four," "five," and "six"; and a few genuinely important poems, "Economic Man" first of all.

Also here, thanks to the editors' care and spadework, reside about sixty pages of "Previously Uncollected Poems." Many are epigrams or miniature odes—to a pocket calculator, to a slide show, to a meerschaum pipe, to Bishop, to "Philip Larkin (1922–1985)," and to Merrill's onetime teacher Marius Bewley. Here, too, are a few more substantial, successful poems. In "Key West Aquarium: The Sawfish," the trapped fish becomes the poet fighting solipsism and age. Can he see himself in the glass? Can he see us?

Now if I speak for him,

A fellow captive, lips that kissed and told
Declare me—well, almost—
Not of this world, transparently a ghost

Into whom still the bright shaft glides. One old
Disproven saw sinks out of mind:
Love's but a dream and only death is kind.

Last, and most important, come the poems Merrill wrote at the end
of his life. "Christmas Tree," shaped typographically like its subject, becomes the final and perhaps most moving among all Merrill's versions
of himself. "Brought down at last / From the cold sighing mountain,"
Merrill says he has been cherished, kept warm, "wound in jewels"—
though only for "a matter of weeks":

<blockquote>

                                        what lay ahead
Was clear: the stripping, the cold street, my chemicals
Plowed back into the Earth for lives to come—
No doubt a blessing, a harvest, but one that doesn't bear,
Now or ever, dwelling upon. To have grown so thin.
Needles and bone. The little boy's hands meeting
About my spine. The mother's voice: *Holding up wonderfully!*
No dread. No bitterness. The end beginning. Today's
        Dusk room aglow
        For the last time
        With candlelight.

</blockquote>

Despite its sugary end (which I have not quoted), it is a deathbed poem
to set beside Stevens's or Keats's.

I keep meeting people who think they won't like Merrill because he
grew up with money. This is as silly as rejecting Proust because he grew
up with money or Whitman because he grew up with none. People who
think Merrill's poems record only the life of his own social class need
to read, ASAP, his poems about Greek men and Greece, which mask
neither his American privileges nor his adopted families' lack of same.
Other readers have found the poems overelaborate, or else complain
that the poems' ranges of reference excludes them. Such objections
can reveal the objectors' ressentiment (or their homophobia), but they
can also contain some truth. Merrill's lesser verse can become mere
"decoration" (as one objector has called it), his tangles of clauses and

high-culture references ends in themselves: all good poets—Merrill is no exception—have written bad or failed poems similar on their surface to their successes. Merrill's sometime frivolousness, his inside jokes, his grammatical tangles are the defects of his qualities; it makes no sense to wish his poems without them.

Merrill's greatest formal achievements are longish poems integrating remembered narratives: among these, new readers should start at "The Broken Home" and "An Urban Convalescence." They can then move on to "Days of 1935," "Strato in Plaster," "Up and Down," "Matinees," "Lost in Translation," "Chimes for Yahya," "Bronze," "Losing the Marbles," "Nine Lives," "Rhapsody on Czech Themes," and "Self-Portrait in Tyvek Windbreaker." The best short poems include "Mirror," "The Water Hyacinth," "Lorelei," "Willowware Cup," "The Victor Dog," "Manos Karastefanís," "b o d y," and "Christmas Tree"; nearly as good are "The Black Swan," "Marsyas," "The Country of a Thousand Years of Peace," "Remora," "The School Play," "To the Reader," "164 E. 72nd St," "An Upward Look," "Economic Man," and "In the Pink."

Moreover (this is the great thing about a *Collected*), after you wear those pages out, plenty of witty or delightful or striking poems, or parts of poems, remain. Memorable images emerge even from failed or precious poems: a seaside town can boast an outdoor lamp "lit even / In sunshine, like a freethinker in heaven." Merrill also offers nearly unmatched formal variety. No one in American English has done more kinds of things with an eight-line stanza, with *rime riche*, with sonnets in series, with a pentameter line—Merrill's grow, almost unpredictably, solemn, quizzical, wry, racy, tongue in cheek; legato, staccato, allegro; even (to switch analogies) pentimento, displaying the process by which we change our minds. Merrill's corpus offers, as few do, the whole life of a whole individual, a man who combined exceptional formal skill with exceptional self-knowledge and exceptional curiosity about all sorts of bits of the world. If certain parts of Merrill's oeuvre make readers laugh, smile, or wince, the major poems are finally comic not as stand-up comics are "comic," but as *Twelfth Night* is comic: xenophilic, sociable, friendly to disguises, and mindful of loss, they nevertheless manage to imagine what a happy life might be.

One fluent passage from "Nine Lives" does as well as any to recommend, as I want to recommend, the whole great, sprawling, wonderful body of work:

> There is a moment comedies beget
> When escapade and hubbub die away,
> Vows are renewed, masks dropped, La Folle Journée
> Arriving star by star at a septet.
> It's then the connoisseur of your bouquet
> (Who sits dry-eyed through *Oedipus* or *Lear*)
> Will shed, O Happiness, a furtive tear.

A. R. Ammons

Marvelous Devising

"I have found the world / so marvelous," A. R. Ammons once declared, "that nothing would surprise me." Many poets make it distressingly hard to find the best way into their work. Reading A. R. Ammons, on the other hand, you can begin almost anywhere and find, at most a marvel, at least a surprise: that's especially lucky since his vast oeuvre offers so many places to start. Ammons was not a fox but a hedgehog, exploring the same large truths and the same winsome or homely tones over and over. And yet the one general thing his poetry knew, and kept explaining, grew from his attention to specialized—often to scientific—points of view. These points of view, in turn, led him to emphasize the littleness of everything we can know: Ammons sought and found humility, flux, provisional order, and homeostasis wherever he looked—in the human mind and in the body, in forests and rivers, on earth and in space.

Ammons explored these preoccupations in a broad array of free verse forms. A palm-width (but thick) 1991 volume, *The Really Short Poems of A. R. Ammons,* offered several works as short, and as permanently memorable, as "Small Song":

> The reeds give
> way to the
>
> wind and give
> the wind away

Then there are his really long poems. Ammons's first book-length work, *Tape for the Turn of the Year,* took its name from the roll of narrow adding machine tape on which he wrote it over a few months in 1963–64. It aspired to include all the thoughts Ammons entertained while writing it, plus anything else a reader happened to bring in: the poem asked, early on,

> who
> are you?
> can I help? is there any
> thing I can do:
> are things
> working out
> all right for you? what
> are those black areas?
> are they parts
> of you that can't
> fall into place,
> come into light?

Later book-length poems included 1974's *Sphere: The Form of a Motion; The Snow Poems,* a 1977 verse diary; the consistently self-deprecating, usually funny, unusually wise *Garbage* (1993); and its semisequel, *Glare.*

Ammons also wrote lyric and essayistic poems of more ordinary lengths. Until the early 1970s some of those poems identified their author with Old Testament or even Sumerian prophets, carrying words to the skies and the winds' high places. (Sometimes the skies or the winds replied.) Ammons's other characteristic modes remained with him throughout his five decades of writing. One such mode makes whole poems from natural scenes:

The ice-bound spruce boughs
point downward
as if to
slide their sheathes off:

Another mode ties poems together from strings of "sayings":

        people are
losing propositions: what
they build flakes away,

even when they don't
take it with them . . .

So says one poem; another ends, "a worm cores this world's doings, look out."

In several-page "walk poems" and verse essays like "Corsons Inlet," these modes of saying and seeing interacted, as Ammons described his thoughts while passing uphill, around a lake, or down the road.

Those modes found raw materials in Ammons's life. The poet grew up on a farm in North Carolina where (he later wrote) "the only book we had at home was the Bible." Poems drawn from his childhood remember horses, mules, pine woods, and two younger brothers who died in infancy; "I saw his coffin being made," Ammons has written of one, "and I watched as he was taken away, his coffin astraddle the open rumble seat of a Model A." *Snow Poems* included a capsule autobiography:

Redneck Kid Grows Up On
Farm Goes Through Depression
But Thanks to Being In
Big War Goes To College
Gets Big Job Making
Big Money
    (relatively speaking) . . .

MAKE NO MONEY
BUT

WRITE NICE
(tries hard)

Ammons entered Wake Forest College (now University) on the G.I. Bill as a premed student; there he met the future Phyllis Ammons. In May 1949 he graduated; in November they married. During the early fifties he served as principal of an elementary school on Cape Hatteras, then pursued graduate study in English at the University of California–Berkeley (where the poet and critic Josephine Miles encouraged him). From 1952 to 1961, Ammons worked for a biological glass company in New Jersey; there he wrote most of *Ommateum, with Doxology* (1955), printed by a vanity publisher in Philadelphia. *Expressions of Sea Level* (1961) began his rise to prominence; the mid-1960s brought a job at Cornell University, in hilly, snowy Ithaca, New York, along with several more volumes of short poems. By the late 1960s, Harold Bloom (a friend from Cornell) had joined other critics in championing his verse. Ammons remained in Ithaca for most of the rest of his life, observing "snow / sifty as fog" and "ice's bruise-glimmer"; the lakes, heights, and heavy weather of upstate New York inform his later poems as North Carolina informed his earliest.

Most young poets assimilate many styles before they discover their own; Ammons instead learned a lot from a few. From the Old Testament he took the elevated sense of vocation that he first imitated, then reversed. From Wordsworth he took his devotion to nature and solitude, and the idea that (in Ammons's words) "a poem is a walk." From Whitman he took the idea of a poem and a line as extensions of personality, able (as he put it) to "reach out broadly across the page in space-hungry gesture." Finally, in William Carlos Williams Ammons found most of his technical tools: irregular lines and thin-sliced stanzas; a variable, enjambment-dependent cadence; and the idea that a short poem can mimic, or equal, a reed, streambed, or tree. (A somewhat later influence was Ralph Waldo Emerson, whom Ammons claimed he read on advice from Bloom: Emersonian concepts and attitudes color most of his longer poems.) "I've written most of my poetry more or less in isolation," Ammons once said: his oeuvre remained at a great distance from the schools and movements that dominated much U.S. poetry during his lifetime.

Ammons's most important backgrounds were neither literary nor regional but scientific. "Most of my study was in the sciences," he told one interviewer. Helen Vendler once explained that Ammons's work "speak[s] from the processes of science"; he "habitually thinks of the world in scientific terms, and sees us very much at the edge of the galaxy, and by no means at the center of the universe." The natural sciences' methods and attitudes (in other words) do much of the work for Ammons that religious, cultural, political, or art-historical models do for other poets; Ammons takes advantage both of the hard sciences' perspectives, and of their unusual verbal properties. After a windy night

> I thought, my word, icicles
> summarize the rate of melt
> and wind direction, are a glacio-spiral
> version of a wind-rose: nature
> that will uproot an eavesload
> of history
> can be so careful of history

The mid-1960s series "Guitar Recitativos" keeps one eye on youth culture's breathless lusts, and the other on Ammons's own chemical models, with deliberately, irreproducibly comic results:

> Baby, there are times when the mixture becomes immiscible
> and other times we get so stirred up I can't tell
> whether I'm you or me
> and then I have this fear of a surprising reaction in which
> we both turn into something else
>
> powdery or gaseous or slightly metallic

Whether he's trying for laughs or for ontology, Ammons's attention to his own thought goes hand in hand with his attention to the nonthinking, nonspeaking, nonhuman objects and scenes he so liked to contemplate. "If people (cruel / and insensitive, survival pluses) ail / you nature is a rescue, go to it," *Snow Poems* declared. For all his chattiness, Ammons often seemed more comfortable with the sciences' nonhuman world than with society, preferring forests' or galaxies' systems to ours. In consequence, Ammons both liked and understood ideas of nonteleological, nonhierarchical, hidden order. One early poem comes close to installing chance as God, complete with Urim and Thummim (but also with "coefficients of friction"):

> My dice are crystal inlaid with gold
> and possess
>   spatial symmetry
> about their centers and
> mechanical symmetry and
>   are of uniform density
> and all surfaces have equal
> coefficients of friction for
>
> my dice are not loaded
>   Thy will be done

If the young Ammons found religious tropes attractive, the older poet found that he neither needed nor wanted "celestial guidance systems." Ammons's beliefs, as they inform his verse, grew at once from a democratic temperament and from a scientific worldview (indeed, they argue that the two are linked). Like Whitman, Ammons went out of his way to exalt the lowly, not through any Christian program but as part of the spirit of inquiry: one poem invites us to

> Honor the maggot,
>   supreme catalyst:
> he spurs the rate of change:
> (all scavengers are honorable: I love them
> all,
> will scribble hard as I can for them)

Ammons's attraction to nonhuman systems, his understanding of forms we find but do not make, also made him a poet of ecology: "in an enclosure like earth's there's no place to dump stuff off."

Ammons titled his most ambitious (and most nearly political) long poem *Sphere* partly because it imagined the earth seen from space, and partly because the "sphere" in the astronauts' photos offered Ammons an alternative to older, "pyramidal hierarchies" in representing knowledge or life as wholes. No poet has ever been more alert to the ways in which the material world resists our desires and our plans. Yet Ammons saw, and preferred to stress, not the gaps between ourselves and clouds or lichens, but the continuities—we are, as they are, homeostatic systems: "Honor a going thing," he wrote in "Mechanism," "goldfinch, corporation, tree / morality: any working order, / animate or inanimate."

Ammons saw his own poems as "going things," too. *Brink Road* defined poems as "Evasive Actions"; as "swerving (lessening and / swelling) elongations"; as "connecting misses"; as "reminder[s] not of keeping but of not keeping." In *Lake Effect Country* (1983), poems were "Dismantlings," "Measuring Points," ways to "let / the quibble speak." His prose claims that "poetry resembles other actions such as ice-skating or football," and that "writing poetry is like surfing . . . If we miss or if the wave isn't right or fulfilling—that is, if the wave is not a whole motion of unfolding, an integrated action—we spill." Yet any spill, Ammons realized, could itself fit into a large enough "whole motion"; he learned to take into his orderly actions, or unities, all manner of random, by-the-way discoveries of "multiplicity" (his term). The much-anthologized "Corsons Inlet" celebrates just such self-revising incorporations of error and mess:

> I see narrow orders, limited tightness, but will
> not run to that easy victory:
> still around the looser, wider forces work:
> I will try
> to fasten into order enlarging grasps of disorder, widening
> scope, but enjoying the freedom that
> Scope eludes my grasp, that there is no finality of vision,
> that I have perceived nothing completely,
> that tomorrow a new walk is a new walk.

A poet who viewed all poems as "action and // action's pleasure," all things as processes, all particles (in a conscious echo of quantum theory) as waves, Ammons liked turning nouns into verbs, and vice versa: in the late, careful "Minutial Impress," "is" means being and "being" means becoming—"even the / biggest is, returning, plays out through / history extraordinary ragged changes." As critics have started to notice, Ammons's poems about fluctuating systems can also evoke the "extreme dependence on initial conditions" that came to define chaos theory. The older disciplines of cybernetics and systems theory, which view all patterns as patterns of information (and which developed early enough for the young Ammons to assimilate them) explain some of these striking coincidences, which let him celebrate, at once, the forms he found and the chaos they failed to contain.

Ammons's smaller-scale formal choices grow from the same open ongoingness that dictates his poems' overall shapes. He tends to alternate details with abstractions, as if to illustrate the interdependence he likes to invoke: "the exception sharply noticed / becomes the groundwork / of the next familiar." Rejecting most devices (rhyme, for instance) that set poems apart from prose, Ammons favors the rhetorical figures poems can share with other speech, especially chiasmus ("poison earth, eat poison"). His aural arrangements rely on tone and phrase-based rhythms, rather than on any intricate euphony; they emphasize interdependences and apparently improvised movement, rather than completing preset shapes. Ammons also depicts his beloved complexities by keeping lines and arguments in overlapping motion, never allowing one aspect of form (a meter, a syntactic figure) to control all the others. Even Ammons's peculiar punctuation gets into this self-revising, ongoing act. Sometimes he eschews punctuation entirely. Usually, though, he simply avoids periods, or uses just one (at the end of the poem): everywhere else, he uses not . but : The colon itself comes to stand for his attitude, since it is (as he is) never conclusive, always moving on, ever ready to introduce a new topic, or a list, or a ratio.

Ammons's antihierarchical informality also governed his whimsical choice of topics. *Snow Poems* comprehends football, ecology, weather, farts, weather, sex, cooking, grief, wit, and weather, weather, weather.

Sphere included "the autopsy and the worm," "an isoceles trian-
gle," "a piece of pie," "dandelion, protozoan, bushmaster and lady-
bird," hydrology, sexuality, elegy, "desk chair, wheel-back side chair,"
"glassware, software and willow ware," all within one hundred lines.
Ammons's diction also advertises his inclusive outlook: he especially
likes the extremely abstract, and the colloquial or scatological, registers most poets avoid:

> lucky for the pheasant they
> have a big ass and long
> tail to sustain them above the
> snow when their legs blop through

Ammons's sense of himself as a physical, natural body, and his
sense of himself as finally inconsequential, made him a funny, wry poet
of old age. Near the beginning of *Garbage,* he considered adopting a
frugal diet based on soybeans ("more protein by weight than meat"):
what else would a poet in retirement need? "Social Security can provide / the beans, soys enough," Ammons wrote there; "my house, paid
for for // twenty years, is paid for" (another chiasmus); "my young'un /
is raised: nothing one can pay cash for seems // very valuable." One late,
short poem decided that "Teeth are distressing only / if you try to save
them." Another, "A Part for the Whole," exercised its synecdoche on
Ammons's feet, their "arches bone-sprung crack flat":

> feet, good feet,
> don't leave me up here with
>
> the one place to go
> and no way to keep from going.

Against such quiet or folksy lines, we might set serious passages like
this from *Sphere:* "I expect to die in terror: / my mother did: old songs
(hymns) erupted from her dying / imagination: they say she sang them
blurred for two nights."

Even before he wrote his poems of old age, Ammons's cosmic contexts let him become a major poet of memento mori, even of *contemptus mundi;* "earth, no heavier / with me here, will be no / lighter when I'm gone." He liked, and meant, both his declarations of wonder and his statements of resignation, his lowerings and modifications of once-salient prophetic ambitions. His poems frequently compare (or contrast) lives to seconds, hours to aeons, geological and cosmic to quotidian time. Many of his strongest passages remind us how little we mean, how little we do, how much we fail to see: they tell us, in other words, how to react to the inhumanity of nature's laws, the fact that the real ground rules of our time on earth come neither from us, nor for us:

> when we learn we are trash
> flimsy, flowable, our holding
> trivial and slight, we must
> not say, if that's what
> the universe thinks of us, so
> much for the universe:
> it should be the benefit of our
> experience here to realize trash
> the just groundwork
> of marvelous devising

Ammons has exerted little stylistic influence on younger poets: his inventions have proved inseparable from his peculiar (and charming) way of seeing the world. Ammons's greatest achievements arise in his longer poems—partly because the long poems are simply more original (their closest precedents remain distant indeed), partly because in the shorter poems, although many of them turned out fine indeed, Ammons's sense of the poem as "saying," as action, could keep him from loading every rift with ore. (The lesser short poems, and there are many, tend to end cute: "drinking this sweet rain, consuming this green.") Of the many self-explanations his poetry offers, my favorite may be "The Put Down Come On," whose sixteen lines encompass both his humility and his wonder, his scientific predilections and his characteristic light touch:

You would think I'd be a specialist in contemporary
literature: novels, short stories, books of poetry,
my friends write many of them: I don't read much
and some drinks are too strong for me: my empty-headed

contemplation is still where the ideas of permanence
and transience fuse in a single body: ice, for example,
or a leaf: green pushes white up the slope: a maple
leaf gets the wobbles in a light wind and comes loose

half-ready: where what has always happened and what
has never happened before seem for an instant reconciled:
that takes up most of my time and keeps me uninformed:
but the slope, after maybe a thousand years, may spill

and the ice have a very different look withdrawing into
the lofts of cold: only a little of that kind of
thinking flashes through: but turning the permanent also
into the transient takes up all the time that's left.

Stanley Kunitz

Out of Glacial Time

Even before his appointment in 2001 as U.S. poet laureate, Stanley Kunitz was famous (as poets go) for his longevity (at ninety-five, he still gave sold-out readings; he died in 2005, as a centenarian) and for his work as a mentor, an institution builder (at, for example, the Provincetown Fine Arts Work Center), and a teacher (preeminently at Columbia University's School of the Arts). These reputations, by the end of his life, risked eclipsing his seven decades of poems. Like the laureateship, the 2002 *Collected Poems* was largely an honor and an expression of gratitude, since it offers no new work: the first half restores his long-unavailable early poems, and the second half reprints 1995's wonderful *Passing Through: New & Selected Later Poems*. Although Kunitz never acknowledged a sharp distinction between his early and late styles, the collection tells the story of that break: it is the story of a movement from intelligence and craft to what lies beyond— and cannot be reached without—them.

Kunitz's father committed suicide before Kunitz was born; the poet was raised in Worcester, Massachusetts, by his hardworking, entrepreneurial mother, and (later) by a gentle stepfather. He attended Harvard in the early 1920s, staying on for an MA, but was told that his Jewish background would keep him from teaching there. Working as a reporter and in the obscurer reaches of publishing, Kunitz lived mostly outside the poetry world, and entirely outside academia, for the first decades of his career. It would be easy to credit prejudice for the lack of notice that his early poems received, but the truth is that most of them weren't very good. The young Kunitz was a more than usually ornate, more than usually sincere, much more than usually mystical Old Formalist, and never more deliberate than when announcing (with nods to Blake, Yeats, and Hart Crane) that he had been seized by a visionary passion, as in "Night-Piece":

> So bear with me, and if I thrash and groan
> In the throes of sleep, believe me that I saw
> The great fish tunneling the purple sea,
> Earth-darkening bird that harries man alone.

I don't believe him: did he see a fish, or a bird? When the early poems address his father, they do so with stilted melancholy: "Father, the darkness of the self goes out / And spreads contagion on the flowing air." Another poem tells its beloved: "Listen! we make a world! I hear the sound / Of Matter pouring through eternal forms." (How does matter sound? How loud does it get?)

Kunitz's contemporaries–from Dylan Thomas to Richard Wilbur— could work with high diction in "eternal forms" and still sound like they meant it; Kunitz seems to have discovered that he could not, even as his last work in his old high way, 1958's *Selected Poems,* won him a Pulitzer. He changed his style during the 1960s. On the evidence of *The Testing-Tree* (1971), Kunitz was reacting (as were many of his contemporaries) to the era's political pressures, to the foreign poets he was translating, and to Robert Lowell's *Life Studies.* Yet he had been asking, even praying, for rawness and vividness since his most controlled early poems: one poem turns away from "the wisdom of another age" to realize that "the thing that eats the heart is mostly heart." In later interviews, he minimized his stylistic change—"Given the kind of person I am," he wrote in the 1970s, "I came to see the need for a middle style"—but it was drastic, and all for the good. What he kept from his old work, and needed, was its compression; what he learned, and needed, was understatement and comedy—the last knotted with awe and horror:

> My mother never forgave my father
> for killing himself,
> especially at such an awkward time
> and in a public park,
> that spring
> when I was waiting to be born.

Is the unforgivable sin in "The Portrait" suicide? Or public suicide? Or suicide at an inconvenient juncture? The grown-up and fatherless child here tells us, as economically as he can, that he will never be in a position to know.

The tones and modes of *The Testing-Tree*—meditative, oracular, sometimes grief stricken, sometimes gently comic—continued through Kunitz's mature poems; collectively they are a spiritual autobiography. Kunitz insists that each poem be an important event in the psychic life of its author—one reason his depth seems connected to his slow output. His short lines convey the effort it took to write them, and seem acutely conscious of the potential silence after every phrase. In his hands, the negative space between lines can represent speechless grief, or the strain of finding a word, or (as in "After the Last Dynasty") room left wistfully for a lover's reply:

> Pet, spitfire, blue-eyed pony,
> here is a new note
> I want to pin on your door,
> though I am ten years late
> and you are nowhere:
> Tell me,
> are you still mistress of the valley,
> what trophies drift downriver,
> why did you keep me waiting?

Even more than he likes pauses and silences, Kunitz likes to end poems with unanswerable questions: "What do we know / beyond the rapture and the dread?" Other poems end by declaring that some long-ago feeling persists, without being able to say (though having shown) why: "In my sixty-fourth year / I can feel my cheek / still burning." Both gestures appeal from the words on a page out into the history of the poet, and to the poet's sense of his own life. "One of my convictions," Kunitz has written, "is that at the center of every poetic imagination is a cluster of key images that go back to the poet's childhood and that are usually associated with pivotal experiences, not necessarily traumatic." In Kunitz's own poetry the experiences remembered are brief, hard glimpses of an indelible past, or else of an inhuman natural order: his images are those experiences' shadows, the coded things to which his life is the key.

As one would expect from a poet so concerned with memory and with ghosts, Kunitz loves refrains and verbal recurrences. "River Road" begins, "That year of the cloud, when my marriage failed," and begins again, on the same line, midway through: moving from sky to earth, Kunitz steadies himself by recollecting "the woods I made . . . through the deep litter of the years." Litter, layers, digging, archaeology, are surely among Kunitz's own "key images": if he has a manifesto it is surely the moving, if slightly predictable, poem called "The Layers," which sorts through his "many lives, / some of them my own," in order to ask (one can hear the crack in his voice), "How shall the heart be reconciled / to its feast of losses?"

Those so-often-invoked layers, and the litter that half-conceals them, can represent his personal past, or the history of a locale, or the past of the whole human species: in "The Mound Builders," "part, if only part of me, goes down / to the master farmers who built" the prehistoric settlements in Ocmulgee, Georgia—tribes whose ways the poem compares (favorably) to the turbulent South of the nineteenth and twentieth centuries. Kunitz also imagines himself as a wandering excavator, exploring old roads, "fishing in the abandoned reservoir," sorting through muck, or mulch, or potsherds, or leaves. The boy of "The Testing-Tree"

> scuffed in the drainage ditch
>   among the sodden seethe of leaves

hunting for perfect stones
  rolled out of glacial time
    into my pitcher's hand.

In that poem's "abandoned quarry," geological, historical, and auto-biographical time become one. All three, the poet fears, have left him behind.

Even more than they are full of memories, the mature poems are full of totem animals: these are without exception wounded or dying. Here is a mutilated "Robin Redbreast," there the dying salmon called "King of the River," become, horribly, in his last days "a ship for parasites." Here is "Jonathan, the last of the giant tortoises," and there are the diseased and "nervous Leghorns" (chickens) condemned by the farm inspector: "not one of them was spared the cyanide." Although they also remind him of nature's inscrutability, these expiring animals all stand for the poet, who for decades has felt both his kinship with nonhuman fauna and flora, and his (all of our) mortality. Other New England writers, from Melville to Lowell, have made their whales menacing and forever unknowable. But in Kunitz's long, magnificent, and wholly characteristic "The Wellfleet Whale," a beached and dying whale's "unearthly outcry" becomes an all-too-human cry of surprise at our limited powers:

    Master of the whale-roads,
  let the white wings of the gulls
    spread out their cover.
      You have become like us,
  disgraced and mortal.

In that whale (and again in a recent, perfect pair of poems about infected hornworms), the old peddlers, questers, archaeologists, and wounded animals throughout Kunitz's oeuvre find their eventual, restless meeting place: contemplating their lifetime of changes, all these creatures are painfully unable—as few of us are able—to turn at last into what they wanted to be.

Kunitz's poems of self-searching, with their long, narrow, carefully excavated sentences, make him so obviously a poet of grief and gravity that it is easy to overlook what else he can do. Although slow, stichic trimeters became his signature lines, Kunitz also made the ballad stanza his own. A marvel of compression and construction, "Three Floors" begins at the young Kunitz's bedroom ("Mother was a crack of light") and moves, stanza by stanza, "downstairs" and then up: after three stanzas, we find ourselves outside the house and encounter the dead father in a thunderstorm:

> Bolt upright in my bed that night
> I saw my father flying;
> the wind was walking on my neck,
> the windowpanes were crying.

Kunitz can also be a compelling interpreter of visual art, from the carvings of "unknown makers" to a disturbing late painting by his longtime friend Philip Guston. And he became, in his fifties and sixties, a convincing and funny—convincing because funny—poet of married love: "Let's jump into the car, honey, / and head straight for the Cape," "Route Six" proposes. What stands in the way? Only the past, the inevitable layers, and the poem knows what to do with those:

> As for those passions left
> that flare past understanding,
> like bundles of dead letters
> out of our previous lives
> that amaze us with their fevers,
> we can stow them in the rear
> along with ziggurats of luggage
> and Celia, our transcendental cat . . .

It is as silly, as personal, and as convincing as any show of long-lived affection can be.

Kunitz's mortally wounded creatures; his mounds, layers, litter; and his succession of ghosts and portents make perfect fits with the techniques (refrains, heavy trimeters, impossible questions) by which we also recognize his work. His short lines balance long sentences, and the ordinary words he chooses yield their densely packed implications, as the poems peer slowly into the depths of being. Some of his best poems, besides those I've quoted, are "King of the River," "Quinnapoxet," "Words for the Unknown Makers," "The Abduction," "Halley's Comet," "Touch Me," and the two "Hornworm" poems. Kunitz makes up for his small formal range with great warmth, with moral seriousness and tragic dignity, and (a virtue without which the others would vanish) with indefatigable attention at once to each word in a poem and to the experience behind it.

Frank O'Hara

Hi, Louise!

Open Frank O'Hara's *Collected Poems* at random, somewhere in the middle, and you may get what looks like a telegram to a friend, or versified notes on a Jackson Pollock painting, a James Dean movie, or "the music of Adolphe Deutsch." You may also get one of many enticing, informal, secretly complex poems that sound like nobody else's ever have:

> How can you start hating me when I'm so comfortable in your
> raincoat
> the apples kept bumping off the old gnarled banged-up biddy-
> assed tree
> and I kept ducking and hugging and bobbing as if you were a tub
> of water
> on Hallowe'en it was fun but you threw yourself into reverse like
> a tractor
> hugging the ground in spring that was nice too more rain more
> raincoat

Who was O'Hara, and how did he learn to write like that? He was born in 1926 and grew up in small towns in Massachusetts, studied piano seriously throughout high school, and served in the navy at the close of World War II. He attended Harvard, where he began a close friendship with his classmate John Ashbery. After a year (1950–51) in Michigan writing and translating poetry, he moved to New York, where he rejoined his Harvard friends and their friends—among them the poets Kenneth Koch, James Schuyler, and Barbara Guest— becoming part of a social circle that was soon dominated by painters. In 1951 and again from 1955 until his death, O'Hara worked at the Museum of Modern Art, where he became a curator of exhibitions and a well-known figure in the New York art world. In 1959 he embarked on a tumultuous love affair with Vincent Warren, the dancer.

Through the early 1960s, O'Hara's commitments at MOMA increased (so did his drinking). He also became a hero for younger bohemian poets who moved into New York scenes he'd helped establish. Even so, until City Lights published *Lunch Poems* (still the best introduction to his work) in 1964, his books appeared in limited editions that were hard to obtain outside New York. In July 1966, O'Hara was hit by a beach buggy on Fire Island; he died a few days later. (Brad Gooch's 1993 biography, *City Poet,* adorned these facts with lurid guesswork and even speculated that O'Hara had wanted to get killed.) A wider world of readers discovered O'Hara's verse when his enormous posthumous *Collected* won the National Book Award for 1971; its editor, Donald Allen, later brought out more volumes of prose and verse.

O'Hara in his adult years lived surrounded by other artists and by the other arts. During the 1950s, he reviewed painting, sculpture, and contemporary classical music. He wrote at least seven poems called "On Rachmaninoff's Birthday," and many others in which music matters. Yet he will always be more strongly linked to the visual arts: American artists made sure of that. "In Memory of My Feelings" is the name of a 1956 O'Hara poem; a haunting 1961 painting by Jasper Johns; a 1967 art world all-star anthology commemorating O'Hara; and a 1999 exhibit at the Los Angeles County Museum of Contemporary Art, curated by Russell Ferguson. O'Hara collaborated with the action painters and the proto-pop artists Joe Brainard, Norman Bluhm, Mike Goldberg, Franz Kline, Al Leslie, and Larry Rivers, on paintings, prints, collages, "artists' books," and short films: these comprise the core of the exhibition. There are also portraits and other works linked to O'Hara: Johns's big black canvas, with silverware attached, now looks like a work of proleptic mourning, its dangling fork and spoon marking a grave.

That gravity makes it atypical. Works in which the poet himself had a hand are almost always playful, exuberantly or reluctantly so. The best known and liveliest are the series *Stones,* by O'Hara and Rivers, and another, rougher series with Bluhm, who recalls his work with O'Hara as "instantaneous, like a conversation between friends." Bluhm and O'Hara's "This Is the First" (1960) offers a scrawled text— "this is the first person / I ever went to bed / with"—over a teasing, ambiguous duo of brown arcs: breast and thigh? pear and leaf? a foreshortened phallus? In runny paint below the lower arc, the artists have added: "wow!"

O'Hara and his friends worked together not only on visual art but on poetic sequences, and on mock-critical documents like O'Hara and Rivers's "How to Proceed in the Arts": "If you're the type of person who thinks in words—paint!" Most of all—with Ashbery, Bill Berkson, Koch, Rivers, and others—O'Hara collaborated on plays, most of which reappeared in *Amorous Nightmares of Delay* (1996). A few of the plays had theatrical runs; more were privately staged at parties, as masques or eclogues in which his friends played outrageously torqued, accentuated, or childish versions of themselves or one another: "I'm Jane, I'm Jimmy, I'm Larry, I'm Kenneth, I'm John, I'm Barbara, I'm Bob, how are you, folks?"

Joe LeSueur (O'Hara's longtime flatmate and sometime lover), writes that one collaboration "might remind the reader of nothing so much as children at play, dressing up in grown-ups' clothes and putting on a show in the backyard." Another, "bitchy and gossipy," "audaciously evokes some of the atmosphere" of the writers' and artists' favorite bars, among them the Cedar Tavern and the San Remo. It can be hard to distinguish backyard and bar: the fun of the plays often lies in their overlap. Stock characters become "real" people, real people become one another (Ashbery plays "Jimmy Schuyler"), and all are conflated with works of art:

GIRL: John has this new Bessarabian poet he wants to publish
    who's not as good as Jimmy's novel. He paints gravel poems!

JOHN MYERS: Jimmy's novel isn't a person and you know it. And
neither is the Bessarabian, for that matter.

The play *Awake in Spain* is a hodgepodge of shepherds; Audenesque,
pastoral airmen; urban gay camp; Shakespearean aristocrats in the
woods; and what William Empson called the child as swain:

TWO SHEPHERDS: We love the country, that's why we're hand-
some, it's love love love love love. We only quarrel over sheep.
We're terribly natural, aren't we? Well, is the sky blue? What
did you expect, a couple of Air Force Cadets? Not that we
couldn't if we wanted to!
SHEEP: Sure you could.
GRANDMOTHER: Would you boys like to take sandwiches to
school or come home at noon?
KING: I'll get back into that palace, I know I will.
SHEEP: Sure you will.

The poets' apparent independence from worldly concerns, their elaborate self-reference and slippery in jokes, can make the world of the
Cedar Tavern seem, in retrospect, a sort of Arcadia in itself.

David Lehman's *The Last Avant-Garde* offers a guided tour.
Chapters on Ashbery, O'Hara, Koch ("our funniest poet . . . a pro-
tean comic genius"), and Schuyler ("the best-kept secret in American
poetry") precede chapters on the concept of movements in art and of
an "avant-garde," a term Lehman knows they would not have used for
themselves. Lehman's book anticipates a very broad audience, one that
won't necessarily know the poems. Those who do should enjoy the
fruits of his biographical research. It's neat to learn, for example, that
Ashbery and O'Hara could imitate each other's voices without trying:
on the telephone "both Ashbery's mother and . . . LeSueur were fooled
into thinking that one was the other."

Lehman writes that in O'Hara's poems "one feels the romance of
cheap digs in Greenwich Village, chinos and sneakers, a constant flow
of adrenaline, taxis, drinks, an opening at the Museum of Modern
Art, a party at a painter's loft, poems written on the run between the
San Remo bar and the New York City Ballet." To show what makes

O'Hara more than just a diarist of a particularly fertile bohemia would be to show how his poems work, why they sound as they do. Marjorie Perloff took on that job in *Frank O'Hara: Poet among Painters* (1977), the first academic book on O'Hara. Her new introduction to the re-issued volume considers recent scholarly accounts of his work, scores a number of important points against reductive readings, and goes on to suggest that O'Hara's "aesthetic is closer to the conceptualism" of Johns, or of John Cage, or of more recent poets she champions than to the expressivism of his friends. This intriguing argument can look like special pleading when it's set beside "Personism: A Manifesto," the closest O'Hara came to a statement of his own aesthetic. A spoof of pretentious manifestos like those of Charles Olson, the 1959 prose piece was also a real declaration of purpose: O'Hara's poems would try to record, though never to stand in for, the idiosyncracies of human relationships: "While I was writing 'a love poem' I was realizing that if I wanted to I could use the telephone instead of writing the poem, and so Personism was born."

The close relations between the poems and the man, between the man and the artists and writers around him, have made it easy, even too easy, to see him in terms of a movement, a New York school. (The art impresario John Bernard Myers coined the term with the "New York school" of painters in mind.) School or no school, O'Hara certainly made himself a New York poet: the poems admire and try to mimic the city, where "however exaggerated at least something's going on / and the quick oxygen in the air will not go neglected." The sun itself, in "A True Account of Talking to the Sun at Fire Island," tells the poet with cheeky authority:

> I know you love Manhattan, but
> you ought to look up more often.
>   And
> always embrace things, people earth
> sky stars, as I do, freely and with
> the appropriate sense of space.

O'Hara wanted his space to be welcoming, vivid, and crowded: "One need never leave . . . New York to get all the greenery one wishes: I can't even enjoy a blade of grass unless I know there's a subway handy, or a record store or some other sign that people do not totally regret life." This often-quoted sentence comes from "Meditations in an Emergency," the best-known and best of his prose poems, whose self-contradictory title also suggests a specifically urban pace. Even in other landscapes (Long Island or Spain), O'Hara's sometimes jagged associative manner recalls the visual field of Manhattan, where anything—hubcaps, actors, potholes, emeralds—might turn up next to anything else: as "Walking" has it, "the country is no good for us / there's nothing / to bump into . . . there's not enough / poured concrete." The lesser poems, scattered or rushed (and there are plenty), create a sense of great potential never quite realized, in part because they include so many distractions; one can have the same feeling about New York City itself.

It took attention, work, and time for O'Hara to become a New York poet—his "'I do this I do that'/poems" (as he called them) start in about 1954. Even before then, he could be a superb poet of what we are pleased to call immaturity, creating young people at once touchingly needy, quite serious, and crashingly ridiculous:

> However the mounting wail of adolescence crashes
> upon the amusement park he is not confused, the boy,
>
> he is not discountenanced by any number of silences
> or natural events like bombs. "Be mine some day!" he
>
> admonishes automobiles and palatial residences
> as well as the ocean and Catholicism.

For every such moment, though, the earlier poems offer yards of flat surrealism and stacks of failed attempts at shock or high camp: "our ensembles must never let down the supreme Decorator, who has habituated the course in stars."

Perloff rightly insists on O'Hara's early and conscious study—of Williams, Gertrude Stein, and the modern French poets. Russians, perhaps, became just as important. "A True Account" responds to a poem by Vladimir Mayakovsky; O'Hara elsewhere praised Mayakovsky's verse and saw in himself the Soviet poet's fragility, writing in a poem called "Mayakovsky":

Now I am quietly waiting for
the catastrophe of my personality
to seem beautiful again,
and interesting, and modern.

O'Hara's longest published essay about literature concerns Boris Pasternak and quotes from *Doctor Zhivago:* "However far back you go in your memory, it is always in some external active manifestation of yourself that you come across your identity—in the work of your hands, in your family, in other people. And now listen carefully. You in others—this is your soul. This is what you are."

Those lines might have been O'Hara's motto. So thoroughly animated by other people, by conversational and social relations, he became a great and almost compulsive poet of occasions—birthdays, parties, dates and missed dates, other people's poems, paintings, musical performances, good weather, even the chance discovery of a body louse:

> There it is stranded in the blue
> gaze. And the gaze is astonished, eye
> to eye: a speck, and a vastness staring
> back at it. Why it's Louise! Hi, Louise.

A poet who could transform such nonevents into mock celebrations could also turn public occasions to intimate ones:

Khrushchev is coming on the right day!
                                    the cool graced light
is pushed off the enormous glass piers by hard wind
and everything is tossing, hurrying on up
                              this country
has everything but *politesse,* a Puerto Rican cab driver says
and five different girls I see
                        look like Piedie Gimbel
with her blonde hair tossing too,
                              as she looked when I pushed
her little daughter on the swing on the lawn it was also windy

Concentrate on O'Hara's "I" for too long and it threatens to—no, it very much wants to—dissolve into a network of encounters with others. To this end, O'Hara even conceives of himself as Grand Central Station: "if they are not thundering into me / they are thundering across me . . . On rainy days I ache as if a train / were about to arrive, I switch my tracks." His own Dejection Ode is the subtle and painful poem "Essay on Style," in which he speaks of his feeling that his friends have abandoned him. Language is collapsing—adverbs have lost their function, and so has the adjective "well,"

> since it has no
> application whatsoever neither as a state
> of being or a rest for the mind no such
> thing available . . .
> no I am not going
> to have you "in" for dinner nor am I going "out"
> I am going to eat alone for the rest of my life

For the author of *Lunch Poems* hardly a worse fate exists.

Russell Ferguson is correct to say that "O'Hara's very sense of self was constantly refracted through his relationships with other people": if this was so of the man, it remains so of the poems, whose most astonishing formal qualities almost always emerge from O'Hara's shimmering social life. He describes himself insistently in terms of what goes on around him, zipping back and forth between two present tenses, one for the eternal truths, one for the present moment, as in "John Button Birthday":

> You know how
> I feel about painters. I sometimes think poetry
> only describes.
> Now I have taken down the underwear
> I washed last night from the various light fixtures
> and can proceed.

O'Hara can flatten unwary readers with a blitz of proper nouns: Who is John Button? Who is Piedie Gimbel? Who are "Blanche Yurka, 'Bones'

Mifflin, Vera-Ellen and Alice Pearce"? The poems, Perloff declares, traverse "an elaborate network of cross-references to personal friends, artists, film stars, city streets, bars, exotic places, titles of books." Is it the poetry of an in-group, then? Not at its frequent best, though it is a poetry of what it feels like to be, and to want to be, part of an in group, or even at its center: we feel the excitement and the mental agility that allowed O'Hara to navigate the vast network, even though we may not know all its nodes. He was, as Lytle Shaw has suggested, a "coterie poet" in some of the ways that Donne was one. Like Donne, he became an energetic poet of intimacy. And like Donne's, his work is addressed both to a public, populous world (which includes his future readers) and to the poet's close friends (encouraging them to believe that they're the ones who matter). This tension between the demands of strangers and the needs of friends is one most of us know. "Chez William Kramps" has no other subject:

What I really love is people, and I don't much care whom
except for a few favorites who fit, which you understand.
It's like the sky being above the earth. It isn't above
the moon, is it? Nor do I like anyone but you and you.

Some academics make much of O'Hara's poems as gay code, which narrowly misses the point. When he wanted to write about sex, he did: "I suck off / every man in the Manhattan Storage & / Warehouse Co. Then, refreshed, again / to the streets!" To write like that he needed, and had, not a movement but an inner circle. The poem "Homosexuality" responds to James Ensor's painting *Self-Portrait with Masks:* "So we are taking off our masks, our we, and keeping / our mouths shut? as if we'd been pierced by a glance." The poem ends with bittersweet drama and public sex:

The good

love a park and the inept a railway station,
and there are the divine ones who drag themselves up

and down the lengthening shadow of an Abyssinian head
in the dust, trailing their long elegant heels of hot air

crying to confuse the brave "It's a summer's day
and I want to be wanted more than anything else in the world."

Written in 1954, "Homosexuality" was published only after the poet's
death—but so was most of his verse: he did not want to become, and
did not become, a poet (like Ginsberg) of public gay identity, nor a public poet of any kind.

O'Hara did want to be, and became, a wonderful poet of erotic
love—of promises, crushes, attractions of all sorts. "I am the least
difficult of men," "Meditations" not quite joked: "all I want is
boundless love." "Having a Coke with You" pursues the very traditional theme in which every alternative pleasure pales beside the
presence of the beloved: "Having a Coke With You / is even more fun
than going to San Sebastian, Irún, Hendaye, Biarritz, Bayonne / or
being sick to my stomach on the Traversá Gracia in Barcelona . . ."
The poems flirt with bathos as they flirt with their listeners, and are
saved from sentimentality by continual oddities. "Weather near St.
Bridget's Steeples" leaves us to decide whether it describes an atmosphere or a person or both:

You are so beautiful and trusting
lying there on the sky

through the leaves
you seem to be breathing softly
you look slightly nude, as if the clouds had parted

when the wind comes
you speak of an itch or a tickle

In the love poems (especially those dedicated to Vincent Warren), all of
O'Hara's inventions bear fruit, among them the subgenre he called the
"anthology," a string of one or two-line minipoems. "The Anthology
of Lonely Days" shuttles between the flirtatious and the wistful:

XII PAINTER
Meet you at the Frick please don't wear pants

XIII FRICK MUSEUM
I'm tired too, of receiving pants, and the pants always say they're tired
of being worn . . .

Such digressive, distracted, flirty poems might well be called celebrations of whim. Taken seriously, they celebrate the freedom to make
a range of affective and aesthetic decisions and associations. (Thus
Parisian "chestnut trees are refusing to bloom / as they should refuse
if they don't want to.") The "true point of contact," Ferguson concludes, "between New York School painting and O'Hara's poetry . . .
is to be found . . . in the idea of the spontaneous." And "Personism" is
both a display and a celebration of spontaneity: "If someone's chasing you down the street with a knife," O'Hara explains, "you just
run, you don't turn around and shout 'Give it up! I was a track star
for Mineola Prep' . . . As for measure and other technical apparatus,
that's just common sense: if you're going to buy a pair of pants you
want them to be tight enough so everyone will want to go to bed with
you." (Why, of course!)

Such prose—like so many of O'Hara's poems—reflects the poet's
exuberance even as it strives to entertain. Yet even the poems of emotional distress (like "Essay on Style") are, or try to be, quick on their
feet; they are full of startling cuts, asides, direct addresses to somebody
nearby (as if the poem really were a telephone), and streams of particu-
lars that don't seem to stand for anything. These effects produce what
Perloff describes as "the sense that we are eavesdropping on an ongoing conversation, that we are present." Alertness, "presence," immediacy, become not only pleasurable pursuits but ethical ones (as they
were for Walter Pater): alertness in life, to works of art, to weather, or
to one's friends has its formal equivalent in the shifts of attention and
enjambment that are found throughout the work:

Yes, it's necessary, I'll do
what you say, put everything
aside but what is here. The frail
instant needs us and the cautious

breath, so easily drowned in Liszt
or sucked out by a vulgar soprano.

Nothing of O'Hara's life—not a "frail instant"—seems excluded from his poetry: what isn't there in the poems wasn't there for him. Many of his poems (and most of his plays) have the odd effect of simulating writing that we can never quite judge because we know and like the author too well. And this effect is not just part of O'Hara's legend, but part of the work his style does on us.

O'Hara will remain best known for poems of extraordinary happiness, though he was quite as good, and more obviously powerful, with disappointment, apprehension, and pain. It has become a standard critical exercise to take an "I do this I do that" poem and show how its pile of minutiae defers or responds to some troubling event—"A Step Away from Them" (a frequent and apposite example) is mostly given up to the pleasant ephemera of lunchtime New York: "On / to Times Square, where the sign / blows smoke over my head . . ." Then the poem reaches its crucial lines: "First / Bunny died, then John Latouche, / then Jackson Pollock. But is the / earth as full as life was full, of them?" Only in O'Hara's Manhattan can life seem to go on undamaged by such losses. Understating deep grief and overemphasizing momentary pleasure or present company became for him not just a tonal technique but a way of life—even a way of thinking about one's own death:

When I die, don't come, I wouldn't want a leaf
to turn away from the sun—it loves it there.
There's nothing so spiritual about being happy
but you can't miss a day of it, because it doesn't last.

The happiness, social and otherwise, in O'Hara depended on his sense of belonging and his need to belong. In the same way, his feeling for moment-by-moment experience—and his ability to assimilate the poetry to an array of crisp encounters—depended on his sense of time passing, and heading toward death. He told his readers as much, in his poems and prose, in famous works like "Meditations" and in others less well known, among them his review of George Balanchine's *Roma* in 1955. That ballet, he wrote, was "something you may live with the dancers, a vital, social, exhausting, and vivacious exchange between you and them, like trying to keep up with an exciting conversation in a foreign language." The experience carried throughout, he added, "an undercurrent of poignancy and regret, the inexplicable melancholy of a place where you are feeling perfectly happy and do not yet know that your visa has just been cancelled. You want to belong to it, you want to stay."

Lorine Niedecker

Raking Leaves in New Madrid

"William Carlos Williams said that I am the Emily Dickinson of my time." So Lorine Niedecker (1903–1970) told a neighbor late in life, and so her readers have often felt, not without reason. Given her life of frequent isolation, and her gnomic poems, often in slippery rhyming stanzas, about traditionally "feminine" subjects (domestic work, family, local flora), it can be hard *not* to compare her to Dickinson. And yet her achievement recalls other masters as well, as Jenny Penberthy's majestic edition shows: if she belongs with Dickinson as a poet of inwardness, compression, and spiritual autobiography, she also belongs with Robert Burns as a poet of rural space, hardship, and humor, and with Williams himself as a maker of new kinds of line.

We can read her without knowing the life, but it helps: she spent most of it in the lake country of central Wisconsin, in and around Fort Atkinson and Blackhawk Island (not a true island but a peninsula on a lake). Her father fished and managed real estate; her mother, Daisy, went deaf during Lorine's childhood, and after two years at nearby Beloit College, Lorine moved back home to care for her. In 1928 Lorine married and went to work in the town library: two years later the job, and the marriage, ended. By then she had placed work in *Poetry*

(Chicago), but her serious apprenticeship began when she discovered the February 1931 "Objectivist" issue of *Poetry,* edited by Louis Zukofsky and featuring Williams, Pound, Basil Bunting, George Oppen, Charles Reznikoff, and Zukofsky himself. In 1933 Niedecker moved to New York to visit Zukofsky, learned all he had to teach her, became his lover, and nearly bore his child (he allegedly insisted on an abortion).

After travels between her home and Zukofsky's metropolis, Niedecker settled on Blackhawk Island, where she cared for Daisy, by then "quite deaf . . . religious and straitlaced," a friend of Lorine's recalled. Niedecker nicknamed her mother Bean Pole and compared her sayings to Mother Goose. In 1938 she joined the Federal Writers' Project, contributing to the Wisconsin installment in its now-famed series of guides to U.S. states. The project's left-wing documentary aesthetic influenced her first collection, *New Goose* (1946), which combined lessons from Williams, Zukofsky, and Dickinson with folk sayings and rural-populist protest: its interpolated quotations and dense rhyming would carry over into her later work.

Niedecker's distance from metropolitan centers and networks made it hard for her to publish what was already challenging (and uneven) poetry; her next project, the sequence *For Paul* (Zukofsky's young son), exists in several conflicting forms, of which only fractions appeared in her lifetime. In 1957 she took a job as Fort Atkinson's "hospital floor-washer" (her term). The next few years saw interest in her work from a transatlantic network of poets and small-press editors, including Ian Hamilton Finlay, Jonathan Williams, Bunting, and Cid Corman (later her literary executor). In 1963 Niedecker married Al Millen, a hard-drinking industrial painter she met when he bought land from her. United with Millen, Niedecker quit her hospital job and split her time between rural Wisconsin and Milwaukee. ("I live among the folk who couldn't understand and it's where I want to live," she wrote in 1966.) Those years brought new short poems, longer homages to historical figures (Thomas Jefferson, William Morris, Charles Darwin with his "holy / slowly / mulled over / matter"), and sequences about her own life and her region. A small-press collected poems, *T & G,* appeared in 1968; another, *My Life by Water,* was in press when she died.

The decades since have seen an academic industry, and a stack of poetic tributes, rise around a poet whose work largely remained hard to find. In 1985 Corman produced *The Granite Pail: The Selected Poems,* whose choices Donald Davie—a Niedecker admirer—excoriated as sentimental and simplifying. Williams's Jargon Press offered (also in 1985) another *Collected,* scarcely distributed and apparently filled with errors; the letters to Corman appeared in 1986. There followed *Niedecker and the Correspondence with Zukofsky* (1993) and *Lorine Niedecker: Woman and Poet* (1996), both assembled by Penberthy, who has devoted much of her life to compiling the *Collected Works,* the first chance to see all of Niedecker's writings more or less as she wrote them.

Niedecker's life was distinguished by its places and people, its interests and duties. Her poetry—like any significant poetry—is distinguished by its style, by the arrangements of sounds and meanings it offers, even or especially for readers who never cared much about central Wisconsin, nor about the objectivists as a group. Niedecker prized, as all the objectivists did, the deliberately fragmentary, the unfinished, the rough, and, sometimes, the twee; she differs from her peers (especially from her mentor, Zukofsky) in her small scales and her fidelity to prose sense. She is never programmatically difficult, but rarely spells everything out; "I can't be entirely content, it seems, without some puzzlement, some sharpness, a bit of word-play," she told Corman. Niedecker offers compression, precision, enticing omissions, and rhythmic balance; sometimes she offers local color and left-wing protest as well. Beyond all these, her work encompasses a sadness amounting perhaps to a tragic sense—a sense that the line of poets from Pound and Williams on would likely lack without her.

"Future studies," an early poem declared, "will throw much darkness on the home-talk." Niedecker's "home-talk" included the complaints of her mother and the speech of others around Fort Atkinson: together these became the basis of her first achievement. Niedecker's "folk project," Penberthy writes, began in 1936, when she (like lots of other writers) tried to represent working-class Americans and their practical misfortunes. She stood far apart from almost all those other writers in the semantic and aural subtleties with which she did so. Niedecker's stanzas recorded a way of life whose scrimps and economies matched her own concision:

> For sun and moon and radio
> farmers pay dearly;
> their natural resource: turn
> the world off early.

Is radio a "natural resource"? Is the sun? Both seem external, and hard to control, to these farmers, who claim—in the off-rhymed space between "dearly" and "early"—just one decision as "naturally" theirs: the choice of when to go to bed.

Resignation remained at least as essential to her outlook as protest: her ruminations and linguistic skills did nothing to set her apart from the neighbors who lacked them, whose daily tasks her family shared:

> The clothesline post is set
> yet no totem-carvings distinguish the Niedecker tribe
> from the rest; every seventh day they wash:
> worship sun; fear rain, their neighbors' eyes;
> raise their hands from ground to sky,
> and hang or fall by the whiteness of their all.

Elsewhere Niedecker routes her resignation, and her equal and opposite sense of frustration, through overheard working-class speakers: "That woman!—eyeing houses. / She's moved in on my own poor guy. / She held his hand and told him where to sign." The most explicitly political poems in *New Goose* take place *after* injustice has been done, presenting neither a struggle nor a debate but a fait accompli. Niedecker identifies herself with wronged figures—from jilted housewives to Native American leaders—whose wisdom proved of no practical use:

> Black Hawk held: In reason
> land cannot be sold,
> only things to be carried away,
> and I am old.

> Young Lincoln's general moved,
> pawpaw in bloom,

and to this day, Black Hawk,
reason has small room.

Niedecker's style explored a broad range of relations between its own carefully pleasing aural constraints and the painful, practical limits which gave her verse its subjects. Sometimes the formal logic of rhyme mimics the iron logic of economic necessity, a long-delayed closure bringing home the uglier closure of sustenance denied:

I was job-certified
to rake leaves
                    in New Madrid.

Now they tell me my girls
should support me again
and they're not out of debt
            from the last time they did.

Sometimes the poems present their fragile formalities as the verbal measure of their characters' resourcefulness or endurance. Both Niedecker's poems, and her people, have learned how to do more with less:

The land of four o'clocks is here
the five of us together
            looking for our supper.
Half past endive, quarter to beets,
seven milks, ten cents cheese,
            lost, our land, forever.

Along with household economies, Niedecker's later poems bring in facts from botany, ornithology, geology, limnology, other life sciences. Niedecker associated these close studies of small things, in her language as in her landscape, both with value-neutral observation and with tropes for democratic equality. One poem reads, in toto: "Asa Gray wrote Increase Lapham: / pay particular attention / to my pets, the grasses." If Whitman saw himself in a field of grass, Niedecker sees herself as one of the blades. Like the American botanist Asa Gray, like any expert on small flora, she challenged the thoughtless equation of size or power with transcendental or moral importance. A later poem about grass offers both a Jacob's ladder of internal rhymes, and a rare case in which Niedecker ventriloquizes figures of social authority:

> We physicians watch the juices rise
> > as we tend
> > to bend her
> toward the soft-blowing air.
> Girl, personal grass,
> > we saved you
> > waved you
> closer. Don't despise us
> > if we ask
> > or do not ask:
> what for?

These lines could depict a sick child in a country hospital, a farmer ruminating on profitless crops, or Niedecker's reflections on her own art in a world where poems subsist without visible consequence.

As a matter of literary history, Niedecker's isolation has been overstated. Much of *New Goose* appeared in *New Directions;* she saw print later in *Granta* and *Paris Review.* And yet, as a matter of emotion and disposition, she seems as isolated as any modern poet has been. Niedecker made that partly chosen isolation one of her principal subjects:

> What bird would light
> in a moving tree
> the tree I carry
> for privacy?

The poet Edwin Honig recalled that Niedecker "at home in Fort Atkinson . . . was closely identified with the rural scene—trees, foliage, birds, game, fish—more than with people." Her interests in evolution and biogeography let her compare human to nonhuman nature without prejudice to either side:

> Pigeons
> (I miss the gulls)
>
> mourn the loss
> of people
> no wild bird does

From the late 1930s to the late 1950s, most of her best work depends on rhymed quatrains and couplets; afterward she relied on triadic dimeters like those above, and on a five-line, partly rhymed stanza like a serious limerick. These three- and five-line units permitted new combinations for Niedecker's dense euphonies. A poem about fishermen concludes

> Sure they drink
> —full foamy folk—
> till asleep.
> The place is asleep
> on one leg in the weeds.

By the anticlimactic not-quite-rhyme in "weeds," both the drunk men and the drinking herons they resemble have called it a night.

Niedecker also depicted her life more directly; she depicted, too, the individuals with whom she shared it. One poem elides an unanswerable question with a brushstroke's description of Millen:

> Why can't I be happy
> in my sorrow
>
> my drinking man
> today
>
> my quiet
> tomorrow

Earlier poems depict Daisy, "the woman moored to this low shore by deafness," whose remarks make us feel bad for her, but worse for the daughter who tends her: "My man's got nothing but leaky boats. / My daughter, writer, sits and floats." A harsher poem adapts Daisy's last words:

> Death from the heart,
>   a thimble in her purse.
>
> "It's a long day since last night.
>   Give me space. I need
> floors. Wash the floors, Lorine!—
>   wash clothes! Weed!"

Niedecker wrote, more sparingly, of her father:

> He wished his only daughter
>   to work in the bank
>
> but he'd given her a source
>   to sustain her—
> a weedy speech,
>   a marshy retainer.

Words, her poems say, did sustain her, through the sometimes unrewarding years those poems describe, and through the broad range of attitudes these deliberately constricted poems present. "I carry / my clarity / with me," one poem decides; another evinces despair instead, offering, as its emphatic rhyming refrain, the sentence "I've spent my life on nothing." The lines below evidently stem from somebody's remark that Niedecker had done good, or been good, for her family:

> I'm good for people?—
> penetrating?—if you mean
>
> I'm rotting here—
> I'm an alewife
>
> the fish the seagull
> has no taste for

I die along the shore
and send a bad smell in

To match this atypically intemperate tone, Niedecker gives us an atypically unbalanced rhyme—*for* with *shore,* and *in* with the faraway
mean. If all these earlier works bring to mind pieces from a verse autobiography, "Paean to Place" let her fit the pieces together. One of her
last, and longest, poems (and Davie's favorite), "Paean" focuses on her
communion with nonhuman nature, and on her long-endured distance
from like minds:

Grew riding the river
Books
    at home-pier
        Shelley could steer
as he read

I was the solitary plover
a pencil
    for a wing-bone . . .

Seven year molt
for the solitary bird
    and so young
Seven years the one
dress

for town once a week
One for home
    faded blue-striped
as she piped
her cry

Niedecker's major claims on us are her short poems and sets of
poems (from *New Goose* to "Paean") about resignation, frustration,
careful attention, and patience in lives only partly lived. Those poems'
painstaking aural choices suggest a mind attuned to the subtlest of signals, acoustic, sociolinguistic, or ecological. Yet Niedecker's skills let

her write other sorts of poems, too. The historical sequences demonstrate scrupulous engagement with fact, though they sound less personal than her best work. Her shorter late poems on other people's lives, seeking both levity and a political bite, can discover a faux naïf sharpness very like Stevie Smith's:

Who was Mary Shelley?
What was her name
before she married?

She eloped with this Shelley
she rode a donkey
till the donkey had to be carried.

How did this tersely flexible style arise? "I went to school to Objectivism," Niedecker told one correspondent in 1967, "but now I often say *There is something more.*" A whimsical poem of 1951 lists modern heroes: H. D., Williams, Marianne Moore, Stevens, Zukofsky, cummings, Reznikoff. Later Niedecker namechecks Li Po and Basho: a list of writers important to her in the 1960s would also include Corman (whose Japanese interests perhaps sparked her own) and Bunting, whose life Niedecker celebrated in an agreeable eighteen-line "Ballad of Basil." The pre–*New Goose* work Penberthy has assembled, dating between 1928 and 1936, shows Niedecker trying all sorts of other programs, among them a rambling surrealism, unactable chunks of verse drama, and a lengthy "Christmas cacophony": like any good, practical modernist, she tries out a form, then goes on to try something else, learning from each eventually rejected kind. The most mysterious among these experiments must be "Next Year Or I Fly My Rounds Tempestuous" (1934): discovered in the Zukofsky archive in Texas, it consists of twenty-seven sheets from a calendar with mysterious, handwritten texts, one or two sentences each, pasted on: "Wade all life / backwards to its / source which / runs too far / ahead." Penberthy reproduces the actual pages, since "Next Year" is as much an artist's book as it is a set of poems.

Much of Niedecker's mature verse consists of sequences that she several times dismembered and reassembled; some remained in manuscript at her death. Other poems and sequences exist in multiple, overlapping published versions. Penberthy's foreword outlines, and her 102 pages of notes spell out, the textual detective work her edition has entailed; she also provides a useful capsule biography, though some admirers may scratch their heads at mention of Niedecker's allegedly "anti-authorial practice." (Penberthy's effort to honor Niedecker's wishes both about individual poems and about sequences means that some poems appear twice in similar versions.) Penberthy also appends most of Niedecker's surviving efforts in prose: these include a memoir of a generous uncle who failed in local politics; a radio play made from Faulkner's *As I Lay Dying;* and short, snappy, fictionalized memoirs of her workplaces. The prose matters mostly because this poet wrote it, though her long sketch of her uncle sticks in the memory on its own. The prose also includes these stray sentences, prose memorials—though her verse is memorial enough—to her meticulous linguistic practice, and to the attentive life it records: "Often John as a boy was not to be disturbed. . . . Johnny would take a boat, paddle out and lie in it. He would look at a tree in a certain light; his sensations the moment he looked formed the tree, he thought, and no one else would find that tree to be just what he found it."

William Carlos Williams

They Grow Everywhere

"The painters have paid too much attention to the ism and not enough to the painting," William Carlos Williams wrote in 1928. Something similar could be said about Williams's own critics: since his death in 1963, attention to his theories and to his life has been getting in the way of his poems. With Williams, more than the usual number of isms and caricatures need to be cleared away. There is, for example, Williams the spontaneous man who wrote by the seat of his pants, the grandfather (for good or ill) of the Beats; Williams the comical minimalist, who proved that a note on the fridge could be read as a poem; Williams the modernist, a foil for experimental painters, or for his difficult friend Ezra Pound. More recently, we have had Williams the avant-garde sentinel, dislocating sense and meaning in the manner of Gertrude Stein, and Williams the multiculturalist, pitting his Spanish Caribbean heritage against a Eurocentric world. Williams the doctor-poet proved that words can heal; Williams the literary nationalist declared in 1957: "I don't speak English but the American idiom." All these Williamses exist; all of them are to some extent distractions, robbing many subtle poems of the attention they deserve. "It isn't what the poet says that counts," Williams wrote in 1944, "but what he makes." We have yet to see fully what he made.

Williams was born in 1883 and grew up in northern New Jersey, speaking Spanish at home and "the American idiom" everywhere else. His businessman father, of English descent, grew up on St. Thomas in the Virgin Islands; his mother, a frustrated painter, came from Puerto Rico. After high school in Switzerland and New York City, Williams took a degree in medicine at the University of Pennsylvania, where he met Hilda Doolittle (later H.D.) and Pound. In 1912, after a difficult two-year courtship, he married the shy and practical Florence (Flossie) Herman. During the same years he established a medical practice in his hometown of Rutherford; he was also writing bad Keatsian verse, some of it printed in *Poems* (1909). Spurred by Pound and contemporary visual art, he began to form his poetic style during the 1910s; soon he was mixing with Marianne Moore, Mina Loy, Alfred Kreymborg, Alfred Stieglitz, and other modernist artists and writers in Manhattan. His local practice thrived (he later specialized in pediatrics), but still he found time during the next few decades to produce a vast body of work: poems, short poems, short fiction, novels, plays, essays, and manifestos, along with a range of unclassifiable prose.

Despite his reliance on small or fugitive presses, Williams won coterie acclaim by the end of the 1920s; after World War II, with much wider support from critics and trade publishers, he became a preeminent influence on all sorts of American writers. The young Allen Ginsberg paid him homage and copied his style, while Robert Lowell looked to Williams for a freer, more democratic manner than his rivals could offer. Although he remains an acquired taste in Britain, Williams's position in American poetry, at least, seems assured.

That position rests, above all else, on one achievement. Between 1914 and 1923, Williams invented an entirely new way of making and hearing verse lines. He was able to do without conventional meters, rhymes, and stanzas because he had made his own tools. Chief among these was enjambment, in all its kinds and degrees: phrases and clauses splay, leap, or crawl across line and stanza breaks, in deliberate violation of natural pauses and syntactic boundaries. Some poems play frequently enjambed lines against end-stopped stanzas; others build up successively stronger enjambments in order to emphasize one big stop. Williams's readers learn to attend to other devices, too: the new or repeated stress patterns in each line; line lengths, and changes in them;

punctuation, of which Williams became an unrecognized master; and the modulations of speed and emphasis that accompany changes in syntactic direction. The best book about his poetry, Stephen Cushman's *William Carlos Williams and the Meaning of Measure,* concentrates on his lines and his line breaks; almost all the acoustic discoveries in American enjambment-based free verse—from Creeley and Niedecker to Ammons, Armantrout, Kasischke, and Graham (though not, for example, the end-stopped free verse of James Wright)—proceed, so to speak, from Williams's prescription pad.

"To a Poor Old Woman" shows how Williams's line breaks work: the woman is "munching a plum on / the street," and holds a bag of plums in her other hand:

> They taste good to her
> They taste good
> to her. They taste
> good to her

They taste good to her (you might not like them); they taste good (not merely adequate); she tastes them, taking them into her body rather than merely contemplating them. Williams then offers further sensory evidence:

> You can see it by
> the way she gives herself
> to the one half
> sucked out in her hand
>
> Comforted
> a solace of ripe plums
> seeming to fill the air
> They taste good to her

Just outside the frame of the plum lies the women's poverty, the whole social world, for which each bite offers its small solace; against that world, Williams's poem promises a sympathy, and a sensory immediacy, that other kinds of poetry may lack.

Williams's aural tool kit suited motion: cars, trains, pedestrians, runners, fire engines, gulls, robins, swallows, "tideless waves thundering slantwise against / strong embankments," a sheet of cardboard in the wind, a "bargeman raking sand / upon his barge"—all these move through Williams's poems in ways his lines make vivid. The same aural tools made it possible for him to represent perception itself. Many poets notice bits of the world, but Williams's technique allowed him to show how we notice things, how fast, through what details, and in what order. Stanzas follow the movement of eye and mind from road to roadside, through "leafless white birches" to a munitions plant, or to the "beauty, / at the swamp's center: the / dead-end highway, abandoned / when the new bridge went in." "Spring Strains" shows how an observer might scan a young tree:

>   tense blue-grey twigs
> slenderly anchoring them down, drawing
> them in—
>
>   two blue-grey birds chasing
> a third struggle in circles, angles,
> swift convergings to a point that bursts
> instantly!

His rhythmic faculties drive anthology pieces like "The Dance," whose dactyls skip happily over its line breaks:

> In Brueghel's great picture, The Kermess,
> the dancers go round, they go round and
> around, the squeal and the blare and the
> tweedle of bagpipes, a bugle and fiddles
> tipping their bellies . . .

Tour de force poems like "The Dance" or "To a Poor Old Woman" can train us to hear subtler effects elsewhere. "Flowers by the Sea" appeared in three versions between 1930 and 1935; here is the last, and best:

> When over the flowery, sharp pasture's
> edge, unseen, the salt ocean

lifts its form—chicory and daisies
tied, released, seem hardly flowers alone

but color and the movement—or the shape
perhaps—of restlessness, whereas

the sea is circled and sways
peacefully upon its plantlike stem

The one-sentence poem opens with temporal progress—when the ocean lifts, chicory and daisies seem—but ends with logical contrast: flowers seem restless whereas the sea sways peacefully. The grammatical surprise evokes the approach and retreat of the sea it depicts.

In a poem of 1948, Williams called himself a "writer, at one time hipped on / painting"; elsewhere he remembered, "I might easily have become a painter." Instead Williams surrounded himself with painters, especially during the 1910s and 1920s, finding allies among the American moderns—Charles Demuth, Charles Sheeler, Marsden Hartley. Williams's poems can be classified as kinds of paintings: landscapes, seascapes, "genre poems" (in the sense of "genre painting"), still lifes, domestic interiors, street scenes, portraits, even abstractions. "Young Sycamore," as the scholar Bram Dijkstra has shown, describes Alfred Stieglitz's photograph "Spring Showers": the poem's attenuated lines follow the tree from its wet pavement "into the air,"

dividing and waning
sending out
young branches on
all sides—

hung with cocoons—
it thins
till nothing is left of it
but two

eccentric knotted
twigs
bending forward
hornlike at the top

Williams treats his single sentence as the young tree's trunk, "sending out" bits of detail as it strains toward its "eccentric" end.

"I've met a hell of a lot more of all kinds of people than you'll ever get your eyes on," Williams said reproachfully to Pound in 1938, "and I've known them inside and out in ways you'll never know." Medicine offered him access of a sort that few major poets have had to different registers of speech and kinds of life: he used what he learned, and what he overheard, in striking short stories and in talk-based poems. "Portrait of a Woman in Bed" devotes two pages to a patient's speech and gestures—the gap between stanzas mimes the gap between her sick body and her energetic mind:

> There's my things
> drying in the corner:
> that blue skirt
> joined to the grey shirt—
>
> I'm sick of trouble!
> Lift the covers
> if you want me
> and you'll see
> the rest of my clothes—

The aesthetic attention he demanded that we give to the landscapes of poverty—to factories, attics, weeds, broken glass—could not be separated from the moral demands made by these landscapes and by the people who lived in them. "The Forgotten City" recalls a drive through a "curious and industrious" working-class neighborhood, and ends by asking:

> How did they get
> cut off this way from representation in our
> newspapers and other means of publicity
> when so near the metropolis, so closely
> surrounded by the familiar and the famous?

Left politics flowered in Williams's poems even before the 1930s. He admired Soviet communism, early on, because it seemed to express the ideal of human equality: at the same time he refused to take orders, asking in "The Men" (1928), "Wherein is Moscow's dignity / more than Passaic's dignity?" (He wrote poems and essays, too, for liberal causes: Al Smith's 1928 presidential campaign, aid for Republican Spain, monetary reform.)

Williams loved declarations and slogans about what he meant to do and why. At the same time, he was too attentive to his own procedures to remain happy with the explanations he offered, and so his poems, his essays, and even his autobiographical writings kept amending and unfolding his earlier statements, among them his now familiar phrase "no ideas but in things." "The Poet and His Poems" (1939) strings together several slogans until it arrives at this:

> It should
>
> be a song—made of
> particulars, wasps,
> a gentian—something
> immediate, open
>
> scissors, a lady's
> eyes—the particulars
> of a song waking
> upon a bed of sound.

Surprise, specificity, ordinariness, new aural shapes, a bit of household detritus: such a verse manifesto portrays much of what Williams tried to do. It attempts, too, to show order emerging from a neglected realm—the emergence, not the final synthesis. "I've always had the feeling that good things happen to me in March," Williams remarks in one of many marginalia reproduced in the editors' notes to his two-volume *Collected Poems*. He loves to depict, or predict, or invoke advents and startings out—the coming of spring, sex, flower buds, parturition. Enjoying beginnings, distrusting conventional sequence, Williams loves to interrupt himself, to have the pleasure of beginning again. These interruptions also show his (angry or melancholic) sense that no completion, no fruition, can satisfy the hopes that beginnings stir in him. His social conscience and his desire to depict new births merged in brilliant, emblematic poems about small, scrappy, flowering things, from the famous first poem of *Spring and All* ("By the road to the contagious hospital") to the 1935 lyric "To Be Hungry Is to Be Great":

> The small, yellow grass-onion,
> spring's first green, precursor
> to Manhattan's pavements, when
> plucked as it comes, in bunches,
> washed, split and fried in
> a pan, though inclined to be
> a little slimy, if well cooked
> and served hot on rye bread
> is to beer a perfect appetizer—
> and the best part
> of it is they grow everywhere.

Enacting the early appearance of a common plant, spreading from choppy initial lineation into a cleanly wrought last phrase, the poem affirms the equal dignity of persons—and shares a cheap, useful recipe.

Williams's moments of frustration or despair (and there are a lot of them) are moments of spring baffled or held back, of failed birth, of winter prolonged. Such moments control the masterfully disorienting 1928 sequence *The Descent of Winter,* written on shipboard and focused on self-doubt in middle age:

> There are no perfect waves—
> Your writings are a sea
> full of misspellings and
> faulty sentences. Level. Troubled
> . . . .
> This is the sadness of the sea—
> waves like words, all broken—
> a sameness of lifting and falling mood.

A 1944 poem (later expanded) finds figures for Williams's frustrations in "The Clouds," whose "tragic outlines" resemble

> the bodies of horses, mindfilling—but
> visible! against the invisible; actual against
> the imagined and the concocted; unspoiled by hands
> and unshaped also by them but caressed by sight only,
> moving among them, not that that propels
> the eyes from under, while it blinds:

> —upon whose backs the dead ride, high!
> undirtied by the putridity we fasten upon them—
> South to north, for this moment distinct and undeformed,
> into the no-knowledge of their nameless destiny.

Clouds excite him because they perpetually assume new shapes. At the same time they suit his bleaker moods, when he feels that human consciousness spoils what it encounters, so that something can stay "undeformed" only if it is as yet unformed.

Williams knew his own limits, took the measure of his own frustrations, as well as any writer ever has. He kicked, too, against the limits imposed on him by bad luck with publishers: "excellence of any sort is a tree." *The Descent of Winter* continues: "when the leaves fall the tree is naked and the wind thrashes it till it howls it cannot get a book published it can only get poems into certain magazines." (Williams had trouble finding a reliable publisher until 1937, when James Laughlin's fledgling New Directions made him one of its central authors.) Williams could be sensitive, too, about his apparent distaste, or incapacity, for step-by-step arguments: he called himself (in the 1948 poem "Russia") "a poet, uninfluential, with no skill / in polemics—my friends tell me I lack / the intellect."

Yet as a poet he displayed all the intellect he needed—one given to discoveries; short, sharp explanations; single insights; intuitive correspondences and aphorism: "What's wrong with American literature? / You ask me? How much do I get?" His focus on sensory detail and spoken immediacy made it hard for him to carry off extended analysis (of politics or of anything else). Yet the same qualities suited him to political rant, nowhere more so than in "Impromptu: The Suckers" (1927), a triumph of venom and sarcasm that blames all of America, himself included, for the execution of Sacco and Vanzetti:

> Take it out in vile whiskey, take it out
> in lifting your skirts to show your silken
> crotches; it is this that is intended.
> You are it. Your pleas will always be denied.
> You too will always go up with the two guys,
> scapegoats to save the Republic and
> especially the State of Massachusetts. The
> Governor says so and you ain't supposed
> to ask for details—
>
> . . . .
>
> It's no use, you are Americans, just the dregs.
> It's all you deserve. You've got the cash,
> what the hell do you care? You've got
> nothing to lose. You are inheritors of a great
> tradition. My country right or wrong!

Williams's stand against inherited, restrictive forms and his energetic, almost disorientingly large output have elicited comparisons with D. H. Lawrence; when Lawrence died, Williams wrote a substantial elegy. Like Lawrence, he liked to think of himself as breaking society's rules, and like Lawrence, he could rely on unfortunate ideas about sexual difference: man as form, woman as matter; man as intellect, woman as feeling. "Some self-defense seems to rise out of a woman," he complained to one interviewer (a woman), "when a man tries to understand her."

And yet Williams did try not just to understand sexual difference in general but (more fruitfully) to understand himself, and to hear the particular men and women he encountered. Sometimes, his poems of sexual love and lust simply give accurate portraits of his roving eye. He does better, though—as he seems to have realized—when he talks about lust, love, or marriage more subtly. In "The Act" (1948), he rewrites "Gather ye rosebuds" as a conversation between a man and his wife:

> There were the roses, in the rain.
> Don't cut them, I pleaded.
>   They won't last, she said.
> But they're so beautiful
>   where they are.
> Agh, we were all beautiful once, she
>   said,
> and cut them and gave them to me
>   in my hand.

Beside the short poems of (say) Robert Creeley, who learned so much from Williams's attention to speech, Williams's best short poems look not like fragments but like classically compressed wholes. "The Red Wheelbarrow," on which so much depends, is a famous (perhaps too famous) example, but nobody seems to have noticed "The Hurricane":

> The tree lay down
> on the garage roof
> and stretched, You
> have your heaven,
> it said, go to it.

Isn't this tiny poem (among other things) a snapshot of Williams's suburbs, an emblem for secularists, and a demonstration of how it sounds (curt, confident) to take disaster in one's stride?

The pleasure in reading the first hundred pages or so of Williams's two-volume *Collected Poems* lies in watching his style slowly come into being. Because there is so much apprentice work, and because his style finally made such a break with the past, it can be almost unnerving to track the transition—like watching a fish turn into a bird. Volume I skips *Poems* (1909) to begin with *The Tempers* (1913), in which Williams moved on from bad Keats to bad Blake, bad early Pound, bad troubadours in translation: "Now the little by-path / Which leadeth to love / Is again joyful with its many." The early, long poem "The Wanderer" has the thirty-year-old Williams asking, "How shall I be a mirror to this modernity?" A feminine presence provides a partial answer, leading him through a Whitmanesque city of strikes and wharves and citizens, "quartered beeves / And barrels and milk cans and crates of fruit!"

His earliest effective poems stick more or less to the dictates of imagism, visualizing short scenes and colorful objects, and sometimes paying comic tribute to Eastern precedents: "O my grey hairs! / You are truly white as plum blossoms." Sometimes, as in "Stillness" (1916), Williams complains that these imagist rules will not let him to do more:

Heavy white rooves
of Rutherford
sloping west and east
under the fast darkening sky:

What have I to say to you
that you may whisper it to them
in the night?

The poems from about 1916 to 1921 show Williams gradually forging his flexible, energetically enjambed modes from the raw material of ordinary modernist free verse. They reveal, too, a cluster of characteristic images, along with his yearning to show that he really appreciates them. Early spring, with its profusion of petals, buds, mud, weeds; automobiles; girls and women of all ages; "the houses / of the very poor," and the detritus around them: "old chicken wire, ashes"—"No one / will believe this / of vast import to the nation."

The last decade of poetic work—which begins in 1952, when he suffered his first stroke—raises its own questions. He stopped writing for almost a year and then introduced a new form, a three-step line characterized by what he called the "variable foot." The poems that resulted were far more abstract, and more ruminative, than anything he had written before: this style must have seemed to Williams a way to avoid the dependence on description, and on other people's voices, which had marked his older work. Description and ventriloquism, though, were his strengths: without them, the late poems grew weakly sententious, or mushy ("No defeat is made up entirely of defeat—since / the world it opens is always a place / formerly / unsuspected"), or artless in their honesty. Williams wrote that such essayistic poems as "To Daphne and Virginia" gave him "the power / to free myself / and speak of it," and some of them are thoughtful personal documents— one example is the long, tender love poem to his wife, "Asphodel, That Greeny Flower." But none of these works achieves the force, the status as actions, or the verbal assurance that marked Williams's verse from the 1920s through the 1940s. His real powers returned in *Pictures from Brueghel* (1962), whose short, halting poems—many based on paintings—sought "to re-establish / the image," to "rekindle / the violet." "The Chrysanthemum," one of his last and best emblem poems, explains the awe it enacts:

how shall we tell
the bright petals
from the sun in the
sky concentrically

crowding the branch
save that it yields
in its modesty
to that splendor?

V

The Elliptical Poets

"The self was once," I said, "a great, great
Glory." "Oh, sure. But is it still?"
　　　　　　—James Merrill, "The Book of Ephraim"

　　　　　　Is there a new way of looking—
valences and little hooks—inevitabilities, proba-
bilities? It flaps and slaps. Is this body the one
I know as me? How private these words?
　　　　　　—Jorie Graham, "Notes on the Reality of the Self"

If the impersonal made personal isn't personal, then what is there?
　　　　　　—Karen Volkman, "Infidel"

Stephen Dobyns's best poem shows a man and his dog staring into a refrigerator at dawn, looking for "answers to what comes next, and how to like it." In 1997 a British editor asked me to introduce recent American poets to British readers—in effect, to open the poetry fridge: I found myself surprised by how many tactics, strategies, and attitudes most younger poets I liked turned out to share.

Where have younger poets found themselves? Of the three masters and influences into which the scholar Vernon Shetley divided the poetry world of the 1980s, James Merrill is no longer with us (though his followers are). Elizabeth Bishop has become part of the landscape, no more a direct influence on the best new writing than Whitman. And John Ashbery is everywhere, ramifying, still. Language writing has become for many younger writers less phalanx than resource, revealing a "Stein tradition" of dissolve and fracture that less radical work can use. Epistemology and theories of language—how we know what we know, how we say it— have become as central to contemporary lyric as psychoanalysis in the late 1950s, myth and politics in the late '60s; partly in consequence, poets who invoke the line of Stevens, or of Bishop, feel free to get odder, harder, while poets who consider themselves Stein's followers sound friendlier than they once could. And Jorie Graham has become the unavoidable presence in other people's styles, partly because she long taught at Iowa and gets lots of press, but mostly because her cinematic, intellective *The End of Beauty* (1987) established her as the best poet of her contexts, the one her contemporaries have to think about.

The most exciting younger poets have read Graham *and* do not imitate her; like her, they treat voice and self and identity neither as givens nor as illusions, but as problems, phenomena, poems can explore and limn. These poets share goals and tones and attitudes, and the best way to explain *what* they share is, I fear, to coin a term for a school.

I therefore introduce the Elliptical poets. Elliptical poets are always hinting, punning, or swerving away from a never-quite-unfolded backstory; they are easier to process in parts than in wholes. They believe provisionally in identities (in one—or in at least one—"I" per poem), but they suspect the I's they invoke: they admire disjunction and confrontation, but they know how a little can go a long way. Ellipticists seek the authority of the rebellious; they want to challenge their readers, violate decorum, surprise or explode assumptions about what belongs in a poem or what matters in life, and to do so while meeting traditional lyric goals. Their favorite attitudes are desperately extravagant, or tough-guy terse, or defiantly childish: they don't believe in, or seek, a judicious tone. (This rebelliousness and this provisionality—the sense that they might change, that nothing they say counts as final— make many of these poets sound adolescent, or give them the cultural position of youth: why that is so, and how it came to be so, is a long story, one fit for another place.)

Elliptical poets like insistent, bravura forms, forms that can shatter and recoalesce, forms with repetends—sestinas, pantoums, or fantasias on single words, as in Liam Rector's "Saxophone":

You and I, our money. Their money.
Our pleasure and fist full of money.
Laughter over money, serious laughter
over money. Too much, too little,
fluid money. The saxophone, color of wheat,
purchased through Hock Shop money, saxophone
splitting the night, our air, blowing money.

Although he later preferred a clearer approach, Rector's harsh, inci-
sive, occasionally baffling *The Sorrow of Architecture* (1984) may be
the first Elliptical book. (Dear publishers: bring that book back into
print for us, please.) Rector's anger stems from his Brechtian interest in
work, debt, and wages, in what he later called "the ongoing circulation /
Of art and money . . . the hunger, // The hunt, the eat." He may have
invented the fractured sestina forms that pervade poems like "Driving
November," a three-page work with the proportionate strength of a
crime spree film:

We are driving November we turned
October several towns back. We applaud
the passing of all that is innocent we inherit
the road as it is here. You speak of habit
as if things do not change I speak
of sweet repetition. We are driving November, from harm.

Ellipticals love poems that declare "I am X, I am Y, I am Z," where
X, Y, and Z are incompatible things. Mark Levine specializes in such
poems, and shares Rector's interests in money, locality, and work:
Levine's first book, *Debt* (1992), is ellipticism at its most aggressive,
rife with allusion and disillusion. His punky "Work Song" proves him
Berryman's legatee:

I am Henri, mouth full of soda crackers.
I live in Toulouse, which is a piece of cardboard.
Summers the Mayor paints it blue, we fish in it.
Winters we skate on it. Children are always
drowning or falling through cracks. Parents are distraught

but get over it. It's easy to replace a child.
Like my parents' child, Henri.

The self Henri presents seems at once 2-D, replicable, disposable, even staged—the efficient result of a discourse—and yet he sounds like a real speaker, with an explosive will of his own.

Elliptical poets treat literary history with irreverent involvement. They create inversions, homages, takeoffs on old or "classic" poems: they also adapt old subgenres—aubade, elegy, verse letter, and especially ode. Almost all write good prose poems. Lucie Brock-Broido is the most ambitious, most tradition-conscious Elliptical. Her *The Master Letters* (1995) quarries Dickinson, Donne, Romeo and Juliet; exclaims "I am angel, addict, catherine wheel—a piece of work / On fire"; specifies, "At your feet I am a shoemaker's apprentice, / Toxic in a long day of fumes"; titles a poem "You Can't Always Get What You Want," and opens it with backtalk from *Lolita:* "Light of your loins— I have been to the ruins & come back with art." Her prose poems boast menageries of similes—"senseless as crates of fish stacked glimmering, one-eyed & blank, one atop the other of them." The best of Brock-Broido's many personae may be Anne Boleyn, in a poem called (after Wyatt) "And Wylde for to Hold":

Lack of water, lack of light,
Lack of heat, lack of bedding, I should go

On this way forever; it is my wont to go.
Tonight—the wind will be high in its scaffolding,

On the strength. I will listen for its habit
Especially about the throat like an Elizabethan cuff

At the crude nest of the mouth. Our bed
Will be lined with shredded bark from sycamore & hair.

Let them lie broad awake in their nest, scissoring.
None will fly.

Ellipticals caress the technical: there is, as Rebecca Reynolds puts it, "less / [she] can touch now / that isn't technical and reluctant." They mix their affections with alienations. Susan Wheeler's *Smokes* (1998) presents her sometimes as a movie star, sometimes as a "hapless stand-in scripter" with an "impedimented personality," fleeing or seeking love or fame. She, too, makes jangling leaps from low to high diction; likes to interrupt herself; writes "I am X, I am Y" poems; and mixes up old, high allusions with TV and Barbies. Her special talent lies in her kidnapping of familiar forms, as in "Shanked on the Red Bed," an update, perhaps, of Louis MacNeice's "Bagpipe Music"; to read her poems through can be exhilarating—or dizzying, depending on whether you are willing to provide for yourself the transitions and rationales that she leaves out.

We could say the same thing about any of these poets, since Ellipticals almost always delete transitions: one thought, one impression, tailgates another. So did Eliot, Berryman, Hejinian; but the Elliptical fast-forward and cutup is far less likely to represent speech, or stream of consciousness, or a program for breaking up subjects and systems; instead it's performance, and demonstration—if you can hear me through all this noise, I must be real. (Thus neither Rosmarie Waldrop nor Michael Palmer, nor Albert Goldbarth, Frank Bidart, Charles Wright—to name some talented older poets who care for epistemology and disjunction—could count as Elliptical: the first two work too far from an "I" in a real world, the other three too unproblematically close.) C. D. Wright is expert at laying down a series of hints, or residues, of experience, making readers discover what happened, find their way through to her. Wright began publishing in the late 1970s, but her first fully Elliptical work is *String Light* (1991), full of detailed tenderness for, and scorched regret about, her native Arkansas. She, too, has a rebellious "I" poem, "Personals":

> In this humidity, I make repairs by night. I'm not one
> among millions who saw Monroe's face
> in the moon. I go blank looking at that face.
> If I could afford it I'd live in hotels. I won awards
> in spelling and the Australian crawl. Long long ago.
> Grandmother married a man named Ivan. The men called him
> Eve. Stranger, to tell the truth, in dog years I am up there.

Wright's technique of hinting allows her in *Tremble* (1996) to make terse, radiant sketches of bodily, erotic histories, "Key Episodes from an Earthly Life": the poem of that name begins "As surely as there are crumbs on the lips / of the blind   I came for a reason." It ends:

> Around this time of year   especially evening
> I love everything   I sold enough eggs
>
> To buy a new dress   I watched him drink the juice
> of our beets   And render the light liquid
>
> I came to talk you into physical splendor
> I do not wish to speak to your machine

Elliptical poets' challenging unease, their resolve neither to play by the rules nor to scrap them, extends from self and voice, through form and tradition, to grammar. "Syntax is the social aspect of language," wrote the British poet and critic Donald Davie, who remained, almost throughout his long life, ambivalent about the modernist forms that dispensed with it; the elliptical self, uneasily social, grows only uneasily grammatical—each distortion or shock to the syntax means, usually, shock to the self. Brock-Broido nouns verbs and dispenses with prepositions throughout the harrowing "Am Moor," an "I am X, I am Y" poem that manages to ditch the relevant pronoun: it begins, "Am lean against. / Am the heavy hour // Hand at urge, / At the verge of one." Anne Carson's short poems from the 1990s belong (more clearly than her book-length poems from the same years) within the Elliptical force field. Syntactical slips and breaks and unaccompanied suggestion do all the work, for example, in Carson's "Sleepchains":

> Who can sleep when she—
> hundreds of miles away I feel that vast breath
> fan her restless decks.
> Cicatrice by cicatrice
> all the links
> rattle once.
> Here we go mother on the shipless ocean.
> Pity us, pity the ocean, here we go.

Want an Elliptical long poem? Try Wright's book-length *Just Whistle* or her *Deepstep Come Shining*. Or read Claudia Rankine's *The End of the Alphabet* (1998), whose near-impenetrable vignettes and meta-analyses make it a sort of *Modern Love* for the post-Graham generation:

> Who distributes the live or die
> after juice is refused, the egg is fried?
> Faced with its straggering number of runny noses
> the day begins, begins again, talks above
> the motor left running.

But Ellipticist long poems are rare as cubist murals (Rankine herself has since moved on to more-or-less-discursive prose): Ellipticist poems treat self and voice more or less as synthetic cubism treated shapes and things, and the poems' necessarily dense, busy surfaces make it hard for them to gain the momentum or clarity long forms can need.

Is Ellipticism a school or a zeitgeist? It's both: let Wheeler and Brock-Broido stand for the school part, the learnable technique, at (respectively) its brittlest and most irritable, and its most extravagantly lyrical. (Both now have epigones—I won't list them—all over journals I like.) Then let the drifts in August Kleinzahler's poetry show what a wider net might hold. Kleinzahler is an Elliptical in his all-inclusiveness, his casual refusals of authority, his jarring jumps from elevation to slang. Kleinzahler's wry, Californian cadences can encompass anything he sees or hears—the sun from a plane, headlines, Thom Gunn, dogwoods, potato chips, DTs. A ballet he watches prompts "Sapphics in Traffic," which begins, "Festinating rhythm's bothered her axis"; where Larkin wrote "Lines on a Young Lady's Photograph Album," Kleinzahler writes the semirhymed, half-nostalgic quatrains of "Ruined Histories":

Ah, Little Girl Destiny, it's sprung a leak
and the margins are bleeding themselves away.
You and I and the vase and stars won't stay still.
Wild, wild, wild—kudzu's choked the topiary.

Looks like your history is about to turn
random and brutal, much as an inch of soil or duchy.
Not at all that curious hybrid you had in mind:
Jane Austen, high-tech and a measure of Mom.

Thylias Moss belongs to the same zeitgeist, flaunts ellipticism at
its most tonally risky and socially conscious: her registers include
Blakean outrage, African American preaching cadences, and disarm-
ing backtalk. Moss swerves between wisecracks and credos: her uneasy speakers, girls and adults, ground their defiance in local events, as
in "When I Was 'Bout Ten We Didn't Play Baseball":

> It's hot. We might
> sleep on the porch. Next year we really will have it
> screened so we won't ever have to respect mosquitos
> again. I listen to all the emergencies,
> sirens of course, the Cadillac horns of the wedding, a mother
> new to the area calling home her children
> forgetting not to call the names of the ones who don't come
> home anymore on nights like these when all it has to be
> is summer and they're cared for better. The heat does hug.
> It isn't shy and proper. My mother wouldn't want me
> to play with it.

Isn't this poem about a coherent character in a well-defined scene? Yes:
but what a character! (What sentences!) And listen to "Easter" (this is
the whole poem), from Moss's best and strangest book, *Last Chance
for the Tarzan Holler* (1998):

> Dr. Frankenstein feeds his son voltage, juice
> fires up the hormones
>
> on the day of unkillable testosterone
>
> while Mary and Martha heed their spices,
> their urges to preserve, not dulled by the impropriety of the kitchen
> in which slaughter lambs and chickens.

Fragmentation, jumpiness, audacity; performance, grammatical oddity; rebellion, voice, some measure of closure: Ellipticist.

All these extravagant, edgy writers want poems as volatile as real life; they want to remake the self, to pick up their pieces after its (supposed) dissolution. So do their peers. Most Ellipticals are (as of 2009) between forty and sixty, and found their real styles after 1986. If they have a geographical center, it's New York City (though several have taught, or studied, at the University of Michigan). Ellipticals invoke as precedents Dickinson, Berryman, Ashbery, sometimes Auden. All want to convey *both* metaphysical challenge *and* recognizable, seen or tasted, detail. Ellipticals reject: poems written in order to demonstrate theories; scene painting and prettiness as its own end; slogans; authenticity and wholeheartedness; mysticism; straight-up narrative; and extended abstraction (their most obvious difference from Graham). Ellipticals are uneasy about (less often, hostile to) inherited elites and privileges, but they are not populists, and won't write down to, or connect the dots for, their readers; their difficulty conveys respect.

Is Ellipticism just a name for Goldilocks's favorite porridge, neither too dry and challenging nor too cohesively sweet? Maybe; but it seems to me that these poets, whether defined narrowly (poems that feel and sound like Wheeler's, like Levine's) or broadly (as far as Kleinzahler and Moss) share techniques, expectations, reactions, goals. Time will find and polish the best Elliptical verse, as it has with prevailing styles from the Tribe of Ben to the allies of Auden. I wish I had space to quote the bedazzled, lyrical prose poet Killarney Clary; Forrest Gander's careful sequences; Karen Volkman's *Crash's Law*; April Bernard's jittery *Blackbird Bye-Bye*; Reynolds's first book, *Daughter of the Hangnail*; the comic, tender botanizings and "fractal" forms of Alice Fulton; and the Ellipticals' overseas counterparts, Australia's John Tranter, who often visits the United States, and Britain's Mark Ford. For now, these uneasy, very contemporary, difficult poets have written a heap of at-least-pretty-good poems. Vaunting or angry, precise but not pedantic, hip but rarely jaded, they are in all the best (and a few worse) senses, what comes next.

Postscript (2004)

People who follow the arts like to talk about schools; often they prefer talking about schools and trends to talking about individual poets and their poems. The attention this essay seems to have attracted may stem as much from our collective liking for "trend pieces" (if I may steal that term from newspaper editors) as from the accuracy or inaccuracy of its claims. Writers who have taken issue with this essay (most of all, the avant-garde critic Steve Evans) dislike the idea that any poets can ever be grouped into schools, or prefer narrower definitions of "school," or else object that it's not clear where boundaries lie. Is Joshua Clover elliptical? Is D. A. Powell? Brenda Shaughnessy? Michele Leggott? H. L. Hix? Matthea Harvey? David Berman? (Since you asked: yes, yes, yes, no, no, yes, and yes.)

The answers to those questions seem to me less important than the fact that they can now be asked. I aimed not to single out six or eight or ten poets as a distinct group with bright-line boundaries, but instead to describe an emerging set of styles, a family-resemblance notion, a nebula of habits and preoccupations that seemed to me then (and still seems to me now) to enfold currently influential poets (and the poets influenced by them). Ellipticism counts as a school or a movement in the way that "metaphysical poetry," or "confessional poetry," count as movements, not in the way that "Language writing" or the Black Arts movement or New Formalism (each of which had manifestos) count as movements; the so-called Ellipticals (like the so-called Metaphysicals) need not have signed a manifesto, or appeared in one place at one time, in order to share the aesthetic goals I have described. (They do, however, publish in the same magazines.)

If "Ellipticism" in fact defines a reigning style, we might expect both the number of new adherents, and the number of limit cases, to increase over time, at least until another style crops up to replace it. This appears to have happened. We have now, in 2004, more poetry of the sort I'd like to call Elliptical than we had in 1999, and many more first books that exhibit its features. If anything, the Elliptical style seems in danger of becoming too easy, a manner graduate students learn to adopt, then discard, before or after their first books win awards.

The growing numbers of youngish poets who might fit the Elliptical label make it easier to see what they've learned and from whom—hence easier to see which older poets might rightly define their putative school. If I were to rewrite this essay from scratch (rather than appending these belated paragraphs), I would not include August Kleinzahler, whose most disjunctive, least obviously descriptive poems of the 1990s have come to seem (given his subsequent work) like outliers; younger poets have not seized on him as a model. (I sometimes wish they would.) I'm not sure I would have included Thylias Moss, though if *Last Chance for the Tarzan Holler* does not belong in this company it becomes a book with no peers and no close parallels anywhere. (That may be right.) I might have included, instead, Powell, or Liz Waldner, whose playful, all-over-the-place jargon acknowledges Berrymania along with cinematic, and wholly fruitful, forms of artistic attention deficit. And I would certainly continue to maintain that Levine, Brock-Broido, Wright, and Carson have become influences who work *together* on many younger poets' styles (sometimes joined to the corrosively un-serious influences of James Tate and Dean Young). These poets are try-ing (as Graham, more abstractly and grandly, tried just before them) to split the difference between a poetry of descriptive realism on the one hand, and, on the other, a neo-avant-garde. In that split much of the present—if not the future—of American poetry lies.

Whether a school exists, and where its boundaries fall, still seem to me questions both less profound, and less durable, than the questions we can ask about each poet and about individual poems. At the same time, individual poems may respond to their historical moment, and invoke their stylistic affinities with other poems; if many poems do so in similar ways, they might prompt readers to class them together—to decide, even, that those poems belong to a school.

Without Evidence

*Remarks on Reading Contemporary Poetry
and on Reading about It*

for Michael Scharf

1

Formalist criticism wants to make itself unnecessary; historicist criticism, to make itself indispensable.

To do a poem justice, explain what makes it unique; to get a poem noticed, explain what makes it typical.

One can demonstrate to skeptics the explicit rules that govern a skill, or a game, but not those that govern an art. Skeptics thus suspect art forms of possessing rules that are trade secrets, or rules that are really table manners (see, for example, Pierre Bourdieu).

Snobbery in the arts is reverse snobbery.

"A poem is either worth everything, or worth nothing." So say Romantics, equating a life with a poem.

Why value the appearance of effort in poetry? Why value apparent (or actual) effortlessness? The first appears to demonstrate the mastery of a craft: the second, to demonstrate that poetry is not a craft at all.

"I stop somewhere waiting for you" (Whitman): the poet as teacher, or leader, who promises that we will catch up to him later, and knows that we never will. (Although certain exceptionally confident poets— Ginsberg, for example—would later claim to have caught up with him.)

Writers in difficult, or "innovative," modes appear more likely than others to make large claims for the (political or intellectual) importance of their art: to justify greater effort on our part, we may require the promise or hope of a correspondingly greater reward.

Louis Zukofsky wrote that poetry had its upper limit in music, its lower limit in speech. Sometimes the useful contrast is not song vs. speech but song vs. speech vs. writing, since the last discourages, and the first two favor, semantic redundancy. Songs and speeches must be heard again in real time, but poems in writing let us take them home; they can be quickly or slowly reread. (See John Miles Foley, *How to Read an Oral Poem.*) But medieval manuscript poets such as Chaucer cared less for the opposition between speech and writing, perhaps because the absence of print made them less alert to it: harder, therefore, for us—who type and cut and paste and duplicate files—to think in terms appropriate to their craft.

The supposed requirement that a poem justify its existence during political or ethical emergencies (and there is always an emergency) is not the same as the demand that poets take action during such emergencies: we could apply the latter demand to carpenters, but not the former to tables or chairs.

Poems, as such, defend the private life. (What verbal composition does such a notion of "poems" exclude?)

What if the ways in which we can think (or have been taught to think) about lyric poetry do not depend on our tacit acceptance of a liberal individualism (as radical critics allege), but instead support (provide good evidence for) it?

"Modern critics . . . have become oddly resistant to admitting that there is more than one code of morals in the world, whereas the central purpose of reading imaginative literature is to accustom yourself to this basic fact" since "to understand codes other than your own is likely to make your judgments better." William Empson's formulation, as he seems to have recognized, places the central ethical work of literature largely in prose fiction (and perhaps in the feature film). Modern poetry, unless it rejects Empson's liberalism entirely, then gets to answer the question: what else can imaginative writing do?

We overlook the difference between representing (in poetry) an ethical, political, or psychological desideratum and contributing to its achievement.

"We make out of the quarrel with others, rhetoric, but of the quarrel with ourselves, poetry" (Yeats). But rhetoric and poetry are not distinct; each of us bears "others" in ourselves, and hears or speaks for them in all our quarrels.

A. K. Ramanujan, in an interview: "Some people are other people, and can never be themselves." Some people are really, or essentially, imitators. Or readers, rather than writers. Or—alas—critics.

Paratext can become poetic material (as in the work of Kent Johnson). Not "How do we get beyond the name of the poet, the name of the press, the context of discovery, to the actual poem?" but "How can we know if and when we have ever done so?"

"If I am an unknown man, and publish a wonderful book, it will make its way very slowly, or not at all. If I, become a known man, publish that very same book, its praise will echo over both hemispheres. . . . You have to obtain reputation before you can get a fair hearing for that which would justify your repute. . . . If a man can't hit upon any other way of attracting attention, let him dance on his head in the middle of the street; after that he may hope to get consideration for his volume of poems." The character Jasper Milvain, in George Gissing's novel *New Grub Street*, earns our contempt, but can we say with any confidence that he is wrong?

"Fame, the being known, though in itself one of the most dangerous things to man, is nevertheless the true and appointed air, element, and setting of genius and its works" (Gerard Manley Hopkins to Robert Bridges). But "Publication is the auction / Of the mind of man" (Dickinson).

Enter the academy too completely, get a job as a college's poet, and the writing of poetry becomes a job. Stay too far outside it (financial considerations notwithstanding) and you may find yourself (1) without a sense that anyone will read your work, or (2) the captive of a partisan school whose programmatic tastes will damage your work, or (3) surrounded by people who read and praise all, and only, the work of poets they know personally. (But the academy may not prevent those outcomes.)

"Dead poets don't do readings." Contemporary literary culture makes it far easier to "revive" a living author with a new book than a dead one, or one who has vanished from all literary "scenes." Dickinson simply kept going, and Hopkins had Bridges; but what about Rosalie Moore?

Nothing so powerfully prompts the completion or even the start of a piece of writing as the writer's belief that when it is finished, somebody will publish it.

2

A poem has a form, and changes that form (so says, explicitly, Frank Bidart). Any poem is therefore "the exception that proves the rule."

Poetry constitutes a second language within any spoken or written (natural) language; a second language containing its own mutually incomprehensible dialects, to be acquired by visiting the place or the milieu in which they become the norm.

Love poem and elegy (in the modern sense of "mourning poem") both seem central to lyric, as lyric seems central to "modern poetry": why? The lyric project (Allen Grossman explains) makes persons present to one another at the site of reading (which thereby resembles listening). The love poem imagines (or tropes) that project's success within the diegetic world of the poem: reader meets poet as lover meets beloved. "Thy firmness makes my circle just / And makes me end where I begun" (Donne); "The poem / Has set me softly down beside you. The poem is you" (Ashbery). Elegy, on the other hand, appears to describe the same project's failure (the living do not meet the dead). Thus the self-descriptive resonance in W. S. Merwin's one-line "Elegy": the line is "Who would I show it to."

How much does the art that you yourself practice, or make, share with what Sappho made? With what Richard Lovelace made? With what Gertrude Stein made? With what Edward Thomas made? With what these writers thought, or said, they had made?

Certain critics tell us that "I" in 1601 meant something almost entirely unlike what it means now, for us; how could we prove otherwise? The problem of historical reading—especially, but not only, for what we now call lyric—turns out to be the Problem of Other Minds.

Cats are lyric animals: we can never know for sure whether they need us. (Dogs, by contrast, thrive on pursuits and instructions, and can endure boredom amid a long task: they are animals suited to narrative.)

"I am I because my little dog knows me" (Stein). Some poets attend nonstop to their "little dogs," and write the same poem over and over; other poets lack little dogs, and nobody knows, or recognizes, their poems.

Style as persona, but also as reason to live. Bob Kane, who created Bruce Wayne (note the aural overlap), a.k.a. Batman: "I was studying metaphysics then, and had delved into meditation, in order to figure out what I could do if *Batman* ended. This was an especially disturbing problem because I had always felt that Batman and I were one."

"The Burden of the Past" (W. J. Bate). We complain rightly about judges who take, as their prime criterion of value, how well a work reflects or embodies its time. Yet given the variety and the powers of work from other times, given all that previously existing poems have managed to do, should we expect contemporary work to excel in any other way? Reflecting our own time, depicting what's going on now, being "absolutely modern," is one project for which past masters offer the present-day poet no competition.

New poetry must "create the taste by which it is to be admired" (Wordsworth). But not ex nihilo: to distinguish typical from exceptional examples of a new style or school, we appeal tacitly or explicitly to older, or at least other, ways of reading, which the new ways will later modify.

"The question of whether the dismantling of all expectation-satisfying devices isn't in the last analysis the dismantling of the novel" (Frank Kermode). What expectations does a really good, longish, "experimental" poem, such as Lisa Robertson's *Debbie: An Epic* or Bernadette Mayer's *Midwinter Day,* set up and then satisfy? Are those expectations different in kind from the expectations set up, and then satisfied, by *Don Juan* or *In Memoriam?* Or by *Paterson?* Or by somebody's diary?

An interest in poems, as against an interest in poetry. (Contra Ron Silliman.)

The approach to an art (poetry, say) that asks, What next? or What now? may prove incompatible with the approach that says, simply, How does this individual piece of language burn or shine? The first is strategic, the second tactical; or, the first is historicist, the second formalist; or, the first is meretricious, the second genuine; or, the first is realistic, the second willfully ignorant. The first approach makes book reviewing easier, since even the dullest work has a context; the second, in its rarely encountered pure state, makes reviewing bad or mediocre work all but impossible.

Consider a language of criticism that described only successful effects, only what a poem actually managed to do (rather than what it wanted to do, or what it resembled); in such a language, describing bad or mediocre poetry would become impossible, since about such poems there would just be nothing to say.

Our habits, informed by older poetry, give us assumptions about how poems (and, for example, how line breaks) cohere, communicate, mean: that is, about how to derive, from them, propositions. Those assumptions allow us not only to enjoy but to interpret language that does not consist of propositions, or whose propositions would not cohere outside of poems. "Wonderful light / viridian summers / deft boys / no thanks" (Denise Riley); "On lake water our faces stay. / Even the river does not carry them downstream. / Dreaming is local" (Allan Peterson); "We choose our friends as we choose to leave / The window open" (Chris Stroffolino).

Such poems use (and use well) our assumptions about propositions and coherence, assumptions derived from older poems that themselves cohere (make continuous prose sense), as Riley's and Peterson's and Stroffolino's do not. Does such use, or "parasitism" (as the scholar Robert Chodat names it), begin with the High Moderns? With Christopher Smart? Are contemporary uses of this "parasitism" ever different in kind from Eliot's? From Smart's? From Stein's?

So-called "New Critical" desiderata included compression, polysemy, irony as the products of "print culture"; poems that foreground those qualities likely end up as far as possible from the requirements (formulas, low information density, narrative component, audience interaction) that typify oral poetries. If changes in taste since about 1955 have moved most of us further from those onetime desiderata, what have they moved us toward? Is it more "oral"? Or more "visual"? Or more "interactive"?

By the way, who are "we"?

3

Must a poet, nowadays, entertain an unsustainable notion of poetry's importance (to the poet herself, to a community, to the future, to somebody else) in order to put in the time to develop the craft that will make other people, later on, want to bother to reread her poems?

One reason for making aesthetic judgments—for making them and for pursuing arguments about them—is to establish an order of importance (for the works, and at least implicitly for their authors) that runs contrary to the Great World's order, to "the mass and majesty of this world, all / That carries weight and always weighs the same" (Auden). We establish such a contrary order, again and again, when we call one poem better than another, or say that a heretofore obscure poem succeeds as art.

But such contrary orders must remain multiple, incomplete, still controversial: otherwise they will lose their reason for being. The contrary order ceases to exist as such (becomes the only order) if we come to believe either that all works are equally worth our attention—that the equality of all persons before the law implies that all works of art reward our attention in equal ways—or else that all works belong to a single order (or "canon"), an order that, once rightly determined, should never be altered again.

The language of the poem is for A a representation, a version, of the body the poet has, and the poem is better the more it is really like A's body.

For B, the language of the poem becomes instead a better substitute for the body: it is the body that B wishes she had.

For C, on the other hand ("hand"), the poem becomes a better substitute for the body not because it represents C's ideal body, the body C wishes she had, but rather because the poem makes perceptible in its surfaces (that is, in the shapes of its phrases, the sounds of its words) the hopes and pains that would otherwise remain hidden "inside" the body and soul of C, invisible to everyone else, perhaps even invisible to C herself.

"Trust your instincts," wrote Dr. Spock, echoing the young Wordsworth ("Let nature be your teacher"), implying that nature, instinct, intuition, even your body will tell you the right thing to do. What if your own experience suggests that your instincts will tell you no such thing? What if you don't have instincts? What if your instincts tell you to trust someone else?

Under what circumstances can a poem, or any other work of art, or any habit formed by works of art, replace an absent "nature," a missing instinct?

We like to watch sports in part because they promise that, for a few gifted athletes, some of the time, all that we want from human bodies (despite their obvious everyday inadequacies) can be had from human bodies, by means of what some athletes can train their bodies to do. In the same way, we like to read poems in part because they appear to prove—they give the illusion—that, for a few gifted writers, some of the time, all that we want from language (despite its obvious everyday inadequacies) can be had within language, by means of what some poets, some speakers or singers or writers, can train their language to do.

Often what we want, from life as from language, is not so much impossible as what Ambrose Bierce called incompossible, the satisfaction of mutually exclusive conditions: security and adventure, the new and the same, innocence and experience. That is one reason so many critics have believed, as one of them put it, that the language of poetry is the language of paradox—and one reason why so many poets wrote poems that seemed, to those critics, to prove it.

Some poets marry a language; some have affairs with it; some treat it as a parent, some as a child, some as an equal, or as a friend.

A poem is a kind of speech, one speech act within a web of speech acts, each an action responding to another, forever enmeshed in its implicit history. And yet, a poem is a made thing—it aspires to be complete in itself, hence to give the impression (however fallacious) that it can stand outside time. On the one hand, "This hour I tell things in confidence. / I might not tell everybody, but I will tell you" (Walt Whitman). On the other hand, "Not marble nor the gilded monuments / Of princes shall outlive this powerful rime" (Shakespeare, very loosely translating Horace).

Shakespeare's sonnet 55 is a poem (Frank Bidart's "A Coin for Joe in the Image of a Horse" is another) that makes no sense unless we regard it at once in its capacity as something spoken to someone, in response to prior speech, and as a thing (analogous to a bronze monument or a hard coin) likely to remain almost intact long after the occasion for its shaping has passed almost out of mind.

On the one hand, the drive to perfect what we make; on the other, the drive to make nothing, since nothing is perfect. (Thus James Merrill's joke about poems, in successive revisions, diminishing to twenty lines, then ten, "And then imploding in a puff of Zen.")

On the one hand, all poems are in one sense self-portraits. On the other, by the time an artist has finished making her self-portrait, it no longer depicts her as she is—it would not do so even were her inner life (as no inner life is) as fixed, as clear in being A rather than not-A, as almost any work of art must be.

The rough, raw, "process-oriented" strands in recent poetry (O'Hara, Schuyler, Ted Berrigan, Bernadette Mayer) so often connect improvisation (or the appearance of improvisation) to autobiography because the soul that cannot be pinned down, the ever-changing, sensitive "real me," requires a poetry that seems to change as fast as we do.

On the one hand, the insistence that poets need to acquire some hard-to-acquire knowledge, and to learn, by practicing, their art: here we find a professionalism, equally evident now among poets who admire Merrill and Wilbur, and among poets who admire Spicer and Stein, though they would disagree on what knowledge poets should have.

On the other hand, the insistence that poetry is that which cannot be pinned down, that which cannot be reduced to technique, that true poetry displays whatever is left of us after techniques and hetero-nomous demands and institutions are peeled away (either because it reflects our real inner lives, or because it manifests some sort of resis-tance to markets, institutions, social facts): here we find a kind of ama-teurism, an insistence that poets must not be mere professionals.

Thus the pressure on poets—once we can no longer see ourselves as apprentices, nor as students—to be amateur and professional at once: to be both, in each poem, with each word.

Is the making of art bad for us (at least potentially) because it makes us less able, or less willing, to live with our imperfection?

Are the rough, or raw, or supposedly improvised, or "process-oriented" strands within contemporary poetry ethically valuable in that they encourage us to live with imperfection, to move on? Or are they ethically suspect, because they encourage us not to take respon-sibility, not to go back and work with patience in order to fix what we break?

Acknowledgments

I am grateful to all the people who helped produce the journals and the edited volumes where many of these essays first appeared, sometimes in longer or shorter forms, and with different titles:

"Close Calls with Nonsense." *The Believer,* May 2004.

"Where Every Eye's a Guard: Rae Armantrout's Poetry of Suspicion." *Boston Review* 27:2 (2002).

"Lightsource, Aperture, Face: C. D. Wright and Photography." *In the Frame: Women's Ekphrastic Poetry from Marianne Moore to Susan Wheeler,* ed. Nick Halpern, Jane Hedley, and Willard Spiegelman (University of Delaware Press, 2009).

"The Revell Variations." *The Nation,* May 12, 2003; additional material from *Believer,* May 2005, and *Slate,* December 2007.

"The Speed of Life." *Boston Review,* March–April 2008.

"Punk Half Panther." *The New York Times Book Review,* August 10, 2008.

"Witness for the Transit." *The New York Times Book Review,* May 25, 2008.

"Poetry in Review" (Peterson, Hayes). *Yale Review* 95:1 (2007).

"Poetry in Review" (Leader, Hix). *Yale Review* 90:3 (2002).

"'My Name Is Henri': Contemporary Poets Discover John Berryman." *Reading the Middle Generation Anew,* ed. Eric Haralson (University of Iowa Press, 2006).

"'I Do Not Expect You to Like It': The Exhilarating, Stagy, Ambitious, Profound Poetry of James K. Baxter." *The Believer,* April 2005.

"Now for the Hills." *London Review of Books,* March 16, 2000.

"'To be sheer air . . .': The Song of Theory in the Poems of Denise Riley." *Times Literary Supplement,* April 23, 2004.

The Salt Companion to John Tranter, ed. Rod Mengham (Salt, 2009).

"Kinaesthetic Aesthetics: On Thom Gunn's Poems." *Southwest Review* 84:3 (1999).

"Paul Muldoon's *New Selected Poems.*" *Thumbscrew* 7 (1997).

"Connection Charge." *Times Literary Supplement,* November 24, 2006.

"Everything Must Go." *Times Literary Supplement,* March 28, 2008.

"All Styles Recommended." *Poetry Review* 95:1 (2005).

"What Life Says to Us." *London Review of Books,* February 21, 2008.

"Becoming Literature." *Boston Review* 26:3 (2001).

"I Have Found the World So Marvelous: A. R. Ammons." *Poetry Review* 92:4 (2003); *Ruminator Review* 9 (2002).

"The Collected Poems of Stanley Kunitz." *Boston Review* 25:6 (2000).

"Hi, Louise!" *London Review of Books,* July 20, 2000.

"Raking Leaves in New Madrid." *Times Literary Supplement,* July 5, 2002.

"Chicory and Daisies." *London Review of Books,* March 7, 2002.

"The Elliptical Poets." *American Letters and Commentary* 11 (1999); *Poetry Review* 88:1 (1998); *A Poetry Criticism Reader,* ed. Jerry Harp (University of Iowa Press, 2006).

"Without Evidence." *Jacket* 22 (2003).

Some of these essays began as reviews of these books:

Rae Armantrout, *Veil: New and Selected Poems* (Wesleyan University Press, 2000).

John Ashbery, *Notes from the Air: Selected Later Poems* and *A Worldly Country* (Carcanet Press / Ecco, 2007).

Robert Creeley, *Complete Poems 1945–75* (University of California Press, 1983), *Complete Poems 1975–2005* (University of California Press, 2007), *Selected Poems,* ed. Benjamin Friedlander (University of California Press, 2008).

Terrance Hayes, *Wind in a Box* (Penguin, 2006).

Juan Felipe Herrera, *187 Reasons Mexicanos Can't Cross the Border* (City Lights, 2007) and *Half the World in Light* (University of Arizona Press, 2008).

H. L. Hix, *Surely As Birds Fly* (Truman State University Press, 2002)

Laura Kasischke, *Lilies Without* (Ausable Press, 2007).

August Kleinzahler, *Sleeping It Off in Rapid City: New and Selected Poems* (Farrar, Straus & Giroux, 2008).

Stanley Kunitz, *Collected Poems* (W. W. Norton, 2000).

Mary Leader, *The Penultimate Suitor* (University of Iowa Press, 2001).

James Merrill, *Collected Poems* (Alfred A. Knopf, 2001).

Les Murray, *Collected Poems* (Carcanet, 1999) and *Fredy Neptune* (Farrar, Straus & Giroux, 2000).

Paul Muldoon, *New Selected Poems* (Faber and Faber, 2004), *Horse Latitudes* (Farrar, Straus & Giroux, 2007), and *The End of the Poem* (Farrar, Straus & Giroux, 2007).

Lorine Niedecker, *Collected Works,* ed. Jenny Penberthy (University of California Press, 2002).

Allan Peterson, *All the Lavish in Common* (University of Massachusetts Press, 2006).

D. A. Powell, *Cocktails* (Graywolf Press, 2004).

Donald Revell, *My Mojave* (Alice James Books, 2003); *Pennyweight Windows: New and Selected Poems* (Alice James Books, 2005).

Denise Riley, *Selected Poems* (Reality Street Editions, 2000).

Richard Wilbur, *Collected Poems 1943–2004* (Harcourt, 2004).

C. D. Wright, *Steal Away* (Copper Canyon Press, 2005).

Permission Acknowledgments

Stephen Burt is the author of two critical books on poetry as well as two poetry collections, including *Parallel Play*. His essays and reviews have appeared in the *Believer,* the *Nation,* and the *New York Times Book Review.* He is an associate professor of English at Harvard University.

The text of *Close Calls with Nonsense* is set in Sabon. Book design by Rachel Holscher. Composition by BookMobile Design and Publishing Services, Minneapolis, Minnesota. Manufactured by Versa Press on acid-free paper.